SECULARIZATION IN MULTI-RELIGIOUS SOCIETIES

SECULARIZATION IN MULTI-RELIGIOUS SOCIETIES

Indo-Soviet Perspectives

Edited by
S.C. DUBE
V.N. BASILOV

Papers Presented at the Indo-Soviet Symposium
on
Problems of Secularization in Multi-Religious Societies
Tashkent 1978

Indian Council of Social Science Research

CONCEPT PUBLISHING COMPANY
NEW DELHI

The responsibility for the facts stated, conclusions reached and opinions expressed in this book is that of the authors concerned and not of the Indian Council of Social Science Research which has financed the publication.

First Published 1983

Published by

Naurang Rai
Concept Publishing Company
H-13, Bali Nagar
NEW DELHI-110015 (India)

Printed by

A. H. Composing Agency
at Mohan Printing Corporation
Padam Nagar
DELHI-110007

Introduction

THIS volume brings together tweny-one papers presented at the Indo-Soviet Symposium on *Problems of Secularization* held at Tashkent in November 1978.

The Soviet Union and India are both multi-ethnic, multi-lingual, and multi-religious societies. Both have explicitly and implicitly recognized cultural pluralism as an objective to be promoted by state policy. The cultural policy of the Soviet Union, under the leadership of Lenin, granted autonomy to all nationalities and encouraged the articulation of free expression of the cultural aspirations of even small ethnic and religious groups. They were expected, at the same time, to join as equal partners in the massive efforts to bring about structural transformation and all-round development of the Soviet Union. The Soviet experiment of state building, in a framework of complete cultural autonomy, is unique in many ways. In Jawaharlal Nehru India found a leader of great vision and dynamism, endowed with a rare empathy and understanding for the diverse elements that constitute the cultural mosaic that is India. The stress, in this country, was always on national integration, but this was not to be achieved at the expense of the identity of the regional cultures as well as the cultures of the religious and ethnic minorities. The emerging cultural mainstream was not to be allowed to erode the individuality and vitality of its many cultures.

The Soviet and the Indian experience have many parallels, but they also have significant differences. Both merit serious study by students of comparative cultural policy. Contrary to the general impression theological institutions in the Soviet Union continue to receive a measure of state support. In India, the state maintains equal distance from all religions, although it cannot be described as irreligious, unreligious, or even areligious. Both have encountered some problems in dealing with religious and cultural minorities and both have achieved a measure of success in bringing about their integration.

The discussions at Tashkent had historical, sociological, and philosophical dimensions. The free and frank exchange of experiences and analyses began with some semantic difficulties and snags. It appeared that the two sides were using keywords and concepts forming the core of the discussion—religion and secularism, for example—in different senses. Was faith in a Supreme Being a precondition of religion ? The Soviet scholars insisted that it was. But this position raised some vexed questions. Did the practice of animism or animatism by tribal groups constitute religion ? Can Buddhism be described as a religion, if the criterion to belief in a Supreme Being is to be strictly adhered to ? Secularism and secularization also presented some difficulty. Does a secular outlook necessarily mean a non-religious world-view? Or, is the Indian variant of secularism, which emphasizes equality of all religions in so far as the state is concerned, also an acceptable view ? For a meaningful discussion, the two sides had to have an explicit understanding regarding the sense in which they used these and other similar terms.

The styles of scholarship represented by the two sides also made a difference. This would be evident to all perceptive readers who go through the Indian and Soviet contributions in the volume carefully. The two sides did not take time to adjust to the differences of idiom and emphasis in each other's approach. They were engaged in a dialogue aimed at mutual understanding and appreciation, not a debate, nor yet a confrontation. At the conclusion of the Symposium both sides felt that it had been a positive and productive experience.

In a situation of face to face interaction it was relatively easy to overcome the barriers of communication and establish easy rapport, but in editing this volume for the press it has not been so. Slightly amended versions of the Indian contributions had been translated into Russian. I am not in a position to comment on the nature and quality of editorial treatment accorded either to them or to the Soviet contributions in the Russian version of this book. In preparing the English version for publication no substantive changes in the arguments (or, their sequence) presented in the various Indian papers have been made to ensure that the Russian and the English versions are not at variance in any significant manner. Translations of the

Soviet contributions were not done in India, they were supplied by my Soviet counterpart Professor Basilov. It has been assumed that they faithfully represent the position taken up by the authors during the Indo-Soviet dialogue. Any rigorous editing, involving deletion of avoidable duplication and restructuring of sentences possibly leading to significant transfers of meaning, has not been undertaken. It was not always possible to check the authenticity of dates and quotations as well as of interpretations. Stylistic changes have been minimal. In consequence, the Indian and the Soviet streams in this volume may look different, but even in the cold medium of print they succeed in conveying something of the flavour of the original presentations. A bilingual dialogue under more propitious circumstances is difficult to reproduce with total authenticity ; the situation has been complicated further in the case of this volume because of the differences in the styles of scholarship of the two sides involved in the discussions. The purpose of the Symposism was to build bridges of understanding despite the nature, and emphases, of styles of scholarship ; the publication of this volume, it is hoped, will be a second step in this direction.

The byproducts of the Symposium were also interesting and instructive. Some of us, who had seen Tashkent a decade earlier, were struck by the changes in this important city. The old Tashkent had almost been completely replaced by a new and modern Tashkent ; only some parts of the old city were left to remind us of what it had looked like in the past. The visits to historic Bukhara and Samarkhand—centres which had centuries old ties with India—were most enjoyable. Here we had an opportunity of seeing history as the past and also history in the making. The visits to farms and collectives gave us a feel of the new Soviet Central Asia. Particularly instructive was a visit to an Islamic seminary. Talks with Uzbek citizens and visits to their homes were informative. The unsurpassed Soviet hospitality and warmth made a lasting impression on us. The visit to Moscow was the first introduction to the great socialist metropolis to many in the Indian group. Here also we spent a day in an old and renowned Christian theological institution and passed a pleasant evening with Soviet research workers. Altogether the Symposium and the associated sight-seeing provided an opportunity to build bridges of understanding. At least we on the Indian side were richer for the experiences.

As leader of the Indian team, I have to express the appreciation of my colleagues for the excellent preparations made by the ICSSR secretariat for the visit. The arrangements made by the Soviet side were faultless. Indian tradition prohibits me from thanking Soviet friends formally for their understanding warmth, and hospitality.

It is my hope that the contributions included in this volume will be a step forward towards better understanding and appreciation of the Soviet and Indian approaches to the emergence of secular societies in the two countries.

New Delhi
26 January 1981

S.C. DUBE

Contents

PART TWO

SOVIET CONTRIBUTORS

PART ONE

INDIAN CONTRIBUTORS

1

Harmonizing Dimension in Hindu Civilizational Processes

S. C. Dube

THE TEXTURE of Hindu civilization is extremely complex ; it incorporates a wide variety of cultural patterns representing a diversity of social forms, value orientations, and goal definitions. Hinduism is not a religion in the conventional sense—it cannot be attributed to any one divine figure or Messenger of God ; it does not consist of a body of beliefs or doctrines that have not been subjected to or are not open to doubt, debate, and dissent ; and it does not have any regulatory organization capable of enforcing its edicts on the adherents of the faith. Though it has demonstrated its durability and resilience, it cannot be said to have maintained an unbroken continuity, without change from Vedic times to the present. The changes in the structure of belief, forms of worship, and nature of ritual have been many and significant. Hinduism, such as it is, is a loosely structured federation of faiths rather than a faith. Hindu civilization represents a pattern of stabilized pluralism with well developed linkages and patterns of interdependence between its insoluble segments that enjoy varying degrees of autonomy and identity. Birth and minimal cognitive participation are enough to identify one as belonging to the Hindu faith. In its essence Hindu civilization consists of a consciousness that allows varied and variegated moods and modes.

The nearest equivalent to the term religion in Indian languages is *dharma*, but *dharma* is not quite the same thing as religion. *Dharma* does refer to the relationship between man and the mysterious unknown, but it lays equal, if not greater, emphasis on the more mundane aspects of human life. Early texts refer to three *purusharthas* or goals of existence : *dharma*—that which sustains the order and appropriate action towards this end—heads the list and is followed by *artha*—pursuit of economic interests and material goods—and *kama*—the pursuit of sexual, emotional and artistic interests. In a sense *dharma* subsumes the last two for one cannot visualize a natural or social order which ignores pursuits relating to worldly goods and bodily cravings. But it is significant that *artha* and *kama* find separate mention and figure together with *dharma*. These worldly pursuits, though they are governed by socio-religious codes, have nonetheless been rated as independent goals of life. To these three a fourth goal, namely, *moksha* (attainment of salvation) was added later. Over the centuries *moksha* gained in importance, although at every stage it was emphasized that one could not move in the direction of salvation without first having discharged one's obligations implicit in *dharma*, *artha*, and *kama*. *Dharma* was paramount because on it rested the order. However, it did not lay down a rigid code of behaviour binding all Hindus in different spatial and temporal settings. The goals and instrumentalities defined by it permitted considerable variation. In fact, the interpretation of *dharma* had to take account of the contexts of *desha* (land or territory), *kala* (time), and *patra* (individual or category of individuals). The spatial setting made a difference and allowed for the continuance of considerable cultural variations in different regions. Thus, practices like cross-cousin marriage, maternal uncle and niece marriage, matrilineal descent and inheritance, polyandry and so forth, confined to certain territories, were left undisturbed. The code admitted variations in dietary practices that were linked to the resources of different ecological settings. The temporal dimension also made a difference. As we shall see later it was believed that the ethos of each major epoch calls for a different interpretation of *dharma* and for different standards in its application ; when decline and decay become progressively worse, the demands of *dharma* are less and less rigid. Also, the individual under consideration or the social category to which he belongs makes a difference in the application of the socio-religious code. The ruler is outside the pale of normal *dharma* and is governed by a special code designated as *raj dharma.* Similarly, one who has renounced the world is not governed by the code that applies to those who maintain worldly ties and are engaged in earthly pursuits. The *dharma* for the four *varnas* (the principal stages of life) is different. A composite view of appropriate action has also to be taken by considering *varna* and *ashrama* together. The provisions of *dharma* thus have specific reference to *varna*, *ashrama*, and *varnashrama.* In specific contexts it should also refer to attributes of persons involved in action (*guna dharma*) and to the objects of action (*naimittika dharma*).

In addition, of course, there are guidelines regarding appropriate action that apply uniformly to all members of society. The Rigveda refers to *rta* or the universal law regulating the cosmic order. On the empirical plane the regulatory code of universal application is elaborated in *sadharana dharma.* Some of the most commonly referred to components of *sadharana dharma* are discharging ritual obligations to one's ancestors, performance of austerities and cultivation of discipline, pursuit of truth, non-anger, fidelity in marriage, cultivation of purities, acquisition of self-knowledge and equanimity in both happiness and suffering. The Vishnudharmottara Purana lists fourteen attributes : forgiveness, truth, control over senses, purity, almsgiving, control over desires, non-violence, service to the mentor, following those that tread the sacred path, kindness, tenderness, absence of greed, worship of deities and Brahamanas, and absence of envy. The Brahma Vaivarta Purana mentions knowledge, kindness, control over senses, purity, truth, not stealing the possessions of others, practising austerities and discipline, control over the body, absence of anger, and modesty as the ten principal ingredients of *sadharana dharma.* Inventories formulated by other sages cover much the same ground. Gautama, in his Dharma Sutra, lists compassion or love for all beings ; forbearance ; freedom from anger ; purity of body, speech and thought ; absence of painful efforts ; doing what is commended ; not demeaning oneself before others ; and not hankering after sensual pleasures or the possessions of others. Similarly, in his Dharma Sutra, Vasishtha says, "...Avoid backbiting, jealousy, bribe, egoism, unbelief, crookedness, self-praise, abuse of others, deceit, covetousness, delusion, anger, and envy." It is significant that these codes of universal application refer to all men and to their behaviour towards others without any distinction of the latter's status or faith. Those belonging to outgroups are as much entitled to the prescribed considerations as those belonging to the ingroups. Devala, in his *Krityaratnakara*, instructs that one should not do to others what one would dislike being done to oneself. It should also be noted that despite the careful elaboration of a large number of rules of outward conduct, there is always insistence on the necessity to satisfy the "inner man" or an individual's conscience. Manu says, "Assiduously do that which will give satisfaction to the inner self". Thus, we find that while the general rules of conduct have been laid down in considerable detail, their interpretation and application in specific contexts have been left to the individual's better judgement and conscience. These two factors together work towards the promotion of universal codes of conduct without taking into account narrow sectarian or religious differences as well as towards flexibility in their application according to the conscience of individuals.

Time makes a difference in the moral order of a society. As is well known the Hindu view of time is cyclical—the wheel of time moves ceaselessly through four principal epochs, each representing a different ethos. The cycle begins with Krita Yuga (also referred to as Sat Yuga—the Age of Truth) representing a moral order of near perfection. In this epoch truth and righteousness prevail ; all sections of society automatically follow the *dharma* ; no coercive authority is needed to ensure conformity. This idyllic period begins to register a decline because of human frailties, and in time Treta Yuga is ushered in. The moral order registers a definite lowering, but worse is to follow. The degenerative processes continue to operate within society and further decline marks the advent of Dwapara Yuga. The wheel of time continues to move, degeneration is followed by more degeneration and mankind enters Kali Yuga. During this epoch, according to the Vishnu Purana, the moral order will experience a process of continuous decay and will ceaselessly move to a point where the human race approaches its annihilation. Rules governing vocations and orders of life shall be ignored. The minds of men will be wholly occupied in acquiring wealth for selfish gratification. The rulers will, instead of protecting, plunder their subjects. In the new depraved social order property alone will confer rank, wealth will be the only source of devotion, passion will mainly characterize the bond between the sexes, and falsehood will be the principal means of getting justice. In these degenerative processes certain regenerative processes are implicit. When human greed and passion have reached their lowest ebb, there will be cataclysmic transformations which will restart the cycle with Krita Yuga. Such a view of time, investing an element of inevitability in the degenerative and regenerative processes, makes for differentials in the application of socio-religious ethical codes in different epochs. As the sacred texts suggest, in Krita Yuga *dharma* rests on four legs, in Treta on three, in Dwapara on two, and in Kali Yuga it rests on one leg only. Balancing of goals and interests thus becomes increasingly difficult. The Vishnu Purana mentions one great virtue of the otherwise vicious Kali Yuga, "the fruit of penance, of continence, of silent prayer, and the like, practised in the Krita Yuga for ten years, in the Treta for one year, in the Dwapara for a month, is obtained in the Kali Yuga in a day...."

Those approaching Hindu thought and the organization of tradition through sacred works are impressed by their metaphysical heights, logical perfection, and profound generalizations. The achievements of the ancient philosophers in these fields are indeed monumental. But the Hindu social system did not rest only on philosophical speculations and feats of logic, it made important pragmatic adjustments and found philosophic rationale for them. The emphasis on transcendence did not lose sight of the existential component. Other worldly pursuits did not enjoy a pre-eminent position. The Arthashastras and the Kamashastras are as basic to the understanding of Hinduism as the Dharmashastras. The *laukika* (worldly) dimension of the social order was important. The sacred works did not reach down to the common man for an overwhelming majority of the people in the country was not literate and a sizeable section of it was denied access to the holy books. The message from these works that reached them was a relatively simple and popularized version. Passing through many cultural transmitters, who were by no account men of learning, and through several cultural filters, which read into them meanings according to their own prevailing cultural frame of reference, this message was shaped and moulded on the pattern of the beliefs and experience of the people. Thus, there inevitably was a great difference between the Hinduism of the holy books and the Hinduism practised by the common man. To the average Hindu, earthly pursuits were of paramount importance, although he did not altogether ignore his ritual obligations to the spirits of his ancestors and to the gods and spirits in the realm of the mysterious unknown. To him *dharma* consisted of worship of the all-India gods and deities as well as the territorial and the family gods, appeasement of evil spirits, performance of rituals connected with the spirits of his ancestors, and observance of *rites de passage* or *sanskaras* connected with the major crises of life. Divine beings were satisfied with some worship, daily or even occasional. One member of the family could perform the worship on behalf of the rest. This notion of *dharma* also includes observance of fasts and festivals connected with gods and mythological events. Pilgrimages to sacred shrines and temples were undertaken by some to ensure their future after death ; to bathe in holy rivers earned one considerable merit. In everyday life the regulation of behaviour was to aim at avoidance of sin (*papa*) and accumulation of merit (*punya*). The notion of sin has been defined in some detail. Almost everywhere a distinction was made between offences that degrade and those that pollute. But in the ultimate analysis what constituted sin was determined largely by local or regional tradition and there was no uniformity regarding the modes of cleansing oneself of the stigma or pollution implicit in it ; removal of pollution was relatively easy, the procedures for overcoming a degraded status were complex and costly.

The *laukika* tradition must be viewed as an essential and a major part of Hinduism. It had visible and invisible links with the metaphysical Hinduism of the literati but it also continued to maintain a distinct identity and considerable vitality.

It has been mentioned earlier that Hinduism does not have a central authority or a hierarchy of functionaries to preach or enforce religion. The enforcement function, at best, is vested in near autonomous communities that are loosely fitted into the framework of Hinduism. Most offences that are punishable through the intervention of human agencies are social in character. Gods and deities as well as ancestors and other spirits are capable of avenging the wrongs done to them and of inflicting punishments on those who are guilty of neglecting them. The enforcement agencies invariably interpret the code according to the local and regional cultural emphases. In general, the ruler had to oversee the maintenance of order and punish the wrongdoer. In Krita Yuga there was no need for kingship or for any kind of coercive authority for the observance of the code of *dharma* was automatic. However, as the wheel of time moved and moral order declined the institution of kingship, invested with coercive powers became necessary. The king was believed to derive elements from several gods, especially Indra, Maruta, Yama, and Surya. But he was only a representative of the gods and was in no sense a god himself. His principal duties were to protect his subjects, to enforce the observance of the code of *varnashrama dharma*, to punish the wicked, and to administer justice. The success of a ruler was to be judged by the degree of contentment among his subjects. No king could regard himself as above the order that he was to uphold and the codes that he was to enforce. A king, failing in his duties and committing atrocities on his subjects, could be killed by the Brahmanas or his subjects without attracting any penalty for murder. The sacred texts do not mention any instance in which the king could justify discrimination between different sections of his subjects on the grounds of their religious belief.

The high degree of flexibility permitted in Hinduism, on the one hand, promoted autonomy and integrity of communities pursuing faiths of divergent characters, but on the other hand it could also legitimize the tyranny of those controlling the social order by virtue of their control over the economy and the polity. Some aspects of Hinduism were definitely exploitative and unjust. The twice-born castes had the upper hand ; the Brahmanas had fashioned the system to suit their interests. Nonetheless the system was not without a safety-valve. Within its framework there was room for dissent, protest, and reform. Over the centuries a number of dissent groups and reformist sects emerged which de-emphasized ritual, questioned the supremacy of the Brahmana, and generally preached and practised an egalitarian social pattern. These dissent and reformist groups emerged from within the Hindu society and continued to be a part of it. The leaders of many of these movements belonged to the lower castes and the lower classes.

Accommodation, pragmatic adjustments and tolerance characterize the Hindu civilizational processes. Hinduism aimed at absorption rather than at conversion and in the process of absorption its own character underwent several transformations. Several territorial and regional gods and goddesses were elevated to the all-India pantheon of Hinduism ; several of the gods and goddesses of all-India Hinduism were fitted into local and regional pantheons alongside analogous deities. The worshippers of Shiva, of Shakti, and of Vishnu and his several incarnations are all Hindus. Of course, there are many who worship them all along with a host of other territorial gods and goddesses. Many of the gods who find prominent mention in Vedic Hinduism are today only remembered and not worshipped. The materialism of the Lokayatas is a part of Hinduism ; so are the esoteric rituals and associated practices of the Tantriks. As suggested earlier, sects could multiply and flourish within the framework of Hinduism. Even religious orders of considerable power such as Jainism, Buddhism, and Sikhism could never delink themselves completely from Hinduism and continued to be treated as offshoots of the parent religion with a strong identity of their own.

Religious faiths of foreign origin could co-exist peacefully with Hinduism so long as they did not totally reject Hindu doctrines and try to substitute for it. The Zoroastrians, for example, thrived despite their separateness. The Ben Israelis of western India are indistinguishable from the neighbouring Hindu communities, except in their faith and forms of worship. Early Christian communities in south India did not encounter much hostility for they adopted a part of the Hindu idiom. On the other hand, the encounter between Islam and Hinduism was not easy whenever the former sought to reject Hinduism totally and replace it. However, Muslim rulers were accepted when they approximated to the traditional image of the king and offered protection to the subjects, promoted their well-being and contentment and did not interfere with the faith and worship of the common people. It has to be noted that some Muslim sects like the Sufis, who meaningfully interacted with Hindu thought and tried to develop a common idiom, attracted veneration from the Hindus. Christianity encountered stiff opposition when it joined hands with the ruling power and adopted an aggressive proselytizing posture.

Hinduism has been able to endure because of its flexibility and adaptability. In the process, it has become somewhat amorphous, but this lack of rigidity has enabled it to respond to the challenges implicit in environments. From early times, the Hindus have believed that Truth is one but its exposition by men of learning can take many forms.

Ancient Hindu logicians adopted the method of elimination —*neti*, *neti*; not this, not this—but Hindu civilizational processes were characterized by *iti eva, iti eva*; also this, also this. In respect of differences in religious beliefs and practices its guiding principle was *samvaya*—moving together with well worked out linkages and patterns of interdependence between groups and communities with distinct identities.

2

The Historical Significance of Secularism in India

T. N. Madan

THE PREAMBLE to the Constitution of India identifies the Indian state as a democratic, socialist and secular republic. I have chosen to open these notes with a reference to the Constitution in order to emphasize the fact that secularism is a *movement*, that is, it is the effort of a certain section of the Indian political leadership to establish a particular ideological position among the peoples of India in so far as the relationship of the state with the religious faiths prevalent in the country is concerned. The essence of this movement is that the relationship of the citizens to the state—the citizens' rights and obligations vis-a-vis the state—shall not be allowed to be affected in any substantial manner by the religious faith of any individual or community. Secularism in India does not stand for the abolition of religion but only for the separation of state and religion. It is important to point out here that a similar separation of politics and religion is not envisaged as the people are free to form political parties, the membership of which is confined to a particular religion in some cases, in principle as well as in fact ; in other cases, in fact if not in principle.

The Constitution of India reflects in this regard the efforts of the Indian National Congress during the national movement to carry on the struggle against colonialism by refusing to acknowledge the political significance of religious differences. The partition of India was a repudiation of this principle and leaders of the Congress—including Jawaharlal Nehru—were a party to this decision. They accepted partition as an inevitable event but reaffirmed their faith in secularism by proclaiming India as a secular state. Pakistan since its inception was avowedly a religion based state. While there is general agreement among independent observers that India has succeeded in establishing a secular state (see, *e.g.*, Smith 1963), there can be no denial of the fact that religion continues to be a major factor in Indian politics as it is in Indian life. This contradiction between politics and the state is a matter of concern and demands critical attention.

The central place of religion in Indian life having been mentioned, two important observations must be made to place the contemporary situation in the right historical perspective.

First, it is important to remember that the traditional conception of religion in India—if at all one may speak in these terms—equates it with the totality of life. Put differently one can say that religion is here constitutive of society (see Dumont 1970a : 94). Politics and economics are neither autonomous domains nor are they contradictory of religion : they are simply encompassed by religion (see Dumont 1970b). The religious and the secular cannot be separated, therefore, in other words, religion cannot be in any meaningful sense privatized.

Two, such a traditional conception had existed in India for millennia alongside of another fundamental principle, namely, that while social life is religious life for everybody, not everybody may subscribe to the same religious faith. Hence the traditional Hindu principle that an alien religious faith is not to be imposed upon anyone—that one is born into a community and its religious faith and, therefore, one cannot acquire a new social identity or religion. In other words, those within the Hindu fold were given no freedom except by opting out of Hindu society. Kautilya's *Arthashastra* is pre-eminently a document of brahmanically controlled state and a popular religion. Cultural pluralism within the state was an accepted fact and the Hindu king was everybody's protector within the kingdom. The basis of a common state was the recognition of the *legitimacy* of cultural difference : agreement between the followers of different religious faiths consisted in acceptance of mutual exclusion. In such a situation secularism (as we understand this term today) had no relevance.

A break in the tradition occurred when Muslim kingdoms and empires were established in South Asia. Practice varied from king to king, but, generally speaking, the Islamic state did distinguish between the rights and obligations of Muslim and non-Muslim subjects. The readiness of common people among the Hindus to render unto Caesar, Caesar's due, irrespective of his religious faith, has been an interesting element in India's social history and manifests itself even today. Some groups of Hindus have been known to acknowledge the Agā Khan, head of the Ismaili Muslims, as an incarnation of god ; it is also known that Queen Victoria was hailed as an incarnation of the goddess Durga. Similarly, as recently as 1975, some Hindus in a north Indian village defended the visit of a Muslim chief minister of an Indian state to a Hindu temple, which had traditionally denied admission to non-Hindus, on the ground that the fact of his having become the head of the government established his superior moral character.

This break in tradition acquired significance when the notion that the people themselves can discharge the kingly role (through their representatives) gained ground. This happened in the course of the national movement. Cultural difference was now transformed into political difference. Nationalism generated communalism which in turn generated secularism. The movements are dialectically related, but secularism is far from being a synthesis because communalism was not the antithesis of nationalism, though this has often been strongly suggested (see Bipan Chandra, 1969), but only a particular manifestation of it.

It has become an intellectually fashionable practice now in India to say that the capacity of some sections of the Indian people to harbour secular and nationalist sentiments, and the incapacity of others to rise above a narrow, communal outlook, can be traced to their level of socio-economic development. Secularization is thus seen as one aspect of modernization. Nationalism is judged as not merely good and progressive but also historically valid, in the sense that it is forward-looking, and therefore true, *per contra* communalism is judged as not merely bad and retrogressive but also as untrue in the sense of false consciousness. Religious conflict is seen as an expression of an immature class conflict. I find this analysis difficult to accept. We must look at the course of recent Indian history more closely before we can pronounce judgement on the historical significance of communalism and secularism.

Raja Rammohan Roy (1772-1833), often referred to as the first "modern man" in India, could well be a starting point in this necessarily brief examination. He had great faith in the civilizing influence of the contact with western civilization, as represented by the British in India. An important element in the political awakening of India was the growing liberalism in Europe itself. Modern education became the principal vehicle of this influence. The nationalist urges of Indian middle classes found their utterance not only in English but also, significantly, in the regional literatures of India. The latter had long used religious symbols and idioms and these were now put to new uses. Thus, Bankim Chandra Chatterji, a great figure in Bengali literature, published a novel in 1876 called *Anand Math* in which he gave sharp expression to the Hindu aversion to aliens, Muslim as well as British, and to the opposition to their cultural and political domination of India. The novel contains the famous Sanskrit poem *Vande Mataram* (I bow to thee, Mother) which identified India with a mother goddess. This poem became the national song of the Indian freedom movement, and India became Mother India.

The Indian National Congress was, as is well known, founded by, among others, a retired British civil servant Allan Hume in 1885, with moderate political goals; its membership had nothing to do with religion. Its president in 1887 was a Muslim, Badruddin Tyabji. The organization was, nevertheless, dominated by Hindus, and the number of Muslim delegates attending its annual sessions, which never exceeded 25 per cent of all delegates, fell from year to year. The attitude of Muslim Congressmen as well as that of their co-religionists who remained outside it was influenced by a factional power struggle within the Congress. The moderates who, though not devoid of religious faith in their personal lives, maintained a secular stance in politics, finally lost to the extremists led by the Bengali Aurobindo Ghose and the Maharashtrian Tilak. Tilak combined the western ideas of nationalism and patriotism with an activist interpretation of the religious philosophy of Hinduism. Ghose proclaimed: "Nationalism is not a mere political programme; nationalism is a religion that has come from God" (de Barry 1959, Vol. II: 727).

Tilak played a particularly notable part in the weaving together of Hindu nationalist and religious sentiment. He used traditional occasions like the annual ten-day festival of the Hindu deity, Ganesh, for intensifying anti-British propaganda in an atmosphere of fervid religious enthusiasm. The "holy" cow was even more deeply involved in politics than before by the combination of an anti-cow killing agitation with larger political goals. The seventeenth-century Maratha hero Shivaji, who had challenged the Moghul empire, was also honoured with a festival. Appeal to Hindu religious sentiment undoubtedly helped to draw Hindus together on an all-India level, but it also alienated the Muslims (Smith 1963 : 87-94 ; Dumont 1970a : 89-110). Originating in a complex historical situation, Muslim separatism was strengthened by the manner in which the Congress developed its campaign against British rule by emphasizing Hindu solidarity. Ultimately, coinciding with the victory of the extremist elements, a group of Muslim leaders founded the Muslim League in 1906 with the blessings of the British Government of India. The seal was placed on this act of separation by the British Parliament's India Council Act of 1909, which provided for separate electorates (Smith 1963 : 84-87).

The leadership of the Congress passed into the hands of Gandhi on the death of Tilak in 1920. Gandhi genuinely respected all religions and his outlook on life was much influenced by Jainism and Christianity. He also drew inspiration from the teachings of Islam. Though he proclaimed all religions to be equally true, the "centre of his being", in the words of his admiring Christian friend Charlie Andrews, ever remained "fixed in Hinduism" (Bondurant 1950 : 121). Gandhi used subtleties of logic—all religions being equally true, it would be inconsistent to convert from one to another—to defend his absolute adherence to his own ancestral faith. In fact, he concerned himself with the cleansing of the social and moral life of Hindus in a manner in which he never interfered with other Indian communities. Thus, he considered his campaign for the eradication of "untouchability" from Hindu society as an inseparable element of his programme of action for the attainment of independence from British rule. His zeal as a religious reformer was unbounded, and he repeatedly declared that he was prepared to repudiate scriptural and canonical texts if these appeared to him to be repugnant to moral reason. It has been rightly suggested by Louis Dumont (1970a: 104) that Gandhi had a double objective in view—"to attain independence and to save Hinduism".

The attainment of independence, however, became Gandhi's predominant concern, which was the national concern affecting Hindus and Muslims alike. To woo the Muslims into the national movement, he made sincere efforts and in the bargain some bad mistakes too. The most glaring of these mistakes was his decision, at almost the very beginning of his political leadership of India, to include opposition to the abolition of the Khilafat (caliphate) in Turkey as one of the political objectives of the Congress, for this made him an ally of reactionary elements among the Muslims. The Khilafat was a traditional symbol of the universal brotherhood of the adherents of Islam, and Gandhi wanted to use it to involve Indian Muslims in the national movement.

Gandhi's support to the Khilafat movement was in conformity with his strategy throughout : to use traditional Indian (Hindu, Jain, Buddhist) ideas and symbols for the promotion of modern ends (Bondurant 1959 : 105 et seq.). He employed these ideas—for example, and notably, truth, non-violence, and soul force—in a manner that was readily comprehensible to even common, illiterate people and thereby succeeded in enrolling the masses into the Congress. To take the national movement out of the "drawing rooms" of the educated middle classes and make it a mass movement inevitably meant Hinduizing it too, given the predominance of Hindus in the country's population. He used such expressions as *daridra-Narayana* (God is the poor, or the poor are God) and *Harijan* (the people of God) to refer to Hindu untouchables, and *Rama Rajya* (God's kingdom) to visualize the independent India of his dreams (Narayana, Hari, and Rama are names of the supreme God in Hindu mythology). On their part, the masses responded to Gandhi as to a *mahatma*—a man of religion, a holy person with spiritual attainments. True to his Hindu sensibility, Gandhi saw nothing wrong in such a combination of the religious and the secular ; on the contrary he asserted : "Those who say that religion has nothing to do with politics do not know what religion means" (Smith 1963 : 91).

Gandhi's efforts to unite Hindus and Muslims in the pursuit of the national goal of independence failed. Extremist elements among Hindus and Muslims alike repudiated his leadership : to the former he was a foe of Hinduism, to the latter, an enemy of their political aspiration for separation. The Congress continued to count Muslims among its followers, but the majority of them gave their allegiance to the Muslim League, which demanded, in 1940, a separate homeland for Indian Muslims to be carved out of the subcontinent. Hindu opposition to this demand became strident under the leadership of the exclusive political party, the Hindu Mahasabha, and the militant and fanatical socio-religious organization called the Rashtriya Swayamsevak Sangh (RSS) (Smith, 1963). Nationalism in India became polarized, with Hindus and Muslims pitted against each other, and the two turbulent streams of communalism flowed their separate courses toward independence. Communalism, in the sense of the conduct of struggle for independence and power on the basis of religious identity rather than the principle of territory—the usual basis of nationalism—thus came to dominate the internal politics of India.

Gandhi and the Congress could not stem the tide of communalism. India was partitioned in the middle of 1947 and the Islamic state of Pakistan was born in the midst of communal riots on an unprecedented scale resulting in the killing of thousands of Hindus, Muslims and Sikhs in many parts of the country, but most of all in Bengal and Punjab. Millions became refugees and crossed the newly created international frontiers. Gandhi was in deep anguish ; his life's work lay in shambles around him. He did not have to suffer long as he was assassinated early in 1948 by a group of Hindu conspirators owing allegiance to the Hindu Mahasabha and the RSS.

Religion, instead of cleansing politics of its unsavoury aspects, as men of faith such as Mahatma Gandhi and Rabindranath Tagore had believed it would, and instead of being reduced in the political arena to a mere "sign" of distinction between human groups, a "shadow" of itself (Dumont, 1970a : 90-91), in the end fouled them. The failure of Gandhiji was the failure of Vivekananda too : Hinduism could no more serve Hindu society, nor would itself be saved by reformism or revivalism. There would still be Hindus in India, and even Hindu political parties and religious and social organizations ; but the leaders of independent India were to look elsewhere for inspiration and guidance.

Jawaharlal Nehru committed independent India to the custody of a modern secular state ; and he entrusted this state with the principal task of modernizing the country through the application of science and technology for the removal of ignorance, ill health and poverty. Or so he hoped he could do. Nehru was by no means against religion as such, but he was deeply conscious of the harm which religiosity had done in India.

Nehru lost no time in having a very detailed Constitution framed for free India and the same was inaugurated in 1950. The ideal of secularism was clearly embodied in the document; the main relevant clause guaranteed "freedom of conscience and free profession, practice and propagation of religion." Religion was not debarred from public life but it was dissociated from the State, which was required to treat followers of all religions equally, favouring or disfavouring no citizen on the ground of his faith. Secularization in India does not mean privatization of religion ; nor does it mean that the State will have nothing to do with the religious life of the people.

Political scientists seem to be generally agreed that, unfavourable circumstances notwithstanding, the governance of free India has been largely free of religious intolerance. They even venture the opinion that Hinduism is "on the whole favourable to the development of a secular state" and draw attention to "its strong tradition of freedom of conscience and tolerance of religious diversity" (Smith 1963 : 493). It is also pointed out that, though the dissociation of the secular from the spiritual components of Indian civilization took place a long time ago, the temporal-ecclesiastical feuds, characteristic of the history of the West, did not occur here. On the contrary, there has been "a constant interplay and cross-cutting between these two polarities" (Kothari, 1970 : 251).

Other students of Indian history arrive at a similar conclusion about the contemporary situation but, along different lines of argument. Thus, a Hindu social philosopher writes (Saran, 1972 : 32) :

> The step from religious fanaticism, corruption and persecution to science and technology which the West took, and which was unique and significant in being a solution not so much against as outside religion and faith, was a step not taken in India independently of the Western encounter and conquest. While in this sense it is external, it is internal in the sense that it is part of India's history, as also of the history of Hindu tradition.

Most analysts seem to concur, however, that the secular state in India cannot be taken for granted, and that the major threat it has faced since independence is from Hindu communalism.

The above brief discussion points to two conclusions. First, nationalism in India could not rise above religious considerations because it derived sustenance from it directly or indirectly. Hindu communalism found expression in two ways : (1) A blatant communalism which would drive the Muslims out of India and establish a Hindu state ; this was the mirror image of the Muslim demand for partition and Pakistan ; and (2) a refined communalism which sought Muslim support to the national movement without abandoning a Hindu weltanschauung, which in fact was imposed upon the national movement. Those elements which either represented the traditional Hindu attitude of acceptance of religious difference and a consequent respect for it or the Western liberal or socialist attitude of privatization of religion found no alternative but to join hands with the "refined" Hindu communalists. By the time Marxism arrived on the scene, notably in the person of M.N. Roy, the character of the national movement had already been established. The Marxist approach, therefore, remained totally peripheral. Even M.N. Roy himself came to be identified (interestingly enough by an American political scientist) as a "secular Brahman" and his Marxism was transformed into Radical Humanism. That is a story for another day, however.

Second, the future of secularism in India remains uncertain. Will the socialist state, which the Preamble to the Constitution envisages, guarantee it ? This is difficult to tell ; in any case the socialist state remains at the moment no more than a distant hope. A reassertion of the traditional Hindu attitude of acceptance of cultural difference also is to be ruled out because the conditions which generated it have changed beyond recall. Is secularism then a social myth in the sense in which Peter Glesner (1977) uses this notion —an ideological weapon rather than a state of existence ? If so, what does it serve as a mask for ? This is a very important question but one that is not even asked. Unless we ask such uncomfortable questions, it seems to me, we will not be able to go to the roots of the problem ; and without going to the roots of problems there can be no radical solutions.

REFERENCES

Bondurant, J.A., 1969. *Conquest of Violence, the Gandhian Philosophy of Conflict*: Bombay : Oxford University Press.

de Barry, W.P., ed. 1958. *Sources of Indian Tradition*, Vol. II compiled by S.N. Hay and I.H. Qureshi. New York : Columbia University Press.

Chandra, Bipan 1969. Historians of Modern India and Communalism. In : R. Thapar, H. Mukhia and Bipan Chandra, *Communalism and the Writing of Indian History*. New Delhi : People's Publishing House.

Dumont, Louis, 1970a. *Religion, Politics and History in India*. Paris : Mouton.

Dumont, Louis, 1970b. *Homo Hierarchicus* : *Implications of the Caste*. London : Weidenfeld and Nicholson.

Glesner, Peter, 1977. *The Sociology of Secularisation*. London : Routledge and Kegan Paul.

Kothari, Rajni, 1970. *Politics in India*. New Delhi : Orient Longman, Ltd.

Saran, A.K. 1972. The two contexts of secularisation : Western and India. *Islam and the Modern Age*. Vol. 2.

Smith, Donald E., 1969. *India as a Secular State*. Princeton, N.J. Princeton University Press.

3

Secularism in a Multi-Religious Society . The Indian Context

Ravinder Kumar

AN INQUIRY into the significance of secularism in a multi-religious community like India can commence profitably by looking at the meaning given to terms like "secular" and "religious" in different political societies. Such an inquiry can also profitably touch upon the relationship between religious belief and political commitment, on the one hand, and the public and private spheres of social action, on the other. All this merits the most serious consideration, partly because of the intrinsic significance of the terms in question, and partly also because of the prescriptive importance of secularism in a society like India, which embraces a number of religious communities.

Perhaps it would be no exaggeration to state that there are as many varieties of secularism as there are political societies which claim to be secular in their texture. It is, nevertheless, necessary to start with a working definition of the term secularism. Broadly speaking, a secular society is one in which religion, in particular, organized religion, has been completely displaced from the formal as well as the informal arenas of politics, and relegated to the sphere of personal belief and private commitment.[1] However, if this definition of secularism were to be taken rigorously, then it would be impossible for any polity to qualify for such an ascription. In practice, polities which regard themselves as secular, as distinct from polities which are professedly theocratic in character, exhibit considerable variety in their attitude towards religion and religious phenomena.

At one end of the scale, there are polities which are hostile to religion, and seek to undermine religious values and institutions through the means that are available to them. At the other end of the scale, there are polities which content themselves with a stance of neutrality towards such values and institutions. In between, there exist societies whose secularism falls within the two polarities which we have sketched out earlier. In all this, it is important to remember, that the nature and quality of religious belief and practice in a society are important considerations, and we shall have occasion to refer to these factors later in this essay.[2]

Our brief review of secularism, as ideally conceived, and as it obtains in practice, enables us to take a critical look at the significance of this term for a society like India, with its complex social organization, its differentiated economic character, and its plurality of religious belief and commitment. To ascertain the meaning and relevance of secularism for India, it is necessary to examine the structure of society and the quality of social consciousness in the country, contemporaneously as well as in the recent past, just as it is also necessary to examine the relationship between the latter and the modalities of ideological articulation and political mobilization. Such an examination will not only throw light upon the prevailing state of religious belief, and its relationship with the political order, but it will also facilitate the formulation of prescriptive values which can conjure into existence the "good society" in India.

Even if we confine ourselves to only two of the religions of India, namely, Hinduism and Islam, we are at first blush confronted with a bewildering variety of belief and practice among the followers of these religions. Let us look at Hinduism, in the first instance. Sociologically speaking, the term Hinduism refers to a loosely articulated religious ideology which embraces a variety of *jatis*, sects, orders, denominations, populist movements and animistic cults, without any sharp institutional focus. The essentials of Hindu belief and practice are to be found in a relatively small number of philosophical and sacerdotal texts. Yet the wide range of Hindu belief, and the even wider range of Hindu practice, as they obtain empirically, would defy categorization by any scholar.

If we can discern any overall unity in Hinduism, then this unity is to be found in the structural rather than in the intellectual identity of the social groups which thrive under its dispensation. What we mean by the structural identity of Hinduism requires a little clarification. The organization of Hindu society is characterized by a number of endogamous social units called *jatis*, which are located in specific regions. The *jatis* in a particular region are linked to each other through an ideal scheme of social organization called the *varna* system. What gives its specific character to Hindu society is the fact that the life-style of the individual within a *jati* is determined by rigorous usage, just as the hierarchical relationship between different *jatis* in a region is determined with reference to the *varna* order of society.[3] The resulting configuration of society has been compared to an enormous beehive, in which the hive as a whole represents the overall structure of the Hindu social order, while the individual cells in the hive are comparable to the *jatis* of Hindu society.[4]

Since we have approached Hindu society through the values which inform its social constituents, we have identified in *jatis* and *varna* the institutions which characterize the Hindu social order. It would have been equally legitimate to seek to understand Hindu social organization through the economic institutions of society : in particular, through the organization of agricultural production, and also through the control and distribution of this product amongst different social classes. Indeed, without regarding religious values and social institutions as derivative in any vulgar sense of the term, we can still look upon the values and institutions of Hindu society, as the values and institutions of a feudal society, using the word "feudal" in the most extended sense of the term. We would also like to emphasize here that the picture which emerges as a result of looking at Hindu society as a society organized for agricultural production is, in its essentials, not different from the picture which emerges from its examination from the standpoint of institutions like *varna* and *jati*. These two complementary pictures of Hindu society not only deepen our understanding of its social character, but they also raise an interesting question about the relationship between material and ideal factors as determinants of the social order, although we do not propose to linger over this question in the present context.

The basic unit of Hindu society, as it was organized for agricultural production, was the village. This unit consisted of a dominant class or *jati* of zamindars, and a lowly class or *jati* of cultivators, who stood in the relationship of share croppers, or tenants-at-will, or agrestic serfs, or casual labourers, to the former. In some parts of the subcontinent, like Kerala, this simple two tiered society gave way to a more complex three tiered agrarian order. In other parts of the subcontinent, like the regions inhabitated by the Jats in the north, the two tiers fused into a single strata of peasants and cultivators.

These classes in the village, which were involved in the ownership of land and in agricultural production, rested upon *jatis* which performed a variety of roles designed to impart substantial economic self-sufficiency to the village. Such *jatis* were linked to the zamindars drawn from the dominant *jati* through ties of prescription and tradition.

The village, as a unit of social production, was integrated into a locality comprising a number of similarly organized rural communities. Further, such a locality often coincided with the dispersal in space of a *jati* of zamindars, spread over a block of villages varying in number from ten to thirty or forty villages. We have also reason to believe that the elder of a *jati* acted as "superior landlord" of the locality, and that this individual has come down to us through the ages as a "Raja", or a "Rai", or a "Choudhry" (the list is suggestive rather than exhaustive). For the purposes of this essay, we shall call the latter "superior zamindars", to differentiate them from their lesser brethren living within the villages, whom we shall call "village zamindars". More often than not, these localities, which were characterized by the spatial dispersal of a dominant *jati* of village zamindars, also constituted the basic administrative units of the regional or imperial polity with which we are all too familiar. Indeed, if we can generalize on such a scale, we would suggest that the polities of varying orders of complexity were federations of greater or lesser zamindaris, in the sense referred to above, held together by bureaucracies, whose main function was the collection of a tax on the land, and by armies, organized for defence against external aggression and for the maintenance of internal order. The strength of such polities rested upon the strength of the bureaucracies and the armies which they controlled. Hence the fact that the most enduring polities in India were polities which successfully institutionalized bureaucratic and military power, like the Mauryan *imperium*, the Mughal *imperium*, or the British *imperium*.[5]

To carry our analysis of the locality a little further, we would like to dwell a little more upon this segment of the polity. While the myth of self-sufficiency in the village has been set at rest sometime ago, we would like to focus upon the substantially autonomous character of the locality—as an economic unit, and as a social, potitical and administrative unit—by describing the generation and distribution of wealth within it, and by dwelling upon its linkages, on the one hand, with the villages which were its constituents, and on the other, with the larger world of the regional or the imperial polity.

The focal point of social and economic activity in the locality was a township, often called the *cusbah*, which could be only marginally bigger than the more substantial villages in the region. In this township resided a few members of the superior zamindari *jati* of the area. The township could also serve as a market for surplus agricultural produce and for consumer goods fabricated by the local artisans ; as a base for the lowermost echelons of bureaucracy ; and as a religious or cultural centre of greater or lesser importance. The economic life of the *cusbah* revolved around the agricultural surplus siphoned off by the superior zamindars of the locality. Yet it would be a mistake to look upon the relationship between the *cusbah* and the surrounding villages as a purely parasitic relationship. For a portion of the surplus produced in the villages was delivered to the *mandi* in the *cusbah* through the mechanism of the market. The latter nexus was reinforced by the ties between the *sowcars* in the *cusbah*, and the petit money-lenders in the neighbouring villages, who extended credit to the zamidars in their communities.

No less important than the economic ties between the *cusbah* and the villages were the political and administrative links between the former and the latter. As we have already indicated, the *cusbah* housed the bureaucrats responsible for collecting the land-tax from the rural communities in the locality on behalf of the state. The importance of this role in a situation where the land-tax constituted the single most important source of revenue for the State can hardly be over-emphasized. What also needs to be stressed here is the relationship of tension between the bureaucrats and the superior zamindars of the locality. Ideally, the bureaucrats sought to eliminate the superior zamindars altogether, by establishing direct fiscal links with the zamindars within the villages. Practically, the bureaucrats relied upon the goodwill, resources and local knowledge of the superior zamindars resident in the *cusbah* to perform their tax collecting role in a satisfactory manner. Yet, whatever be the nature of the relationship between the collectors of taxes and the superior zamindars, the existence of a distinctive bureaucratic machinery in the *cusbah* served to highlight the identity of the locality, just as it also served to link the *cusbah*, on the one hand, with the villages in the neighbourhood, and on the other, with the larger worlds of region and empire.

When we consider the social structure and religious consciousness of Muslim society in India, we are confronted with a situation which is, at one and the same time, simpler and yet more complex than the situation revealed by our analysis of Hindu society. Theoretically speaking, the followers of Islam, in contrast to the followers of Hinduism, constitute an *umma* or a community, held together in close bonds of allegiance to the doctrine set out in the Koran. The actual structure of Muslim society in India, however, displays a fairly complex hierarchy, which can best be understood through an historical survey of the spread of Islam in the subcontinent.

The first Muslim communities in India were established on the littoral of the Arabian Sea, as a result of commercial contacts between this region and West Asia. This link between coastal India and the original homeland of Islam resulted in the conversion of a number of commercial castes to the new religion, although sections of the peasantry, too, opted for Islam. Slightly later, when Muslim invaders from Central Asia and Afghanistan established their sway over the Indo-Gangetic, plain, they were accompanied by bodies of camp-followers—soldiers of fortune ; or a professional and religious intelligentsia—who set themselves up as a landed aristocracy, or more modestly, as a landed gentry, in this part of the subcontinent. While the bulk of the rural classes in the Indo-Gangetic plain clung to the religion of their forefathers, in north-western and north-eastern India, contemporary Pakistan and Bangladesh, the overwhelming majority of the peasantry, too, entered the community of Islam. A similar process of conversion took place in the cities among the artisans and craftsmen, though the mode of their conversion remains something of a mystery at the present state of our knowledge of medieval Indian society.

The religious sensibility of different sections of Muslim society in India showed substantial differences in quality and tone.[6] The dominant class amongst the Muslims, the aristocracy and the gentry of the Indo-Gangetic plain, not only controlled a predominant share of social and economic power, but it was also drawn closely into religious orthodoxy, despite denominational and sectarian differences. The artisans and craftsmen of the cities were separated by a deep gulf from this dominant section of Muslim society. For, apart from their lowly status, the former often retained un-Islamic customs and rituals, which reflected their indigenous origin.

The gulf of wealth, status, and values which separated the Muslim landed classes from the lowly artisans and craftsmen also separated the former from the cultivating classes of the north-west and the north-east of the subcontinent. As is true for the poor urban classes, the social anthropology of Islam as a populist religion in the villages is a subject about which we know very little. Yet it is obvious that the religious sensibility of the Muslim peasant, who married the great tradition of Islam to local cult practices and animistic rituals, was qualitatively different from the religious sensibility of the aristocracy and the gentry. This is also true of the Muslim commercial classes of the western and south-western coastal region, whose Islam rested upon indigenous influences that were largely absent in the Islam of the landed classes of the Indo-Gangetic plain.[7]

How can we sum up our picture of Islam in India ? Despite the ideals held out in classical literature it would be more legitimate to talk of Muslim "communities" in the subcontinent rather than of a single Muslim "community". We have, earlier, given a brief survey of the differentials in wealth, status and sensibility which characterized various Muslim social groups in India. Yet despite these differentials, if Muslim society were to be compared in its social structure and its religious values to Hindu society, certain important contrasts would be observed. Notwithstanding the social gulf between different classes in Muslim society, the religion of Islam is based upon an ideal—the ideal of a closely knit community or *umma* held together in loyalty to the doctrines adumbrated in the Koran—to which Hinduism can offer no parallel. The concept of the *umma* presents a theoretical basis for unity the like of which is conspicuous by its absence in Hinduism. This is so despite the fact that the transformation of India under the British *imperium* generated new solidarities in Hindu society.

Our brief survey of the social structure and the religious consciousness of the two major religious communities in India suffers from a number of inadequacies. But over and above everything else, it presents too static a picture of changing social reality in the subcontinent. We have already hinted at the transformation which the British *imperium* conjured into existence in the material and the intellectual life of the country, and the consequent changes in the quality of social ties which linked men to each other in political society. We shall now dwell some more upon the nature of these changes, which shaped anew the political climate of India, and in doing so, determined the variety of secularism which characterizes contemporary politics in the subcontinent.

We have, earlier in this essay, described political society in India as a federation of greater or lesser zamindaris held together by bureaucracies linked to regional or imperial States. It would, perhaps, be valid to say that this description of the Indian polity is particularly true for centuries prior to the 19th century. Under the British dispensation, a qualitative change took place in this state of affairs. To extract a tribute from her colony, through spacious commerce as well as through an oppressive land-tax, the British devised a more centralized system of administration than had been devised by any of their predecessors. In their initial administrative arrangements in India, the British lacked the political self-confidence to dispossess the superior zamindars. The Permanent Settlement of Bengal, therefore, reaffirmed the "property" rights of such zamindars, though it trenched heavily into their political and judicial prerogatives, and also drew them into close association with the imperial administration.[8] Be that as it may, the centralizing tendency of the British Government found its clearest expression in the administrative systems created in southern, western, and northern India, the so-called *raiyatwari* and *mahalwari* systems.[9] In these areas, the intermediaries who had mediated since times immemorial between villages, on the one hand, and the bureaucratic representatives of the States, on the other, were eliminated, and property in land was settled, on zamindars within villages. The resulting peasant societies resting upon a class of proprietors whom we have hitherto called "village zamindars", were controlled by a centralized bureaucracy novel to the subcontinent, though recent researches have shown the limited authority exercised by this bureaucracy.[10]

The creation of a centralized polity was one facet of the transformation which took place in India under British aegis. The erosion of traditional solidarities, and the widening of economic, political, and intellectual horizons, was yet another facet of this process. Inspired by the aggressive spirit of capitalism in the first flush of its triumph in Great Britain, the Imperial Government in India initiated a number of measures which undermined the insularity of the rural communities in the subcontinent. All this was achieved by creating a new system of laws, and by devising administrative and economic institutions which facilitated the exportation of agricultural products to markets overseas, and the importation of industrial products for internal markets. The tragedy of British rule lay in that these changes took place in a context which impoverished India and linked her in ties of subordination to the economy of Great Britain.

As we have already suggested, the extension of economic horizons in India under British aegis was closely associated with an extension of social and intellectual horizons. The latter transformation has been spelt out in a rich literature dealing with the impact of western ideas upon the Hindu and Muslim intelligentsia ; and their consequent attempts to recast their own intellectual traditions, or to adopt novel values, with the objective of promoting the welfare of the community. We have reason to believe that as a result of those changes, the social consciousness of the individual began to outgrow the worlds of *jati* and *varna*, though it may not be easy to present concrete evidence in support of so tenuous a social transformation.

It is in this context of social flux and economic change that we propose to examine the growth of secular politics in our country, both the politics of nationalism prior to 1947, and the politics of independent India since 1947. Such an examination will not only illuminate this politics, but will also throw light upon the quality of secularism which has taken root in the soil of India, and upon the strengths as well as the weaknesses of this secularism.

Even outside the formal arena of politics, some members of the Hindu intelligentsia had, in the second half of the 19th century, advanced the concept of an overarching Hindu community as the true basis of a movement for national regeneration in the subcontinent.[11] But in the formal sphere of politics, the first theory of secular nationalism to be put forward was the "liberal plural" theory, which was advanced by the moderate nationalists in the closing decades of the 19th century.[12] The principles of this theory can be summed up in two sentences : Religion ought to be divorced from politics, and relegated to the sphere of private belief and commitment. If such a state of affairs was attained, then even in a multi-religious society like India, individuals owing allegiance to different religions would face no difficulty in extending their loyalty to the nation.

The liberal plural theory of social action was elegantly couched in the idiom of modern politics. But as an ideology of nationalism in India, it suffered from some fatal flaws. Only the upper middle classes and the westernized intelligentsia possessed the sort of education that enabled them to respond positively to such an ideology. Inevitably, therefore, the liberal plural theory became the ideology of the upper middle classes, and was unable to gain acceptability among wider social circles.

When we consider the limitations of the liberal plural theory of secular nationalism, it should occasion no surprise that it was soon displaced by other ideologies. A theory of nationalism resting upon religious symbols held the possibility of making a deeper impact upon the community, despite the wide range of belief and practice which characterized both Hinduism and Isiam in the subcontinent.

The "orthodox plural" theory of secular nationalism, first enunciated as an integral whole by Gandhi, was precisely such an ideology. While the moderate nationalists tried to relegate religion to the sphere of private belief, Gandhi deliberately picked upon religion as the basis for political action and national identity.[13] The "nation-to-be" that was India, so Gandhi argued, should draw upon the religious sensibility of the Hindus, the Muslims and other communities, to attract the masses to the politics of nationalism. Once the use of popular religious symbols had drawn the masses into nationalist politics, the experience of participation in a common struggle would conjure into existence an overarching national identity that would be all the more strong because it rested upon religious belief and commitment.

It need hardly be pointed out that our exposition of the orthodox plural theory of secular nationalism is brief to the point of a caricature. It distorts Gandhi's subtle concept of religion and his lofty vision of the intimate link between religion and politics as the basis for an enduring national identity for India. Gandhi's spirituality took active cognizance of the problem of poverty in India, and it had little use for the empty formalism of institutionalized religion. All these qualifications notwithstanding, the spiritual underpinning of Gandhian politics, and his belief in the religious basis of a national identity for India, stand out as distinctive characteristics of the orthodox plural theory of secular nationalism.

If a theory of politics is to be judged by its ability to inspire social action, then the orthodox plural theory of Gandhi has to be looked upon as a successful theory in the context of nationalism in the subcontinent. By appealing to different religious communities through issues dear to their followers, and by marrying such appeals to policies reassuring to the rich and the powerful in the subcontinent, Gandhi was able to force a formidable nationalist alliance, the strength of which was reflected in a number of epic agitations against the British Government in India. Yet the success of orthodox pluralism, a success confined to the sphere of political mobilization, left two problems as a legacy for politics in India after 1947. First, Gandhi's belief that religious cleavages could be healed by using religious loyalties as the basis for nationhood proved to be a miscalculation. With the British Government anxious to exploit every division within society in India, the ideology of orthodox pluralism heightened instead of reducing the gulf between different religious communities.[14] Even in the decades after 1947, therefore, religious and communitarian solidarities continue to plague politics in India, though it is important to remember that such solidarities often provide a mask for the promotion of class interests. Secondly, the device of drawing the rich and the powerful into the nationalist struggle, often through policies which more than protected their interests, ensured that these classes would assume a dominating position in politics after independence. Neither of these consequences, we would emphasize, was of Gandhi's seeking. Yet their presence in the structure of contemporary politics in India is a fact which cannot be easily denied.

Even as Gandhi was drawing new classes in Indian society to the cause of nationalism, through appealing to their religious loyalties, a rival theory of politics made its appearance in the field. Inspired by the ideology of socialism, a new generation of nationalists tried to conjure into existence a theory of secular politics resting upon the aspirations of the poor classes in the cities as well as in the villages. Like the liberal plural theory of secular nationalism, the advocates of the "radical socialist" view refused to look upon religious loyalties, prescriptively or existentially, as related to social action or to national identity.[15] The only basis for an enduring national identity, so they believed, rested upon a politics which linked the social and the economic welfare of the poor to the existential reality of nationhood. Religion, they further believed, should be free to play its role in the private life of the citizen, but it should not be permitted to intrude in the formal arena of politics. The radical socialist view of religion, as we have suggested earlier, was closely related to the liberal plural view of religion. But unlike the advocates of the latter, the advocates of the former addressed themselves to the poorer classes in society, and their efforts were directed towards bringing about a redistribution of wealth and power amongst various social groups in the subcontinent.

The radical socialist theory of secular nationalism was articulated both within and without the Indian National Congress, the premier party of nationalism in India, during the second quarter of the 20th century. But despite its potential appeal for the poor classes in rural as well as in urban society, particularly in a country where wealth was as unequally distributed as it was in India, the advocates of the radical socialist view were unable to gain much support for their standpoint, in the face of the overwhelming popularity of the ideas propagated by Gandhi.

The popularity of the orthodox plural theory of secular nationalism can be attributed to a variety of reasons. First and foremost, it owed its popularity to the strength of religious feeling among different classes and communities in India. This religious feeling, as pointed out earlier, was utilized by Gandhi to provide a popular base for nationalism. Equally powerful a reason for the popularity of the orthodox plural viewpoint was the fact that, despite its appeal for the lowly classes, it did not challenge the hold of the rich classes, industrial, commercial, and professional, over the levers of social and economic power. A theory of nationalist politics, which could rally the lowly classes around the demand for national self-determination, without raising awkward question about the ownership and distribution of wealth in the community, commended itself in no uncertain terms to the propertied classes. This is not to imply that Gandhi was willing to subordinate the problems of the poor to the avarice of the rich. This is merely to suggest that the upper and middle classes discerned in the orthodox plural theory a convenient mask for their class interests ; a mask, moreover, which did not come in the way of the political mobilization of the poor classes in society.

While the organization of the poor classes on a radical basis offers formidable problems in any society, the problem was a particularly intractable one so far as India was concerned. Why this was so shall soon become clear. Earlier in this essay, we have compared political society in the subcontinent to a federation of greater or lesser zamindaris, loosely held together by social, political, and economic ties. We have also drawn attention to the extension of social and economic horizons and the strengthening of political and administrative linkages which took place under the British *imperium*, if only to facilitate the exploitation of the subcontinent. Yet despite the integrative processess initiated by the British Government, the residual fragmentation of India into localities and regions continued to thwart those nationalists who wanted to draw the peoples of the subcontinent into the association of nationhood. This fragmentation was equally formidable an obstacle in the way of those leaders who sought to shape the national identity of India on the basis of a politics resting upon a revolutionary transformation of the locus of social and economic power in the community.

If our understanding of the link between the orthodox plural theory of secular nationalism and the emergence of antagonistic communal solidarities in India is legitimate, then certain logical conclusions can be drawn about the variety of politics best designed to conjure into existence the "good society" in India. Theories of secular nationalism which rest upon a religious or communitarian basis cannot be expected to stimulate a creative politics in India. By the same measure, theories of social action which differentiate between religion and politics can be trusted to yield beneficial results in the arena of politics. Of course, secular politics of the latter variety can either rest upon the interests of the privileged classes, or it can rest upon the interests of the poor classes. We thus have a choice between two alternative courses of social action, both of them genuinely secular, with a clear indication of the consequences cf our choice.

The changes which have taken place in India, since 1947, provide a concrete basis for the prescriptive choice which we have posed earlier. The growth of an industrial economy, and the commercialization of the rural economy, have greatly undermined the structural isolation of the traditional units of society in India, thereby removing one of the major obstacles to the organization of the poor classes on the basis of a radical politics. The way is thus clear for the emergence of a truly secular society in India ; a society which combines religious freedom with social equity and economic democracy ; a society, moreover, in which the creativity of the individual can express itself in a climate free of irrationality and communal strife.

NOTES AND REFERENCES

1. Perhaps the best definition of secularism which I have come acress is the one given by Professor S. Alam Khundmiri : "Secularism is not a philosophy of life which excludes all other alternative explanations of reality or human situation; it is simply an attitude of mind which is compatible with any metaphysical theory and religious doctrine in so far as they do not usurp the right of man to solve the problems of his earthly existence in the light of his own reason and in the guidance of the principle of human happiness". See S.A. Khundmiri, "Secularism, Religion and Education in India", in V.K. Sinha (ed.) *Secularism in India* (Bombay, 1968).
2. D.E. Smith, *India as a Secular State* (Princeton, 1963). Professor Smith's pioneering study of secularism in India suggests that India falls midway between the two polarities which we have suggested. See in particular pp. 499-501 of his book.
3. For the portrayal of Hindu social structure, I have relied upon the writings of the distinguished sociologist, Professor M.N. Srinivas. See in particular M.N. Srinivas, *Caste in Modern India and Other Essays* (London, 1962); his *Social Change in Modern India* (Berkeley, 1968), and his (ed.) *India's Villages* (Bombay, 1960).
4. Barrington Moore, *Social Origins of Democracy and Dictatorship*. (London, 1960) p.458.
5. The structural model of the Indian polity which I have drawn is culled from two different sources. First, the distinguished work done by Aligarh historians on late medieval society, see in particular, Saiyid Nurul Hasan, *Thoughts on Agrarian Problems in Mughal India* (New Delhi, 1973) and his *Zamindars Under the Mughals* in R.E. Fryken-

berg *Land Control aud Social Structure in Indian Society* (Madison, 1973) also I. Habib, *The Agrarian System of Mughal India* (New York, 1963). Secondly, the researches of B.Cohn and his associates at the University of Chicago, see, in particular, B. Cohn, "Political Systems in Eighteenth Century India : The Benaras Region" in *Journal of American Oriental Society*, Vol. LXXX, pp. 312-320.

6. On this see M.Mujeeb, *The Indian Muslims* (London, 1967). In the "Introduction" to this book (pp. 9-20) Mujeeb shows the wide range of Muslim belief and practice in India.
7. For two excellent studies of social differentiation and social structure in Muslim India see :
   (*a*) T.N. Madan (ed.) *Muslim Communities of South Asia* (New Delhi, 1976).
   (*b*) I.Ahmad (ed.) *Caste and Social Stratification among the Muslim* (New Delhi, 1973).
8. For the Permanent Settlement and its effects see :
   (*a*) S.Gopal, *The Permanent Settlement in Bengal and its Results* (London, 1949).
   (*b*) *Report of the Land Revenue Commission, Bengal* (Calcutta, 1949); E. Stokes, *English Utilitarians and India* (Oxford, 1959); and finally, N.K. Sinha, "Administration 1793-1833" in N.K. Sinha (ed.) *The History of Bengal* (1757-1905) (Calcutta, 1967).
9. For survey of the ryotwari and associated land-systems see :
   (*a*) N. Mukherjee, *The Ryotwari System of Madras* (Calcutta, 1962) ;
   (*b*) R. Kumar, *Western India in the Nineteenth Century* (London, 1968) ;
   (*c*) T.R. Metcalf, *The Aftermath of Revolt* (Princeton, 1964).
10. Vide R.E. Frykenberg, *Guntur District 1788-1848* (Oxford, 1965).
11. See Bankimchandra's *Letters on Hinduism* reproduced in J.C. Bogal (ed.) *Bankim Bachnavali* (Calcutta, 1969).
12. This argument rests partly on Professor D.E. Smith's book entitled *India as a Secular Society* quoted earlier, and partly also in A. Seal, *The Emergence of Indian Nationalism* (Cambridge, 1968).
13. The most sophisticated statement of this argument is to be found in R.N. Iyer, *The Moral and Political Thought of Mahatma Gandhi*, (Delhi, 1973).
14. This is the main thesis of my "Introduction" in R. Kumar, *Essays on Gandhian Politics* (Oxford, 1971).
15. The most distinguished exponent of this view in the Indian political scene was Jawaharlal Nehru. See his most recent biography, the monumental work by S. Gopal, entitled *Jawaharlal Nehru : A Biography, Volume One 1889-1947* (Bombay, 1976).

4

Towards Secularization : Nationalism in Nineteenth Century India

Sudhir Chandra

NATIONALISM transforms itself, in every historical setting, from a conjunction of material interests to an autonomous force swaying masses of human beings through appeals to their emotions. Beginning with promises to satify the material interests of the few, it grows to invoke the ideal interests of the many; of course without ceasing to perform the former function. In its essence a secular force, in its ideological manifestations nationalism tends to transgress its own essence.

In India the emergence of nationalism meant the introduction of a new kind of community orientation in a religion-bound traditional society organized on the basis of all-embracing social units. By inducing group formations that cut across traditional solidarities, it tended to secularize aspects of Indian society. But its ideological rationalizations—its transformation from a matter of interest to a matter of sentiment—took place in circumstances that were not always conducive to secularism. An attempt is here made to sketch the possibilities and limitations of secularization in modern India by focussing attention on the situation in which nationalist politics and ideology took shape.

Nationalism in India was stirred into being by the discovery of the damage that was being done to certain material interests by British rule. It was a gradual discovery that occurred at different levels over a period of time. Naturally the sections which first noticed an adverse effect on their interests took the lead in organizing political associations for seeking redress. The early political associations, though not exclusive in their membership, were dominated by an upper middle class oligarchal leadership to an extent that transmission of hereditary assets often included political leadership also. Stress on dominant interests created tensions. Representatives of political awakening, but less privileged and organized sections, began to insist on widening the social base and concerns of these associations. Tussles for leadership ensued.

These tussles meant, until the 1880s, a definite broadening of nationalist politics on secular lines. Motivated basically by their secular corporate interests, rival groups buttressed their claims on the ground that they really represented the interests of the "people" vis-a-vis sectional interests. This was done without invoking religious sentiments. An example may be cited. Unhappy with the sleepy and selfish character of the Bombay Association, some persons led by Pherozeshah Mehta and K.T. Telang decided to form "a political association of active character". But Mehta, a Parsi, and Telang, a Hindu, thought it prudent to approach Badruddin Tyabji, a Muslim, and seek his cooperation "as the representative of the third community to which he belonged" in order that the proposed Bombay Presidency Association might be acceptable to all sections of society without reference to denominational distinctions.[1]

The conscious care taken to project a secular image and the manner of implementing this care constituted a pattern that was later perfected by the Indian National Congress. It revealed both the secular concern of nineteenth century nationalist politics and the ill-preparedness of contemporary Indian society for secular politics. For, evidently, among the determinants of its prospective following were not only the aims and objectives of an association or movement but also the religious affiliations of its organizers and leaders.

Alliances prompted by coalescence of material interests were secular in that they were formed in response to felt economic and political needs. But the very logic of their formation tended to make them fluid. If demands of self-interest could induce a person to opt into a group, so could they, in a different situation, induce him to opt out of it. Moreover, these alliances—even when formally organized in the form of a political association—possessed few effective sanctions, material or moral, to enforce continued loyalty on their members.

The situation, however, was not altogether hopeless. In its cohesive role material interest was curbing its own freedom of separative motivation. Influential and articulate sections had, in the tussle for leadership and promotion of their own interests, rationalized group interests as national interests. Such rationalization invested with some respectability the alliances that these interests had brought about. A none too vague unity of sentiment also came to attach gradually to these alliances.

Freedom of material motivation was particularly curbed as greater stress came to be laid on issues that pointed towards a fundamental antagonism between "national" and "imperial" interests. As demonstrated in British Indian politics relating to such matters as taxation, famine, racialism, employment, or the drain, this antagonism seemed invariably to operate against Indians. Stress on this aspect of British rule imparted to the growing public opinion a moral force that it became progressively difficult to disregard.

Instances may be given to illustrate the increasing effectiveness of material interests as a cohesive force. Faced with an unprecedented depletion of finances after 1857, the government was obliged to raise the import duties in 1859. This was generally looked upon by Indians as a belated and partial redress of an old injustice that had been done by the adoption of free trade. But two prominent members of the British Indian Association, the premier political association in the country at that time, struck a discordant note by opposing the enhanced tariffs. They even joined an agitation launched by resident Europeans, and did so without any ostensible damage to their reputation as public men.[2] As businessmen these two members, Ram Gopal Ghosh and Durga Charan Law, were bothered by the likely reduction in the margin of their profits from the sale of imported articles.

By the 1870s, however, it was no longer possible to adopt an unabashedly selfish stance in regard to public issues. Thus the British Indian Association opposed Lytton's statutory civil service scheme even though the class it represented was likely to be benefited by the scheme. Of course, self-interest was not submerged by nationalist sentiment. But the kind of freedom enjoyed by Ghosh and Law in the 1850s was no longer available.

It was now safer and more prudent to respect public opinion—even contribute to its making and promotion—and at the same time devise ways of circumventing it to promote self-interest. This is exemplified by Bharatendu Harishchandra. He preached *swadeshi*—economic autarky as part of nationalist tactics and ideology—even as he advertised in his own *Magazine* that his firm had "received various goods direct from England...consisting of new and choicest novelties of the season that are not to be had in the Indian markets."[3]

The connection between material interests and nationalism and the mode of its early political organization provided and strengthened the secular potential of Indian nationalism. At the level of ideology this was propped up by the principles of equality, democracy, and freedom which educated Indians were quick to employ—even when they were not demanding the severance of the British connection—as ideological ballast for constitutional agitations. Nor were they slow to comprehend the possibilities of associational politics within the autocratic structure of British colonial administration. This comprehension found, with one notable exception, a largely secular manifestation during the nineteenth century.

Its secular springs and props notwithstanding, it was within a specific traditional ambience that nationalism developed in India. It certainly represented a new group consciousness that tended to transcend the existing social divisions. Yet, circumstanced as it was, it could not but be influenced by the very social anastomosis that it was poised to transform. Not only was the ideological conception of nationalism attempted within the traditional ambience, the adoption of a particular strategy of political action within a plural colonial society was also encouraged by this ambience.

While nationalism emerged in response to the perception of common material interests, it did not represent a class or classes capable of providing a viable alternative to the existing social divisions based on caste and/or religion. Group formations across caste and religious affiliations on the basis of economic ties did bring people together—but only briefly and for limited specific purposes without supplanting the traditional social unities within which the larger part of people's lives continued to move. These traditional unities, moreover, possessed the advantages of external compulsion which rested on minatory sanctions, capped by the dreaded weapon of excommunication, in addition to the suitably internalized responses of their members which ensured that the sanctions would have to be only rarely employed. True, the facility of this hold was declining progressively. But in the absence of alternative social arrangements that could cater to the basic psychological and social needs of their members, the logic of gregariousness perpetuated the hold of traditional solidarities.

This meant that modernization would take the form of a fusion between a new kind of consciousness and traditional thought processes ; that India, a world in transition, would change and yet stick to its traditions. Thus, it happened that even the best liberal specimens of English education remained emotionally wedded to their own traditions. The whole history of social reform, from Rammohan Roy to Ranade and Malabari, illustrates that, whatever its motivation, change was invariably sought and justified as refurbished tradition.[4] Tactical considerations played but a marginal role in this reliance on tradition. There obtained a general belief, real or simulated, in the richness and ultimate superiority of Indian culture. That enabled Indians to withstand the cultural onslaught which was integral to the colonial relationship.

Revivalism was rooted in a political domination that threatened cultural submersion. Except in his exaggerations, Dayananda was not atypical in being a revivalist. Uninfluenced by him, others also essayed reconstruction of their past in order to overhaul the present. Thus Peary Mohan Mukherji, a member of the staid British Indian Association, was not content to record the greatness of ancient India in theology, philosophy and art ; he hailed as "unparalleled" her "wisdom and excellence" in politics, claiming that the ancients in India had effectively safeguarded their political rights by institutionalizing separation of state powers.[5]

Even in those early times people were so keen about political rights that the question whether legislative powers should be united in the same person or body of persons who exercised executive powers was put in issue in some deadly battles in which Porrosram was at the head of the liberal party. The result was that the legislative power was withdrawn from the hands of the executive and entrusted to Brahmin counsellors.

Even westernized liberal leaders like Surendranath Bannerji saw in glorified history "the strongest incentive to the loftiest patriotism" and employed it to inspire the youth. Addressing the Calcutta Young Men's Association, he said in 1876 :[6]

> ...What Hindoo is there who does not feel himself a nobler being altogether, as he recalls to mind the proud list of his illustrious countrymen, graced by thrice-immortal names of a Valmiki and a Vyasa, a Panini and a Patanjali, a Gautama and a Sankaracharya? For ours was a most glorious past.

The convergence of western liberal and indigenous traditional cultural influences, to offer a rather unexpected but typical case, is epitomized in R.C. Dutt. A member of the covenanted civil service who rose to preside over the Lucknow session of the Indian National Congress in 1900, Dutt was one of the ideologues of economic nationalism who wrote the classic two-volume *exposé* of the material consequences of British rule in India. But he also wrote, apart from *A History of Civilization in Ancient India*, two novels in Bengali—*Maharashtra Jivan Prabhat* and *Rajput Jivan Sandhya*—which so romanticized two periods of Indian history as to invoke the reader's nostalgia, pathos, and patriotism.[7] This interrelation, in Dutt's own person, between secular economic nationalism and historical romance with strong communal overtones represents the fusion of modern and traditional influences in the evolution of nationalism in India.

The impact of the co-existence of political liberalism and cultural conservatism on the evolution of nationalism has not received sufficient attention. Rather, a misleading binary classification of tendencies has gained general acceptance. The following excerpt from an otherwise sensitive scholar like Richard Lannoy is typical of this logically neat but historically simplistic approach :[8]

> The beginnings of nationalism should be viewed against this cultural background of intellectual ferment, with the Westernised elite turning toward liberalism and the conser-

> vatives to Hinduism. The liberal advocates of social and political reform were uncompromising in their disapproval of traditional culture, which they considered a retrogressive force that submerged the masses in superstition.

This kind of categorization presents a sharper differentiation of persons and movements as progressive and reactionary than is warranted by the actual historical situation.

The hold of tradition—refurbished and idealized tradition—imparted to nationalism that necessary emotional appeal which mere conjunction of material interests could not have possessed. But the resultant culturization of nationalism proved inimical to its secularization. Religion could not be kept apart from appeals to history or tradition. Such, indeed, was the popular understanding of the country's past that selection of particular periods of it for glorification depended on one's religious affiliations. Cultural superiority, too, was asserted in terms that introduced religious overtones. When the Hindus remembered their ancient glory, they thought of its eclipse following the Muslim conquest. The Muslims, who could hardly feel attached to an Indian past prior to their arrival, revelled in the remembrance of their ascendancy.

The participation of liberal nationalists like Ranade, Dutt and Bannerji in the reconstruction of an inspiring past lent respectability to the exercise. But the fact of their secular stance in nationalist politics could barely induce the Muslims to be inspired by the past that was being reconstructed, unless it was to undertake a matching exercise of their own. This complicated the situation further. It meant that the projection of religious and sectional loyalties in terms of historical glorification of the Hindus would pass for cultural nationalism. But the projection of similar grandeur would be castigated as communal if undertaken by the Muslims.

This was the upshot of a pervasive and, often, unconscious prejudice. The naturalness with which this kind of historical glorification was undertaken by the Hindus as an exercise in nationalism stemmed largely from the unconscious nature of this prejudice. Complications arose and conscious mending became difficult in proportion as the prejudice operated unconsciously.

A particularly telling example, the kind of which does not easily come an historian's way, relates to Gokhale who symbolized the very essence of liberalism. Speaking on the Seditious Meetings Bill, on 18 October 1907, Gokhale said that what was described by the government as sedition was a creation of repressive official policy. Maintaining that "a policy of steady and courageous conciliation" was the "only way in which the wings of disaffection can be clipped", he said, "With Bengal unconciliated in the matter of Partition there will be no real peace, not only in Bengal but in any other province in India." He conceded that the question had been "complicated by the fact that the Mahomedan population of East Bengal expect certain educational and other advantages to accrue to them from Partition." But he saw no reason to despair and observed :[9]

> But surely it cannot be beyond the resources of statesmanship to devise a scheme whereby while the expected advantages are fully secured to the *Mahomedans*, the *people of Bengal* may also have their grievances removed (Italics added).

What was, in Gokhale's mind, this distinction between the Mahomedans on the one hand and the people of Bengal on the other ? He was obviously unaware of the implications of this distinction like he was unaware of the very fact, perhaps, that he was making a distinction. More than the perceptible expectations of the Muslims it was the imperceptible operation of this unconscious prejudice that hampered the growth of secular nationalism.

But to argue that the secular potential of Indian nationalism was placed under stress only by its culturization in a specific *milieu* would be to miss the complex dynamics of the manifestation of a particular motivation. For even secular motivation could assume non-secular manifestations. Indeed, the very forces that nourished secular Indian nationalism also lay at the root of separative tendencies that sought their basis in a religious identity.

Nor did cultural nationalism *per se* invariably hamper the organization of nationalist politics on secular lines. After all, in spite of the hold on them of a romanticized past, people like

Ranade, Dutt, and Bannerji did remain steadfast in their commitment to secular nationalist politics. Hence the co-existence of political liberalism and cultural conservatism, its unintended fall-out notwithstanding.

It was, paradoxically enough, secular motivation relating to material interest and power that contributed to the activization of the latent conflict between secular nationalist politics and culturized nationalist ideology, and subjected their co-existence to increasing tensions. It was not a coincidence that group conflicts relating to material interest and tussle for leadership were, until the 1880s, mainly carried in a secular idiom. But during the 1890s religion came to be in growing use as the "moderate" Congress leadership began to be challenged by its "extremist" opponents.

This change of pattern is substantially explained by an enlargement of the constituency that needed to be addressed, and by the absence of a sharp cleavage in the interests represented by the conflicting groups. During the late 1870s and early 1880s, for example, when the Indian Association was fighting for pre-eminence vis-ā-vis the British Indian Association, the constituency to be addressed comprised, apart from the government, a small politically conscious class. Claims were no doubt made by both on behalf of the "people". But in the state of political consciousness then prevailing, this implied little obligation to reach out to the people ; though the Indian Association did go through the motion of holding some meetings of the cultivators while exposing the selfish dominance of the wealthier zamindars over the British Indian Association. Moreover, there was a definite divergence of interests between these zamindars and the educated middle classes ; the latter—however unsatisfactorily defined—having become a category of self-identification in contemporary Indian society.

No such antagonism of interests divided the "extremists" and the "moderates". As before in the growth of associational politics, this time also the challengers thought of unsaddling the established leadership by enlarging the constituency in order to stake their claims to be the representatives of the people. By now, however, this gradual enlargement of constituency had reached a point where further enlargement for buttressing claims of representing the people would entail the obligation of actually reaching out to sections of them. But it seemed hardly prudent to so attempt a reconciliation of the existing plethora of interests as to provide a genuine economic base for popular participation in nationalist politics. Whatever general promises could safely be made to the people by the challengers could be made by the established leadership as well. There were limits beyond which the more or less identical interests represented by the rival groups could not be risked.

This was not necessarily a matter of conscious design. Barring highly organized and clearly articulated corporate interests, nascent group interests had a way of groping toward a course of action that was favourable to them. What was, however, a matter of conscious design was the caution with which the challengers acted in response to the constraints of a colonial situation. For, given the state of national consciousness, they had to devise a programme that would be consonant with the co-existence of nationalism and loyalty to alien rule.

In view of the constraints within which they had to woo the people, the challengers could have differed from the established leadership mainly in their idiom. Naturally, instead of offering a radical programme, they played up cultural nationalism. Far from radicalizing nationalist politics, this kind of politicization of larger sections of people gave it a conservative orientation. Nationalism, consequently, weakened traditional loyalties less than it was strengthened by them.

Considering the factors that influenced the choice of the mode of reaching out to larger sections of people—through cultural-religious appeals rather than through radical economic-political programmes—it seems difficult to accept the usual assertion about the absence of alternatives before the Indian nationalists. It is this failure to explore the nature of motivation that, perhaps, leads to the belief that "Indian nationalist leaders could reach the masses only be communicating new aspirations through familiar symbols like the Mother Goddess";[10] or that unless the nationalists "appealed to religion", nationalism would have remained "limited to the small educated elite, and consequently more or less powerless".[11]

There was nothing imperative about appeals to religion. And the crucial factor related not to the mode of communicating new aspirations to the masses, but to the constraints within which these aspirations were conceived. If, however, invocation of a glorified cultural legacy was imperative, it was not because of the need to enlist the masses but because of the threat of cultural submersion.[12]

This reliance on ideology in a manner that ensured the promotion of certain common interests both weakened and strengthened the secular potential of Indian nationalism. It retarded the general secularization of society by bolstering up traditional solidarities. It created, moreover, tensions which provided psychological sustenance to a parallel nationalism that was beginning to emerge. But, at the same time, it enlarged the constituency which the Indian National Congress as a secular political organization was able to mobilize.

But when a different coalescence of material interests sought to promote itself by appealing to another traditional category of differentiation, a greater stress was placed on the emerging Indian nationalism than it was evidently able to withstand. The beginning of this development lay in the projection of material interests in terms of Muslims as a community. It was natural in a society used to perceiving social phenomena within the framework of caste or religious categories that such projections should enjoy a high degree of credibility. This process was particularly facilitated by the mediation of alien rulers. It was here that the fact of the development of nationalism in a traditional and colonial ambience encouraged secular motivation to assume non-secular manifestations.

In the long run, continuing stress on the ideological aspect of nationalism proved inimical to its secular potential. Indeed, as an eventually conservative force in nationalist politics, it created a vested interest in containing the secularization of nationalism. For, integration at the ideological rather than the economic level held out to the beneficiaries of nationalism the possibility of containing the disruptive potential inherent in a highly segmented and differentiated society. This stress on the ideological aspect did boomerang in a significant respect when a parallel nationalism took root. Within the latter nationalism, too, similar utilization of non-secular forces for secular ends could be discerned. The process, though, was not always conscious, and the two levels were getting inextricably interlinked.

NOTES AND REFERENCES

1. J.R.B. Jeejeebhoy, *Some Unpublished and Later Speeches and Writings of the Hon. Sir Pherozeshah Mehta*, Bombay, 1918, p. 185.
2. *Bengal Hurkaru*, 18, 21, 24, 26, 28, 30 March 1859; *Friend of India*, 31 March 1859.
3. *Haris Chandra's Magazine*, 15 January 1874.
4. See C.Y. Chintamani, ed., *Indian Social Reform*, Madras, 1901; especially the presidential addresses delivered at the annual sessions of the Indian National Social Conference.
5. A paper read in 1869. See *Selections from the Writings and Speeches of Raja Peary Mohan Mukherjee*, pp. 1-2.
6. *Speeches of Surendranath Banerjee*, Madras, not dated, p. 1.
7. How extensive and immediate the effect of Dutt's writings was can be seen from the Diary of a Gujarati graduate who later rose to be an eminent poet and critic. Writing on 1 February 1890, B.K. Thakore recorded in his Diary : "*Jivanprabhat* moved me for days and I could not rest until I beg (sic) a long review of it in Gujarati. I dashed off ten pages but the subject grew as I went on writing and the review proper is not begun yet." H.M. Trivedi, ed., *B.K. Thakore : A Diary Part II : Year 1889-1900*, Baroda, 1976, p. 9. On 20 April 1892 he wrote : "Finished Dutt's Ancient India, I remember the first time, 4 years back, that the reading of Macaulay first awakened me to Nationality and national progress. . . . Dutt's is the first book by an Indian I have read capable of exciting in the sympathetic heart something like the same feeling." *Ibid.*, pp. 42-3.
8. Richard Lannoy, *The Speaking Tree : A Study of Indian Culture and Society*, Oxford University Press, 1971. p. 244. See also D.E. Smith, *India as a Secular State*, Princeton, New Jersey, 1963, pp, 51, 88 ; K.R. Minogue, *Nationalism*, London, 1967, p. 99 ; Charles H. Heimsath, *Indian Nationalism and Hindu Social Reform*, Princeton, 1964, p. 143. Posting a dichotomy between the moderates and the extremists in terms of their political culture, Smith writes : "The Indian National Congress, founded in 1885, reflected principally the values of Victorian liberalism, but for a few years early in this century it came under the control of the Extremists with their Hindu revivalist emphasis." (p. 51).
9. D.G. Karve and D.V. Ambedkar, eds., *Speeches and Writings of Gopal Krishna Gokhale*, Vol. ii, Political, Bombay, 1966, pp. 32-6.
10. Prabha Dixit, "Secularism and Communalism : A Comment", *Economic and Political Weekly*, 1 November 1969, p. 1750. See also Heimsath, *op. cit.*, pp. 131-46.
11. Minogue, *op. cit.*, p. 99.
12. This is the crucial point where scholarship on this subject has unquestioningly accepted the basic assumptions of the Indian nationalist historiography of Indian nationalism. This has had serious repercussions on our understanding of the processes of social and political change in

modern India, thereby obviating the very possibility of a radical perspective. I may make a confession here. Until the time of writing the first draft of this paper, I had myself subscribed to the view that the challengers found it "neither possible nor prudent to attempt a reconciliation of the existing plethora of interests to create an economic base for popular participation in nationalist politics." But, as is clear from the present discussion, it was possible for the challengers to take a genuinely radical stance even within the traditional and colonial ambience. If they did not exercise this option, the reasons did not lie in the non-availability of the option. The relevance of this argument comes down to the Gandhian phase in regard to which, too, a similar spot-blindness has manifested itself. The best example of this is provided by N.K. Bose whose understanding of Gandhi's programme remains the most perceptive. For while realizing the status quo implications of the ideological aspect of Indian nationalism, Bose accepted the assumption that within the colonial framework Gandhi had no option but to defer his more radical ideas of social reconstruction. Bose, too, avoided the question: Why was this particular approach to a national consensus adopted? See his *Problems of Indian Nationalism*, Calcutta, 1969, and *My Days with Gandhi*, Calcutta 1953.

5

Plurality of Religions, Science and Secularism

Mrinal Miri

THE CONCEPT of religion brings together a bewildering variety of phenomena under it. Rituals vary enormously from religion to religion, and even within the same religion. Also, what may be called, for want of a better word, religious "beliefs"—the kind of thing that some would regard as constituting the core of religion—are radically different from religion to religion. Think in this connection of the major religions of the world—namely, Hinduism, Buddhism, Islam and Christianity; and imagine the fantastic variety we have if we add to them further the religious beliefs of the tribal peoples all over the world. This may be thought to present a special difficulty to a philosophical approach to religion.

Philosophy, it will be agreed, is primarily a study of concepts—of their interrelations, of the grounds of their application, of the limits of their intelligible employment and so on. Philosophy of religion would thus be a study of religious concepts as they are presumably embodied in religious beliefs, or, if one prefers a wider term, religious language. But since systems of religious beliefs or religious languages are so widely different from one religion to another it is doubtful, so it may be said—whether a philosophical reflection on the concepts of a religion can really have any important bearing on our understanding of the concepts of another religion. Very often, someone might even say, it may in fact be a hindrance rather than a help. This may be seen to be borne out by the actual practice of philosophers. Philosophers who set out to write about *religion* as such and not about *their* religion, do in fact tend to limit themselves, either tacitly or self-consciously to the confines of their own religious tradition. And this applies both to people who are sympathetic to the claims of religion as well as to those who are hostile.[1] On the other hand, those who look for concepts which, as it were, cut across the boundaries of different religions—in the hope that they might find something which is universal and essential to all of them—invariably fail to produce anything that is truly enlightening—anything that arises much above the level of the trivial. If all this is true, then it might be thought inevitably to point to one thing, namely, that any philosophical approach to religion must be, in some strong sense, tradition-bound. I shall return to this point later.

Let us meanwhile say something about a possible reaction to what has just been said. Someone might say that it is not true that religious languages are so radically different from one another ; it is, of course, the case that while in some religions there is talk of God, in others, such talk is not allowed at all or there is, rather, talk of "pure-consciousness" or "nirvana". And it may also be the case that in translation the religious talk of a tribal people gets assimilated to the religious talk in the translator's language in such a way as to be a hindrance to its proper understanding. All this may be true. Yet, so it may be said, it is undeniable that all religious languages have at least this in common, namely, that, in each of them claims are made which fall outside the bounds of propriety laid down for scientific talk. There are two related, but distinguishable, ways in which this might happen : (*a*) there are truth-claims in them which transcend the logical limits of scientific enquiry ; and (*b*) there are statements which have the look of statements about the empirical world such as scientific statements are, but which grossly violate the norms of propriety of the latter.

Take (*a*) first. In some religions there is talk about "heaven" and "hell" ; Ramakrishna talks of "meeting" Jesus Christ in person ; a devotee of Kali is visited by the goddess ; Sai Baba "materializes" objects out of nothing ; Krishna is claimed to be the incarnation of the god Vishnu. All such talk seems, in an important sense, to be beyond the scope of scientific enquiry. Of course, it cannot be denied that scientific enquiry can be made—indeed has been made—about *people* who indulge in such talk. One has only to think of psycho-analysis in this connection, particularly of the Freudian variety. But any such investigation seems essentially to involve a debunking of the actual truth-claims made. And this is the important point. It seems that the assumptions on the basis of which alone any scientific enquiry can be conducted are quite incompatible with what I call a "serious" view of the kind of religious talk we are concerned with here. These assumptions—if indeed they can be called "assumptions"—include such beliefs as : "One place is spatio-temporally traceable from another" ; "I cannot meet another person, unless either I or he or both can travel through space to the meeting place" ; "You can make an object only from already existing stuff", and so on. But such beliefs form the framework within which alone scientific investigation is conducted. As a paraphraser of Wittgenstein says : "These truths which are beyond question for us in this way form a system, experience does not teach them to us in isolation, and in the system they give one another mutual support. Each is held fast by what lies around it. Testing, confirmation, doubts, and mistakes take place in the system ; our arguments, criticisms and judgements have their life within it. The truths thus held in place are the fixed stars around which these activities revolve ; the movement around them determines their immobility. Each is so anchored in all my questions and answers that I cannot touch it." (Dilman, *Induction and Deduction* : 39-40). But the point about the truth-claims in religious languages that we are considering is that they fall outside the scaffolding of scientific thought.[2] The conclusion to be drawn from this may, however, be radically different according to one's intellectual preferences. Thus someone might say that in so far as any religious language contains truth-claims such as we have mentioned above, it is so much the worse for it. On the other hand, another might say that this only proves that the "assumptions" of scientific investigation are not the same as those of other universes of discourse, and that this fact has nothing to do with the preferability of one universe of discourse to another. This point will concern us a little later.

Meanwhile, let me consider briefly the other point (*b*), that any religious language contains statements which have the look of statements such as could be legitimately made in the sciences, but which nonetheless grossly violate the norms of propriety of scientific statements. In this class are placed beliefs which are called "superstitions". Of course, not all "superstitious beliefs" have religious significance (*e.g.* "The number 13 is bad for you", "X is dying, because his friend Y is secretly and slowly cutting X's picture into shreds", and so on). But in every religion, it may be said, there are such beliefs. Thus, take the belief that praying can cure the sick. But what is there in a belief for it to be "superstitious" ? It may be said that a belief is superstitious, if it is about a supposed empirical correlation which is such that most empirical evidence points against it. Take the belief that if a cat crosses your path while you are driving, you are likely to have an accident. On the face of it, this statement looks like the statement : "If you are driving while under the influence of too much alcohol, you are likely to have an accident." But while for this latter statement, there is substantial empirical evidence ; the evidence against the former is quite overwhelming. Now, take the belief that praying can lead to the cure of the sick. One might say, this has the general form of "Performance of certain kinds of action can lead to the cure of the sick." Thus : "Administering of medicine by a medical practitioner can lead to the cure of the sick," also has the same form. But, it is quite obvious that while this latter statement is a well-established truth, the belief about praying has little or no empirical evidence to support it. To designate a belief superstitious in this way is, of course, to condemn it as a grossly mistaken empirical belief.

But the notion of "superstition" needs examination. When a person believes that if a cat crosses his path while he is driving, he is likely to have an accident, it is not as though he is not aware that there is little or no empirical evidence in support of his belief. If he can successfully handle such a sophisticated piece of machinery as the motor car, it would be absurd to think that he was unaware of the lack of evidence for his belief. He might even be prepared to say that his belief, in this sense, is "irrational". But the important point is that in the life of this belief the notion of "empirical evidence" *has no role to play at all.* Contrast in this connection the belief that the excessive intake of alcoholic drinks tends to give one a headache. Here the availability of empirical evidence determines, as it were, the life of the belief. Once, this difference is grasped, we might realize that it might be wrong to think that the so-called "superstitious" beliefs are *mistaken* empirical beliefs ; in the case of ordinary empirical beliefs, the absence of evidence for it or the presence of evidence against it, is one of the things that determines its mistaken character. But where a belief is such that considerations of supporting empirical evidence or of the lack of it do not play any role in its operations, might it not be the case that its criteria of assessment or appreciation may be quite different from those appropriate for beliefs where such considerations play a vital role ?

In any event, in whatever way we decide the issue about (*a*) and (*b*) above, the fact remains that all religions are in an important way profoundly non-scientific. To this, there may be, as I hinted above, two radically different intellectual reactions.

One of these reactions has come from the side of what has been called the positivist school of philosophers. The main idea behind this reaction is that what I have called above the "scaffolding of scientific thought" contains (*i*) the criteria of intelligibility, and (*ii*) the criteria of rationality of *all* our beliefs about the world or the Universe—what David Hume would have called "matters of fact". Take the first, it has been said that within the framework of scientific investigation, no sentence can have any literal sense, if what it says cannot be verified or falsified in experience. Add to this, the belief, which is shared by many, that all our talk about the world must aspire to the ideal of scientific talk about it. You then have the immediate consequence that any talk about the world must at least satisfy the criteria of intelligibility or meaningfulness, laid down for any talk within science, in order to acquire even a minimal degree of intellectual respectability. This is the famous so-called "verification principle" of meaning. Very few philosophers now-a-days would claim to be "verificationists" in an unqualified fashion. But the influence on many of this line of thinking is undeniable ; and much recent philosophical criticism of religious thought is the direct result of this influence.[3]

There is no need here to enter into any discussion of the verification principle. This was for quite some time the proudly acknowledged "official" theory of meaning. It still continues to be the official theory ; but there is a certain reluctance to acknowledge it in public. What is important, however, is the appearance on the horizon of another theory of meaning, associated with the name of Ludwig Wittgenstein. There are several highly interrelated aspects of the theory ; but I shall here mention only a few. (1) It is a mistake to ask for *the* meaning of a word or a sentence ; it can have a variety of meanings depending on the context of its application. (2) The meaning of a word (given its variety) is determined, more than by anything else, by the use that is made of it ; and its use embodies a (more or less specific) rule or criterion of correctness. (A word has a meaning in so far as there is a criterion of its correct use). (3) Significant use of any bit of language is necessarily a part of a larger human activity ; it is only against the background of human activity that language acquires any life at all.

I do not wish to discuss any of these aspects in detail : much detailed and incisive discussion of the theory of meaning in question is available in recent philosophical literature. The important point for us is its likely impact on the philosophical discussion of religious language(s). Take points (2) and (3) above together. I think it will then be possible to make the following remark about religious language : Words in a religious language may have rules of use which are internal to the language itself, and their criteria of correctness are therefore, to be found also within it, and the complex of human activities within it has its life. To put it slightly differently : one cannot understand a religious claim, unless one understands the concepts involved in such a claim. But the concepts are embodied in the use of words or complex of words corresponding to them. And this use is to be determined by reference to the system of human activities we call religious activities, or, to use Wittgenstein's apt phrase, by reference to the "form of life" we call religious. To take an example : A worshipper lies prostrate in front of an image of Kali, and says, "Mother, you who know everything, why are you still angry with me ? What more can I do to please you?" A crude positivist response to this might be as follows : This involves addressing an entity which cannot ordinarily be seen, heard or felt, and, therefore, also involves the belief that such an entity exists. The confusion is further compounded by calling "this entity", "mother" and by the belief that somehow it exists in the piece of stone or lump of mud in front of the worshipper. Given the verification principle of meaning, these "beliefs" are literally nonsense and, therefore, cannot be taken with any degree of intellectual respectability. But if the theory of meaning, we have just been discussing is correct, a suitable reply to the positivist would be that by assimilating the notion of addressing in worship to the ordinary notion of addressing a person, the positivist misses the whole point of the former. Addressing in the religious context is crucially different from say, addressing a friend or a stranger in the ordinary course of life ; and the positivist laments that the addressee here is not empirically available, in the same way as when I address my friend or my father, is like the child's lament that he cannot eat a number. The concept of an addressee in the religious context is to be understood not by trying to assimilitate it to our ordinary notion of an addressee—although there undoubtedly are connections between the two—but by exploring its use, by discovering the criteria of its correct and incorrect applications in, to use another phrase of Wittgenstein's, the religious "language-game" itself. And since undoubtedly there are such criteria within the language game the religious beliefs where this concept figures cannot be nonsense. As to calling the addressee "mother", although the concept *is* in a way parasitic upon our ordinary concept of mother its use in the religious context has crucial logical differences. For instance, there, its criteria of correct use, rule out the significance of such questions as : "How old is she ?" "Who could be my father ?" "What is her nationality ?" and so on. A realization of this is sufficient, to begin with, to appreciate the possibility that the word can have a distinct and equally legitimate meaning within religious language.

I think, I have said enough to suggest that the positivist response to the "non-scientific" character of religious talk, that it is unintelligible (nonsensical) is perhaps too glib. Religious language may have a kind of autonomy which makes it immune to charges of unintelligibility in terms of criteria appropriate to the language of science.

Let us now look at the other aspect of the positivist reaction, namely, that, whether or not religious language or part of it is meaningless, in any event, most of what goes by the name of religion is *irrational.* The charge of irrationality may be levelled against two things : (1) what may be called religious "dis-course" and (2) religious activities for example, rituals, and so on.

(1) Here I shall consider only *one* way in which the irrationality of a given piece of talk can be determined. Any discussion, whether in ordinary life or in the sciences, makes certain assumptions or takes certain things as given. Take, for example, a discussion about student unrest in our country or in any country. It will take as given that there are educational institutions ; that they impart education to people who are called students ; that distinction could be made between the situation which can be described as one of unrest and a situation which could not be so described ; and so on. It is only against the background of such commonly agreed assumptions that the discussion can proceed. This is, of course, not to say that these assumptions cannot be questioned. But in so far as the discussion is, say, about the *quality* of unrest among students as opposed to the unrest among other sections of the population, those assumptions are, for the purpose of the particular discussion, unquestioned. Now one way of showing that a discussion is irrational may be to show that the assumptions on which it is based are mistaken in one way or another. Thus, for instance, a discussion about whether or not a particular ghost is a kind ghost or a cruel one could be considered irrational if it is the case that the belief in the existence of ghosts is a totally false belief. However, there is a *limit* to our questioning of assumptions. There are certain assumptions—if we can call them that—which, as it were, set the limits of, not just a particular discussion, but an entire universe of discourse. Take the universe of discourse about the external world and beliefs such as : if you throw a stone up, after a little while it will fall to the earth ; water flows downwards ; a physical object just does not disappear : if you have brought a

cabbage from the market, it will not turn into a turnip by the time you have reached home ; and so on. These beliefs are, to use a Kantian phrase *constitutive* of our universe of discourse about the external world. It is against the background of these and similar beliefs that *any* discussion about the external world takes place. To abandon them is also to abandon all talk whether rational or irrational, sound or unsound, plausible or implausible—about the external world. In any discussion about the external world, the rationality/irrationality distinction operates within the bounds of such beliefs. To put it slightly differently, one must take a distinction between my particular discussion and the universe of discourse within which it takes place. A discussion can be shown to be irrational by showing that the assumptions on which it is based are mistaken. But the criticism of these assumptions must take place within the structure of the universe of discourse to which the discussion belongs. And the beliefs which constitute the structure cannot be questioned or criticized in the same way.[1] Now it can be argued that religious language embodies a universe of discourse of its own which is, in many ways, radically different from the universe of discourse of science. Its structure allows and provides for the possibility of criticisms and assumptions of discussions within it on the basis of which they can be judged to be rational or irrational ; but the beliefs which are "constitutive" of the structure are logically immune from such criticism. Take again the devotee of Kali. His belief that Kali exists and enters into relationships with individuals and exercises tremendous power over them, and that she can be infinitely loving as well as unimaginably angry, is, as it were, the pivot round which all his thoughts about the state of himself and the world revolve. The rationality or irrationality of any particular religious belief of his can ultimately be determined only by reference to this immovable centre of his universe of discourse. And this centre itself cannot be the subject of such appreciation. One might thus draw the conclusion that (1) since religious discourse can be regarded as constituting a *universe* of discourse the question of its being rational or irrational does not arise—such questions arise in connection with specific discussions within it, and they can be settled ultimately by reference to the structure of the universe of discourse ; and (2) to think that religious discourse as such can be irrational is to think of it as part of some other universe of discourse, and this is a mistake in logic.

One possible response at this point may be to say that even if we grant that religious thought constitutes a universe of discourse in the above sense, one thing that a universe of discourse must satisfy in order to be considered legitimate at all is that it must not contain any assumptions which are contradictory. And religious thought —so one might continue—does very frequently contain self-contradictory assumptions. This point has to be granted. But is it really the case that religious thought contains such assumptions? It is my view that attempts at showing that religious beliefs are self-contradictory arise almost invariably from an inadequate as well as a distorted understanding of religious concepts. However, to substantiate the point will take me too far afield. I shall content myself by dogmatically asserting that it has not been shown that there are self-contradictory assumptions in every religion.

I want now briefly to comment upon the other aspect of the charge of irrationality that I mentioned above. It is the charge that religious *activities*, for example, rituals, are irrational. It is not only thinking which can be rational or irrational but also human activity, although—so it might be granted—what confers rationality on an action or an activity is the thought behind it. Nevertheless, the idea of applying the concept of rationality to human action is interesting in itself. It might be said that, we have a fairly general idea of rationality of human action, and the positivist might readily agree that this is the idea in terms of which the rationality or otherwise of the behaviour of a scientist may be judged. This idea of rationality of human behaviour can be explained thus : "A piece of behaviour is rational only if the agent is justified in believing that what he does (a) is likely to achieve, or (b) is one possible way (which in certain circumstances may be a very unlikely way) of achieving what he wants to achieve, and (c) is not likely to bring about other consequences more undesirable than the prospective desirability of what it is intended to achieve."[5]

Armed with this analysis of "rationality"' one might say that most, if not all, religious actions are irrational. Take the practice of sacrifice ; one makes a religious sacrifice (an offering) to some "god" so that one's sick child may get well. This may be considered irrational because one is not "justified" in believing that making a sacrifice (*a*) is likely to achieve or (*b*) is one possible way of achieving what one wants to achieve by doing so. One answer to this would be that usually when one makes an offering of this sort, one does not do so to the exclusion of other things where one is "justified" in believing that they would achieve what one wants them to achieve. These other things may include taking the advice of the best available medical practitioner, proper nursing and so on. It might also be said that justification of the belief in the efficacy of sacrifice is to be sought in ways quite other than the ways in which justification for belief in the efficacy of these other kinds of actions is sought. It is a religious belief and it shows itself, as Wittgenstein says, "not by reassuring or by appeal to ordinary grounds of belief, but rather by regulating for all in his (the believer's) life."[6]

Whatever we may think of this answer, the above analysis of rationality is, to say the least, quite inadequate. I have argued elsewhere[7] that this account of rationality rests on the assumption that any human action which can be counted as rational must aim at achieving some end. And this is false. There are countless human actions, and varieties of them, for which it will be difficult to specify any ends except in a trivial way. A painter may paint a picture to achieve all kinds of ends, but he may also do so without believing that he wants to achieve anything by means of it, he may just paint. And yet one can hardly call it irrational for this reason alone. Indeed, the capacity to engage in an activity of this sort is so distinctive of human intelligence, as opposed to that of lower animals, that it would be absurd to call it irrational. Given that, there is an aspect of human life which manifests itself in artistic creations, the question of the rationality of any work of art may simply be a matter of our being able to place it as a feature of this aspect, irrespective of any specific ends which may be sought to be achieved by means of it. I believe that the same may be true of religious activities of various sorts.

What I have said in the preceding section may be summed up as follows : the religious form of life can be taken "seriously". What I mean by this is that logically speaking, it need not be taken as an aspect, distortion, manifestation, and what have you, of some other form of life. This is not to say that there are no connections between the religious language-game and other language-games. Indeed many concepts enter into religious language from a sphere of operation which may be quite non-religious. (Thus take the concept of "mother" I have discussed above.) But having entered it they acquire a life of their own, and this life may be intelligible only in the context of religious language itself. To take an example from games, take the concept of "scoring". While it is common to many games, its meaning for a particular game can be understood only in terms of the rules of that game.

But this brings me back, at last, to plurality of religions. Given that the religious form of life is, in some strong sense of that term, "autonomous", what about the *variety* of religious forms of life that we spoke about in the opening section of the paper ? I think the game example may be helpful even here. Different games may be similar to one another (*e.g.* football, volleyball, basketball) in many ways. But each is bound by its own complex of rules and none is reducible to another, nor is one an inferior or a superior version of another. It is my belief—which I do not have the space here to substantiate—that different religions are also, in the same way, bound by their different networks of rules. Any aspect of a particular religion can be fully understood, assessed, or criticized only in terms of the rules of that religion.

Let me, however, give some assurances : (*i*) I am not ruling out the possibility that a knowledge of one religion may help to throw light on the concepts of another (this often happens in games, especially when one is learning or teaching a new game) ; (*ii*) nor am I ruling out the possibility of cross-religious discussions, whatever their purpose might be ; and (*iii*) it is even possible that in future there might be a religion which is *the* religion of all mankind. But I do regard the following, from a logical point of view, as incorrect : (*a*) *criticism* of the concepts of one religion in terms of rules internal to another religion.

(This has happened in much of the so-called Christian missionary work in the tribal areas of India, particularly, North-East India) ; and (*b*) the idea that religions form a hierarchy where they can be ordered according to the superiority of one over another. Questions of superiority or inferiority just do not arise here. To think that they do is to suffer not only from a logical blindness but also may be from moral insensitivity. It must, however, be admitted that there are difficulties here. Primary among these is the claim of superiority inherent within a religion. Thus think of the Christian claim that there is but only one true God, and that is the God of Christianity ; to believe otherwise is either blasphemous, or to be ignorant or both. There is no space here to discuss these difficulties ; but I do believe that they do not upset the position I have just outlined.

Let me now ask the questions which all this has been leading up to. In view of what I have said about the religious form of life and the variety of religions, what should be the attitude of the secular State to religion ? It is not quite clear what "secularism" really means. I suppose in its normal meaning, it stands for an attitude of mind which reflects an intellectual and practical opposition to religion and the religious, and that this attitude is supposed to be the natural consequence of the acceptance of "modern science and all that is implied by it". But in actual practice, even States which profess secularism do not usually adopt policies—or, at any rate, do not *claim* to adopt policies—which are destructive of the religious form of life. And in India, where secularism is a matter of fundamental policy, the word has been deliberately given a meaning, which is different from its normal meaning, but is in consonance with the practice of non-interference with the religious form of life. In this meaning "secularism", far from reflecting a hostile attitude to religion, stands, in fact, for equal respect for all religions. In a country, where there is a truly fantastic variety of religions, this may be thought of as a matter of political expediency. But I believe that it has really arisen from a conviction that (*i*) religion has an independence which is the consequence of its conceptual autonomy ; and (*ii*) every religion operates within its own more or less independent framework.

I would like to conclude the paper with a quotation from George Santayana : "Any attempt to speak without speaking any particular language is not more hopeless than the attempt to have a religion that shall be no religion in particular ... Thus every living and healthy religion has a marked idiosyncrasy. Its power consists in its special and surprising message and in the bias which that revelation gives to life. The vistas it opens and the mysteries it propounds are another world to live in ; and another world to live in—whether we expect ever to pass wholly over into it or no—is what we mean by having a religion."

NOTES AND REFERENCES

1. See, for example, W.D. Hudson, *A Philosophical Approach to Religion*, London, 1974. D.Z. Phillips, *Death and Immortality*, London, 1971. An exception, in this connection, is R.C. Gandhi, *The Availability of Religious Ideas*, London, 1976.
2. The recent decision by the authoritiesof BangaloreUniversity, in India, to conduct "scientific enquiries" into the various claims made by Sai Baba may be seen as the result of a total failure to appreciate this point about the scientific mode of thinking.
3. To take only two names, A.G.N. Flew and K.Nielsen.
4. See above p.4.
5. H. Mullane, "Psychoanalytic Explanation and Rationality", *The Journal of Philosophy*, 1971.
6. *Philosophical Investigations*, p.54.
7. M. Miri, *Philosophy of Psychoanalysis*, Simla, 1977.

6

Secularism and Islam

S.T. Lokhandwalla

SECULARISM as a movement was basically ethical and, in order to avoid a head-on collision with established churches and religious beliefs it tended to be negative in its relation with religions. It had, as was natural, very pronounced and beneficial philosophic and political aspects. Secularism was intended mainly to provide a certain theory of life and conduct, bereft of divine connections or ordinances and deeds and actions without any relationship with rewards or punishments in the life hereafter. It attempted at fulfilling an hitherto religious function without any religious associations. It was an outcome of the 19th century humanistic radicalism, which was endeavouring to meet the social and political complexities by withdrawing ethics from the fold of religion. There was no doubt an anti-theistic strain in the movement, but it was more or less relegated to the background to make it possible to attract to its social, political, and ethical aims all the liberal elements from the manifold religions and Christian sects which it could muster together if their belief in theism was not disturbed. This also became necessary with the rise of the national States, with their variety of Christian sects and religious groups. It was also argued that just as mathematics, physics, and chemistry were "secular" sciences, so it would be possible on the same lines to establish a secular theory of the conduct and welfare of life. It was also recognized that the relationship of secularism to religion was mutually exclusive and not hostile. Religion with its theology, is left undisturbed to speculate on divinity and to interpret the unknown world whereas secularism is expected to concern itself mainly with the known world interpreted by experience, its refusing to enter into the assertions or negations of another life. If religion has morality, secularism offers a basis for morality independent of any religion, and a plausible solution to multi-religious and multi-cultural societies of countries like the USSR and India.

The central principle of secularism is to seek larger human good through material basis. Secularism was more or less basic to the historical growth of Christianity. At its inception Christianity was faced with vehement social and political antipathy. To soothe the political antagonisms, the new dispensation was prepared to come to terms with it by "rendering unto Caesar what is Caesar's" and leaving to God what was not Caesar's. The medieval conflicts between the Church and the State were power conflicts with emphasis on either religion or secularism, depending on whether the Church or the State was dominant and supreme. Islam, unlike Christianity, had no Caesar to whom to allocate or apportion parts of its domain of influence. Islam, itself, within a period of a score of years, was the all-pervasive force. The Meccan subjugation led to the discomfiture of almost all the opposing elements; and before the death of the Prophet, the Arabian Peninsula was largely under the control of the new might and fresh vigour of Islam. Soon after it prostrated and humbled two doughty and sprawling empires, the Sassanid and the Byzantium. To put it crudely, Islam had taken over the role of Caesar and hence it did not leave unrelegated any sphere of human life. It created political institutions and a political theory to provide indisputable claims to the new emerging political elites. Religion itself being the law giver, morality, ethics, and law were all treated as sets of obligations imposed from above. Social, political, moral, legal, and economic aspects all derived their sanctions from religion. It laid down the code of behaviour *in extenso*, not only for the professors of the religion but also for their relations with the professors of other religions. However, behind the growth of these rules were the social and historical pressures and processes of the Arab society and the speedy expansion of the Arab empire.

The Arabs, even before Islam, were a very conservative people. Being divided into tribes, and living in a hostile environment, the norms of established behaviour within a tribe and between the tribes were the only means of preserving a semblance of law and order in an atmosphere where "a man's hand was against every man and everyman's against him". The protection of one's tribe was the only guarantee for one's safety ; and hence the Arab respect for the accepted norm of behaviour was supreme, the *Sunna* or the traditions of the Arabs was the only acceptable code with the result that any innovation was a breach of the accepted norms and was not easily acceptable. The introduction of Islam was itself a great innovation, and was not at first acceptable to the Arabs of Mecca. The disturbance it caused to the existing balance of equities and inequities was not at all welcome and the principal reason adduced for its non-acceptance was that it was against what their forefathers did or how they behaved. But once it was partially accepted, the Arab notion of *Sunna* reasserted itself and took the sacred and sacrosanct form of the *Sunna* of the Prophet. What the Arabs did was to acquire the religious sanction of the *Sunna* from the Prophet. Being religiously hallowed and declared inviolable, the *Sunna* of the Prophet, which covered all imaginable activities of human life, became the yard-stick for ideal human conduct. A deviation from it became an abhorrent *bid'a*, an innovation.

The political development of Islam, with its mutually antagonistic political theories in the fourth century *hijra* was another factor responsible for its rigidity and religious control. The monolithic unity of the Shi'ite politico-religious theory helped protect the communal uniformity and solidarity, whereas the historicity of the growth of the orthodox religious schools innately tended to split and sectionalize. The Abbasid polity, by the end of the third century *hijra* was extending absolute protection and support to the orthodox schools, whereas the latter were producing political theories to validate the Abbasid political claims and cover them with the aura of religion. The tendency of orthodoxy towards fissure was checked by a strange but necessary decision to assume validity of the four orthodox schools and banning the establishment of any new school. This was sought to be achieved by what is known as closing the gates of *ijtihad*, that is, refusing the right of independent judgement in matters relating to religion. The history of human thought has been a continuous record of conflict between insistence on the maintenance of the status quo and its rigidity and the compulsions of change and evolution. There is always a contest and rivalry between tradition and change. The problems become more complicated when religion imparts sacredness and perpetuity to the doctrines which have otherwise no more than mundane and transitory relevance. The political and social factors of the fourth century *hijra,* involving internal schisms and external challenges led political and religious leaders to declare that the Islamic *Shari'a,* as they had envisaged, was complete and perfect. The social and political causes that led to this rigid and inflexible attitude have been ignored and even forgotten and what remains is the sacredness and sanctity of every minute rule of the *Shari'a.*

> The code of conduct represented by the *Shari'a* was fixed and final in its terms and any modification was regarded as a deviation from the legitimate and valid standard. In other words, the religious code thus established was an all embracing one, in which every aspect of human relationship was regulated with meticulous detail ; the law having once achieved perfection of expression was in principle static and immutable, for Mohammed was the last of the Prophets, and after his death in 632, there could be no further direct communication of the divine will to man. In the Islamic concept, human thought unaided cannot discern the true values and standards of conduct, such knowledge can be attained only through divine mediation, and acts are good or evil exclusively because Allah has attributed this quality to them. Modernity in Islam as an active principle of change forward, which manifested itself in its Golden Age lasting a bare two centuries 900-1100 gives place to traditionalism, defined as the claim, most religious systems have that they alone bear within themselves a deposit consisting of ceremonial myth, dogma or ethics or some of those elements, revealed by some ultimate divine or quasi-divine authority and meant to be handed down to posterity by a succession of duly qualified trustees.

This rigid and inflexible attitude has confronted, in the past as much as it does today, the Muslims, the world over, with the problem inherent in the very nature of Islam, namely, to define the relationship between the standards imposed by the religious faith and the mundane forces that activate society.

The Islamic political theory is centred around the institution of *Imama* and *Khilafa*. Although, in general terms, *Imama* had a religious connotation and *Khilafa* a temporal one, for the orthodoxy both the titles synchronize into a single personality. The growth of Islamic political theory had various other contributing factors. The philosophic excursions of the early Muslims were also attempts at arriving at a synthesis between the Platonic and Islamic concepts in the field of politics. The Shi'ite and, especially, the Ismaili concept of *Imama* was in many respects a Platonic legacy. However, the religious import that the Shi'ite *Imama* had gathered was also appended to the orthodox concept of *Khilafa* and *Imama*. But for the opposition of the Shi'as, with their political theory inflexibly hinged on to religion, the orthodox *Khilafa* would have taken a more liberal turn. Consequently, the *Khilafa* was also to be for Sunni Islam, a God-centred rule and had to conform to the divinely laid down *Shari'a*. The Shi'i *Imama* was to appertain to the descendents of the Prophet and the Sunni was impropriated for a larger group of the tribe of the Prophet to validate the rule of the first four Rightly Guided Caliphs, the Umayyads and the Abbasids.

The first rupture in Islamic political theory occurred when the Shadow Abbasid Caliphate—preserved by the Mamluks in Egypt for nearly three centuries after the debacle against the Mongols who had occupied the lands of the Eastern Caliphate and had put to sword the 37th Abbasid Caliph Mustasimbillah in February 1258—was replaced by the Ottomans. In Cairo, this shadow of the sovereignty of the Caliphate continued till 1517, when Selim I, the Ottoman Sultan, conquered Egypt and compelled the last of the Western Abbasid Caliph Mutawakkil 'ala'llah to abdicate the Caliphate in his favour. The Caliphate then, for the first time, passed from the Quraysh and Arabs to non-Arabs. The very essential qualification that the Caliph should be from the tribe of Quraysh deemed to be supported by the textual prescription as well as the consensus, was vitiated by the Ottoman takeover, but this too had to be accepted by the Muslim jurists as quite in order for nearly four centuries by creating legal fictions and sanctions from the Prophet forecasting the coming of the Ottoman Caliphs. It may be noted, however, that at no given time, from the beginnings of Islam as a political power, has there been a single Caliphate, to whom the whole of the Muslim dominated areas of the world owed allegiance. With the coming of the Ottomans, and the vitiation of the legal requirement, it was easy for those kingdoms, where the Ottomans sway and might did not reach, to refuse allegiance to the Ottomans courts. The Moghuls in India, because of this and other factors also, did not give any recognition to the Caliphate of the Ottomans.

The degeneration of the Ottoman empire and the gradual political subjugation of parts of the Muslim dominated areas was creating a slow consciousness amongst certain strata of Muslim society about the ineptitude and inefficiency of the Caliphate and an apathy towards Islamic political institutions was being built up. The most affected were the Turks themselves on whom it had been imposed and, in spite of its hallowed essence, was incapable of producing a sense of harmony and uniformity, even in the predominantly Muslim areas of the Ottoman empire, in the face of growing nation-state polities and sentiments everywhere. The result was that in November 1922, the Turkish National Assembly abolished the Sultanate and established a shadow Caliphate shorn of all temporal powers. By 1924, Turkey took the decisive step of abolishing an Islamic political institution without the presence of which the pious believed the world would come to an end. The abolition did cause a certain stir in different parts of the Muslim world, but soon people learnt to live without it. The Caliphate was no more than a symbol of religious glorification, and in India it only found its relevance when the Moghul dynasty was already on the decline. Its abolition by the Turks themselves came as the greatest shock in India, where as early as 1919 the *All India Khilafat Committee* for the defence of the Caliphate was formed. They had expected the danger to the Caliphate from Western powers; but it was laid to rest by Muslims themselves. The Khilafat movement in India would have petered out much sooner but for the impetus it received because of its being pinioned to the Indian freedom movement. The echo of the transformation in Turkey reverberated in several places and in several ways. Ali 'Abdu'r-Raziq, following the footsteps of Muhammad 'Abduh, went far ahead of him and asserted that the Caliphate was not an Islamic institution. In his book, *al-Islam wa Usulu'l-Hukm*, he argues that the institution was built up because of purely political factors and the religion had nothing to do with it ; it had neither sanction in the Quran nor in the *Sunna* of the Prophet, 'Ali' Abdu'r-Raziq's ideas failed to have a much impact not only because the orthodoxy opposed them vehemently, but also because there were quite a few aspirants to the Caliphate outside Turkey ; one of them being the then Khedive himself. Since the abolition of the Caliphate, most of the Muslim majority states described themselves as secular, some pendulously alternating between being Islamic and secular, according to the dictates of the internal and external requirements and exigencies, and a few calling themselves Islamic, because of historical or other factors. However, the political dominance of Islam, through its own political institutions had faded with no possibility of its revival. The political creativeness of Islam is more or less confined to drawing parallels between the modern institutions and old traditional ones and making use of the new ones under assumed Islamic nomenclatures. The *Majlis-Shura* of the days of the second Caliph 'Umar takes precedence amongst other parallels.

The ossified and stagnant state of Islamic law and theology, the complete containment and accompanied decline of the political power of Islam, the resulting decay and deterioration of the Muslim society in all matters cultural, economic, and social led to some stray and sporadic attempts to arrest the process of petrification by the reconsideration of the "received content" of the Islamic heritage formulated by its early savants. Ibn Taymiyah and his disciple Ibn Qayyim al-Jawzi, in the wake of the crusades and the establishment of the State of Jerusalem, were battling against orthodoxy for their right to use their own independent judgement, depending on the revealed segments of Islam. Although belonging to the Hanbali school, he refused to follow blindly all the dictates of the school, rejected *Taqlid* and even consensus, *Ijma*, at many points. He claimed to follow the letter of the *Qur'an* and the *Hadith*. He believed that there was nothing wrong in holding an opinion contrary to the consensus and there was no infidelity or impiety involved in it. It was the enunciation of Ibn Taymiyah that inspired the Wahhabi reformist movement of the 18th century in the Arabian Peninsula under the puritanical leadership of 'Abdu'l-Wahhab (1703-

1787). In India, about the same time, the efforts of Sheikh Ahmad Sirhindi, who later came to be known as Mujaddid, the revivalist of the faith, was working against the compromise that was being worked out in the Indian locale between Islam and other indigenous faiths—a movement which had started from the very induction of Islam in India and of which the *Din-i-Ilahi* of Akbar was the climax and Dara Shikoh, the last of its representatives. Sheikh Ahmad Sirhindi's efforts were to infuse old moral values into the fabric of Muslim society and so also were Shah Waliyullah's in the 18th century. The Indian Wahhabi movement of the 19th century was the fusion of the orthodox value system and the militant puritanism of the Arabian Wahhabis.

The reformist trends of the 19th century were very limited. The emphasis was on the purification of Islam from any accretion of superstition, degeneration of belief and practice, free use of *ijtihad* to escape from the arrested development of law and theology formulated by the second and third century (*hijra*) jurists and theologians, and revival of the social and moral values of Islam. The purification process struck mainly against the Sufi orders and folk religion. The result was disbandment of Sufi orders in Turkey and their losing ground in other countries. However, since political subjugation of the Islamic countries was not complete, there was many a militant movement whose aim was to reform Muslim society and save it from the encroaching political occupations from the West. The Sannusis in Libya, the Mahdists in Sudan, the Fulanis in Nigeria, and the Wahhabis in India were fighting their battles with more or less similar motives and ends. The reformist trends were destined to fail in spite of their proper motivation and their reiteration to use their *ijtihad* because of one single reason. The dead weight of the *Sunna* of the Prophet, which in reality reflected the ways and modes of the tribal Arabs and already had the halo of divine inspiration about it and dealt with every human problem, could not be dispensed with that easily. The result was that the 19th century reformist movement did not even touch the periphery.

With the political dominance of the West over almost the whole of the Islamic world by the beginning of the twentieth century, the reformist movement received another stimulus both with the political and economic support of the ruling powers and the percolation of Western ideas. Constitutions were demanded to be framed on the models of the Western democracies and the new educational institutions were divorced from the traditional ones.

Turkey, under Kemal Ataturk, declared itself a secular state, ousted the *Shari'a* and introduced the Western codes of law in its place. The Arabic script was replaced by the Roman script. The Arabic script, without the vowel signs, was neither suited to the genius of the Turkish language nor—being tied securely to the divine word in the *Quran*—would lend itself to the drastic changes needed to bring about proper concord and unison between the spoken and the written word. Besides, because of the mood of disowning the old and ushering in the new, large scale reforms in Turkey became possible.

In other countries, secularism entered through the influences they encountered. The *Shari'a* which was all comprehensive, dealing with laws of property, crime, evidence, procedure and so on, was to come under the survey of the political rulers and slowly most of these were replaced or codified with suitable and resquisite amendments loosening the hold of the *Shari'a.* However, the occupying powers, in the name of religious freedom, refused to take any notice of that portion of the law which came to be known as "Personal Law". Even the term "Personal Law" was a Western legacy and it was a novel palliative for the subjugated people who were led to believe that their religion was not being interfered with. Since the Islamic legal system had closed its doors to any additions or amendments, the conflict between theory and practice was already there, and many parts of the Islamic law were largely substituted by the customary and conventional practices of the place and time. The non-interference in the Personal Law kept away any drastic changes in the social pattern of Muslims, and the application of the *Shari'a* law in this restricted field also created a fantasy and romance of adhering to the whole of *Shari'a.* The reformist groups confined themselves to asking for two major reforms in the Personal Law, namely, abolition of polygamy, and regulation of procedure of divorce. Most of the Muslim countries have adopted measures to either restrict or discourage polygamy. Tunisia has banned it altogether. Restrictions on unilateral repudiation by husband have also been placed in different degrees in several countries.

All these are merely peripheral changes. On the one hand, the *Shari'a* has lost its relevance to life in its entirety and, on the other, where piecemeal reforms do not bring about the desired changes in the social and political framework, the revivalist tendencies gather momentum. The most difficult problem is the relation with other religions. The law that was built up during the period of the Islamic conquest gave the Jews and the Christians the status of "the people of the Book", thereby recognizing their cultural and religious autonomy. The concepts of *Darul-Islam*, *Daru'l-Harb* and *Daru-s-Sulh* are of the times when the Abbasid empire was waging wars every year with the Byzantium, and territories were changing hands all the time. What was Islamic land one year changed into the territory of the Byzantium in another ; what was *Daru-l-Islam* became *Daru'l-Harb* only to be reconquered and assimilated in *Daru'l-Islam*. But these became the immutable rules to be applied for all times to come. With the conquests of Iran and India, the treatment of *Ahlu'l-Kitab* had to be extended to the local inhabitants. But this too was only for political and practical reasons. The strict classical formulations would not even allow this and for them the rule that Islam applied to the early pagans was applicable. The modernists reject the classical formulations and emphasize the equality of status for all the citizens of a given state, irrespective of their religious persuasions, but the classical formulations are not disowned by the orthodox. It may also be remembered here that the capitulations had their beginnings because of such legal formulations where the non-Muslim population was very rightly not prepared to be governed by the Islamic ordinances and articles ; and capitulations made it easier for foreign occupations and interferences in the Muslim states. In a society, where Muslims are in a minority, it is impossible to insist on a separate Muslim cultural and social identity, merely based on religion and that too in the national polity. If any religion claimed the right to determine the cultural, social, political and economic affairs of all its followers, conflicts between religions, and the state and religion cannot be ruled out. Besides, the classical Islamic law, taking into consideration the treatment it meted out to the followers of other religions, dispenses with the following of Islamic law by Muslims in territories which are not ruled by them. But those formulations with their political, social, and cultural background are not applicable to the modern societies and states, where Muslims, along with the followers of other religions, whether in minority or majority, are co-partners. This situation has not been visualized by the law-givers of Islam. In the contemporary historical situation, the Muslim socio-cultural stand will have to mould itself under varied influences and under different geographical and historical contexts. The solution of the classical *Shari'a* under which religious principles were elaborated under a rigid comprehensive scheme of duties becoming the exclusive determinant for the conduct of society cannot be received as such in the present day social set-up. The adoption of secularism, relegating religious principles to the realm of individual conscience and allowing the forces of society unfettered control over the shape of social and political relationships, is the only possible option for the multi-cultural societies of today, where the binding force is no longer religion. Religious control would lead to dualism and hypocrisy, and add another conflict-factor. The world of today, which is searching for a closer union not only on the material plane but also on the intellectual plane, cannot afford more discord and conflict. When one looks at the *Shari'a* as the result of socio-economic growth, one can then realize its mundane character. Religion should place emphasis on devotion to God, cleanliness of spirit, and orderliness of life, but need not be enmeshed in the minute particulars of do's and don'ts.

7

Secularism in a Multi-religious Society : The Sikh Experience

Pritam Singh

THE PROBLEM faced by a religiously plural society can be understood properly if the subject is viewed from the standpoints of the State as well as the religious communities constituting the society. Also, the nature and quantum of the problems and their solutions will vary according to the basic ideology of the State. For instance, under theocratic government, the followers of all non-official religions may be presumed to enjoy less privileged citizenship as compared to those who belong to the State religion. Similarly, a genuinely anti-religious movement may look askance at all its organized religious communities. We do not propose to discuss problems arising in such societies. Our attention will be focussed on the nature of problems that multi-religious secular India faces, in spite of its constitutional provisions assuring equidistance from all religions, non-interference with doctrinal and credal systems, freedom to learn, educate, even proselytize, and non-discrimination on the basis of religious beliefs. For religious minorities these are quite a desirable set of assurances. In fact, who will not like equal operation of law, unprejudiced dispensation of justice, freedom to acquire and disseminate knowledge, and the possibility of occupying even the most strategically sensitive and the most highly responsible public office, on merit?

According to the religious minorities, the trouble lies not so much in the provisions available in the Constitution as in the actual implementation of the promises made therein. We give here a few of their imputations : delimitation of electoral constituencies for parliament and the legislative assemblies is done to the detriment of religious minorities ;[1], boundaries of the federated units are drawn with malicious intentions ;[2] merit has to face hostile prejudice and entrenched privilege ;[3] languages associated with minority religions are suppressed ;[4] development of the areas inhabited by people of the minority religions is delayed or gets postponed ad infinitum ;[5] the proverbial cat's paw is used to bring about breakdown in the law and order so that loss of life, property, and means of livelihood may create panic amongst members of the affected minority ;[6] press campaigns are let loose to misrepresent, denigrate and ridicule religious minorities ;[7] the entire community's patriotism is sought to be made suspect ;[8] assimilation and merger, rather than cultural plurality, are projected as national ideals ;[9] and, wherever possible, even the judicial processes are distorted to rob the religious minorities of their rights.[10]

These may be taken as a specimen of the charges that are levelled against the governments of the federated states and the centre, both of which are imagined by the alleging minorities as being the repositories of the interests of the majority community. The majority community retaliates, through press and platform, with such allegations as tardiness in relinquishing the blatantly confrontational postures developed by the religious minorities during the latter half of the 19th century. They are pictured as people with bloated self-images wanting to be carried on the shoulders of others with the help of weightages, reservations, and special treatments. They are also dubbed as psychotics, typifying a perpetually aggrieved complainant. A cursory survey of the editorial page of only one Urdu newspaper of Jullundur, the *Hind Samachar*, will be enough to provide any number of such accusations against Sikh politics. If we add to these charges and counter-charges, examples of other inter-community and inter-community tensions, the scene as it will present itself to any social scientist, will be one of incrimination, suspicion, lack of mutual accommodation, and non-identification of interests and ideals. Such social and psychological maladjustments, though not uncommon in most of the multi-religious, multi-cultural or multi-racial societies of the world, do call for the attention of psycho-social pathologists, specially because disputes of a religious nature often find expression in outbreaks of violence and vandalism.

In order to establish how well-entrenched and multi dimensional the roots of the problem are, it is proposed to view contemporary behavioural compulsions of one of the Indian religious minorities, the Sikhs, through the prism of its history.

When Guru Nanak, the founder of Sikhism, was born in A.D. 1469, there were in the North-West of India two major religions, namely, Islam and Hinduism. Though in a minority, the rulers were Mussalmans and the majority of the subjects were Hindus. Guru Nanak established his own spiritual-cum-ethical Way of Life, which soon caught the imagination of the people of Punjab. The nascent religion had, from the very beginning, the seeds of political viability. The Sikhs, the followers of Guru Nanak and of his nine spiritual successors, had unflinching faith in the Guru. Economic self-reliance achieved through hard labour, having become an article of faith with the Sikhs, they developed, rather early in their career, a sensitive feel for self-respect. "Damned be the morsel, for which self-respect has to be bartered", is one of Guru Nanak's sayings. The Sikhs devised an inbuilt system for the co-operative provision of free food, accommodation, and security to the needy. Better status was promised to women, tillers of land, and manual workers—the sections of society which had long been denied opportunities for upward social mobility. The affirmation accorded by the Sikh religion to the physical world and to honest worldly pursuits, must have come as a godsend to the commodity-producing sections of society. By the time of Guru Arjan, the fourth successor of Guru Nanak, it became impossible for the government of the day to shut its eyes to the fast-developing sinews of the new faith which, clearly was not just another quietist version of the legion Hindu sects. Sensing danger, the Mughal emperor, Jehangir, who stigmatized the new faith as an "unholy concern" in his autobiography *Tuzk*, passed orders for torturing Guru Arjan Dev to death.

Reacting sharply, Guru Arjan's son and successor Guru Hargobind began sporting all the concomitants of royalty and clashed with the forces of the State a number of times. Many of those who were not on the right side of the government started rallying round him. Understandably, the office of Guru tended to become non-grata with the Mughal administration. One of Guru Hargobind's sons, Guru Tegh Bahadur, who became the ninth Guru of the Sikhs, had to pay with his head the price of his espousal of the cause of the oppressed. Guru Gobind Singh, the tenth and the last Guru, formally legitimatized counter-assertion and armed defence. He succeeded in overhauling the community temperamentally and invested it with an unmistakable personality. Baptized by him into Singhs (Lions), his Sikhs, developed a self-image of great confidence. They were the chosen ones of God and, therefore, always destined to win.[11] They became a full-fledged *tisar-panth*, the third alternative to Hinduism and Islam, with distinctive symbols and rituals and a separate charter of do's and dont's. Already, they had their own places of pilgrimage and a separate Holy Book, the *Granth*, which Guru Gobind Singh willed to be invested with eternal Guruship after his death. Backed by all this, it was natural for the community to nurse political ambitions. Aurangzeb, the last of the Great Mughals, who died in 1707, left a bitter trail of anti-Sikhism behind. The trail was taken up by his successors, otherwise men of no consequence. Each successive occupant of the Indian throne was determined to give the Sikh community a taste of what is meant to make the church of worship a church of socio-political commitment.

The Sikhs reacted by solemnly vowing to accept nothing short of sovereignty. Thus began, during the later Mughal regime, an extremely critical phase in the life of the community. In order to defend themselves, the Sikhs perfected the art of guerilla warfare. It was during the first half of the 18th century that the passion for political liberation crystallized into a corporate attitude of the community, The State struck hard by bringing into active operation all the engines of oppression, including genocide. Hence, the Sikh cause won massive support from the peasantry who went to the extent of offering one male member per family to compensate for the diminishing Sikh manpower. The Sikhs came out victorious from this difficult struggle and carved out for themselves various autonomous principalities under their respective leaders. Later, a loose confederation of the leaders was formed, but the emergence of

Ranjit Singh, an able Sikh leader, put an end to these principalities, except the few which accepted the suzerainty of the British, who after subjugating the rest of India, were now hovering along the south-eastern frontiers of Ranjit Singh's empire between the Sutlej and the Jamuna rivers.

The Sikhs, in spite of their numerical increase, attendant upon political power, continued to be a minority during the Sikh regime. Mercifully, the Sikh leadership exhibited great maturity in not allowing any spillover of their harrowing past to their present. Throughout the period of Sikh hegemony, no case of forcible conversion to Sikhism is reported to have occurred.

The Maharaja died in A.D. 1839. Soon, the British made their presence felt in Lahore, the capital of the Sikh empire, which they were able to annex formally within a decade. With the British, entered in the Punjab Christianity, the religion of the new rulers. Altogether different experiences awaited the Sikh community under the British dispensation. These ranged from near-extinction under the reeling impact of British occupation, to a powerful revival, through the assertion of an autonomous Sikh identity. The heightened consciousness of exclusiveness was in the nature of a defensive measure against the inroads of Christian missionaries. It served also as a counterblast to the aggressively separatist politics, introduced in the Punjab by Hindus and Mussalmans of non-Punjabi extraction. Even before the close of the eighth decade of the nineteenth century, the people of the Punjab were divided into four warring communities—Hindus, Mussalmans, Sikhs, and Christians. Rather than defusing the explosive situation, the British rulers, who were the real wire-pullers, helped accentuate the infighting through devious means, including the conversion of religious communities into electoral colleges for their co-religionists. The idea, mooted much earlier,[12] was tried in 1888 by reserving Hindu and Muslim seats in the Municipal elections of Amritsar City,[13] but came into full operation, through the Montague-Chelmsford Reforms in 1919.[14] This was one of the trump cards which the rulers used against the rise of nationalism in their Indian empire. As intended, community-wise consolidation and inter-community tension touched a new high.[15]

Reverting to the predicament of the Sikhs in the seventies and eighties of the last century, we find them caught up in a vicious web. Till then, they had learnt either to face an antagonistic state or had lived peacefully with other religions under a protective umbrella. But now they were facing inter-community cross-firing, sometimes quite severe, with a not-too-clean third party presiding over the unedifying exercise. Moreover, sheer numbers, which had never mattered much for them, were to become the only determinant for their share in the administration of the State. If they did not get into the strait-jacket of "communal" politics, they faced the danger of being written off as a factor of little consequence, if they accepted it, they had to rest content with a ten per cent share in the administration of their own "homeland". Discretion had the better of valour and they fell in line with the then prevalent pattern of Punjab politics and began to use all the defensive and offensive instruments employed by other communities. Like others, the Sikhs tried to shut themselves up in the security of exclusively Sikh organizations, namely, *Singh Sabhas.* Their places of worship, called the *gurdwaras,* became the centres of all their socio-religious revivalist activity. The Singh Sabha movement threw the leadership of the community in the lap of the upcoming English-educated middle class, delimited its horizon to Sikhism, made the Sikhs more Sikh-minded and fixed the gaze of the community at the glory that was Sikh history. But the net social result of the religious efflorescence among the already segregated communities of the Punjab was sharp accentuation in mutual estrangement.

The British game was being played exactly to the prescribed tune, when the bottled Sikh giant found itself accidentally uncorked in the early twenties of the 20th century. It all started with the Sikh wish to oust the corrupt priests who had sneaked into the control of their historic shrines. In this priest-Sikh confrontation in which the British administration sided with the priests, members of the Sikh community were left with only two options : to be either with their co-religionists or with the administration. A large number opted for the former and as the Sikh plan of passive, non-violent resistance unfolded itself in the face of extremely savage baton charges, firings, torture, jail-terms, and confiscation of property, it brought about unparalleled cohesion among Sikh ranks and earned, for their unflinching faith and perseverence, full-throated encomiums from all quarters at home and abroad. It was a newly-formed Sikh organization, the Shiromani Akali Dal (SAD), founded on 14 December 1920, that provided the Sikhs with excellent leadership throughout this difficult period. The British administration was squarely humbled and the Dal emerged as the most authentic and representative mouthpiece for the socio-political aspirations of the Sikhs.[16] The struggle also brought into existence a central managing body for Sikh gurdwaras, namely, Shiromani Gurdwara Prabandhak Committee (SGPC), to be elected by adult Sikh voters. It came into operation on 1 November 1925. Ever since the induction of popular vote in the management of the *gurdwaras*, religious politics has been the first concern of the Sikh community. Even now, the surest way to Sikh political leadership lies through the SAD and SGPC.

When the British colonialists agreed to part with power, there was hectic political activity among the contending Indian successors. The All India Muslim League agitated for an independent Muslim State of Pakistan. The idea of the bifurcation of India, and that too on the basis of religion, was anathema to the Indian National Congress, but ultimately it fell in line with the League and the British thinking. The SAD also, which had resolved on 22 March 1946 to call upon the "Sikh Nation" to work whole-heartedly for the establishment of an "independent Sikh State",[17] was persuaded to follow the Congress way, in spite of the offer of an autonomous Sikh area within the jurisdiction of the proposed Pakistan.[18] This step was taken in the belief that the solemn assurances given by the Congress leaders, promising an effective role to the Sikhs in the framing of the Constitution of India, would be honoured in letter and spirit after the attainment of freedom.[19] The Muslim League was incensed at this drift in Sikh politics. Then followed the unprecedented massacre as a result of which as many as a million people are reported to have lost their lives on both sides of the border and the whole surviving Sikh population, affluently settled in the territories of the newly-formed Pakistan, had to migrate to India lock, stock, and barrel.

The Great Exodus of 1947 from Pakistan and the equally Great Resettlement in the Indian Punjab and other states of India, had in store for the community more doses of new experiences. The major part of the community was living now in the country of its choice. Hindus, with whom the Sikhs were politically hand-in-glove, were the only other major community left in the Indian Punjab. However, not many months had passed after independence when the Governor of the Punjab issued a secret letter to high government officers directing them to consider all Sikhs as habitual criminals.[20] This letter, which leaked out, upset the Sikhs greatly and hardened their posture against the none-too-sympathetic Central Government. Meanwhile, a notable demographic situation had stabilized in the Indian Punjab, which raised the Sikh percentage to about 33. This concentration of a highly politicized community along a not-too-friendly sensitive international border, was frowned upon by some members of the majority community as an alarming development. Soon, cracks began to appear in the Hindu-Sikh solidarity and the jockeying for power by the two communities fell back into the beaten track of religion-based politics. Among the Sikhs, the SAD and SGPC, both claiming to be defenders of the faith, continued to hold the key to politics.

Immediately after independence, all the strings of political power were controlled by the Congress, both in the Punjab and at the Centre. It was a nationalist party, but veteran Sikh leaders felt that its nationalism had turned out to be a euphemism for assimilation, whereby all regional cultures were required to merge themselves into one giant Indian *i.e.* Hindu culture. The SAD reacted violently against what it regarded as the communalism of the majority.[21] It was already smarting under the belief that it had been cheated out of power and prestige. Its noise, therefore, was loud and its following among the Sikhs, massive. Goaded by a feeling of persecution and deprivation, some Sikh extremists resumed the talk of an independent Sikh state. There were others, the Sikh Homelanders, more sophisticated and subtle, who were successful in selling their idea to the SAD. "Khalsa is a State", was their argument, and "sovereignty is a *sui generis* characteristic of the Khalsa". Their duty, therefore, was "firstly to carve out and establish for themselves a congenial habitat and milieu wherein the guiding impulses and postulates of the Sikh society can freely operate and fructify".[22] The Sikh Homeland was envisaged as an integral part of India, but the idea got a severe drubbing from the urban political publicists of the Punjab state and the Centre, which in turn, served as grist to the SAD mill. After brave, unbending public postures, both the Congress Government and the Dal climbed down to trying a number of midway alternatives, which after half-hearted trials, were rejected by the SAD. The latter had to organize massive agitations to bend a reluctant Central Government into carving out a Punjabi-speaking state within the Indian Union.[23] The SAD was thoroughly dissatisfied, at the exclusion of certain areas from the new state.[24] Interestingly, however, the Punjabi language had come in handy as a secular instrument to achieve a compact Sikh-dominated province.[25]

In the new Punjab State, which came into being in 1966, the Sikhs, for the first time in their history, found themselves in a slender numerical majority. The SAD, as was expected, have had, since then, some occasions of ruling the Punjab State, in collaboration with other parties of the left and the right.

It is little wonder that with such an actionful past the community's reflexes have been trained to be homeo-responsive to its salient historical referents. Appeal to some of these, for example, to Guru Gobind Singh or his martyred sons, have been found to be highly effective community-stimulants.[26] The SAD knows this and has been successfully using such referent to induce wholesale emotional arousal of the community. Simultaneously, however, the community has been experiencing other challenges, so very different from the earlier ones, that neither its dependence on its past exploits nor the recurring exhibitions of danger-signals may be of much help to it in facing these. The religious unconcern of the giant official educational apparatus, the audio-visual mass media, the judiciary, and all official employment agencies on the one hand and the emergence of new socio-economic parameters of consciousness as a sequel to the induction of science and technology in all fields of human activity, on the other, have set in motion a process of recession of social life from the tutelage of institutionalized religion. Slackness in the observance of religious rituals, practices, and injunctions and some cooling off in the sense of belonging is already in evidence among the Sikh youth.[27] The attack mounted by Marxism has a more penetrating thrust than passive secularism, as it claims to provide a materialistic alternative to the institution of religion.[28] Further, the monolithic character of the community is under attack by leftist analysts who revel in proving that religio-political slogans in the past have helped consolidate class interests of only the urban money-bags and the rural landed aristocracy among the Sikhs. Furthermore, the Union and State Governments are taking over the responsibility of welfare programmes, formerly conducted under the banner of religion. On top of it all, the Indian Constitution does not lend itself easily to providing safeguards to any endangered religion. For instance, howsoever angry a SAD Government in the Punjab may be at Sikh young men who choose to violate such religious taboos as shaving or smoking, it may find it genuinely difficult to undertake any legislative measures against defaulters.[29]

We know that irrespective of all other basic urges, the visible bond that binds the Sikhs into a community is that of religion, which is their medium both for self-identification and for distinction from others. But at least, as important as religion is the other contemporary social reality of secularism, with which all religion-based communities have to contend. The notional juxtaposition of religion and secularism is that of two opposites. While religion is God-centred, secularism is man-centred, while one believes in spiritualism, the other believes in materialism, while the one hopes to live after death, the other's earthly journey ends everything for ever, while the one believes in mystical experience, the other pins its faith on empiricism. Secularism also claims to substitute enquiry for reverential belief, change for tradition and nationalism for sectarianism. This is no place for apportioning credibility to the rival claims of either religion or materialistic secularism. If religion is believed by secularists to crouch only in those regions now which have not yet been explored fully by the searchlight of science, the religionists hope that the aridity of pure reason and the profligacy of material surfeit will force the materialists to seek peace of mind in the by-lanes of religion. Even so, in spite of the almost total rejection of secularization as an independent variable by Martin,[30] and serious obfuscation discovered by Glasner[31] among social scientists of the world about the sociology of secularism, it may be admitted that institutionalized religion has been yielding some ground to secularism, either by making workable adjustments with it or wherever found expedient, reserving "the activities of religious organization...to the realm of valutarism and personal conviction".[32] By and large, the Sikhs have also developed similar defensive mechanism against the heavy inroads of secularism, although their non-rejection of the physical world, insistence on family life, and belief in the dignity of labour so soften them towards many aspects of secularism, that they readily appropriate some of its elements, meet others half-way and stand up against a few others. For example, they take very kindly to the pursuit and application of science and technology, their intellectuals now try to explain their faith rationally, they rarely uphold superstition and either disbelieve or give scientific explanation of miracles. Also, they are keen to participate in the production of wealth[33] and make many other suitable adjustments with the changing socio-economic patterns of life. So much so, that few from amongst the most conservative of Sikhs would like to forego the characteristic benefits of modern living, in spite of its commitment to secularism, yet, it will be quite misleading to carry the impression that Sikhism, as an institution, is on the run and unadulterated secularism, equated here with materialism, is going to have an easy run over.

The reasons for the Sikh community's resistance to secularism range from the usual ones that all religions marshall against it, to those that are born of the doctrinal, geo-historical, demographic, international, and even intra-community situations, affecting the main body of the Sikhs. We would leave alone the stock objections and would refer to a few, which can be traced ultimately to the desire for identity, security, and power. It has been mentioned earlier that in the Punjab State the numerical tilt is presently slightly in favour of the Sikhs. The Hindus of the Punjab have not lost much time in developing the psychology of a minority community and in order to encash their minority status, most of them own Hindi, the official language of the Centre, even at the cost of their mother tongue, Punjabi, want education to be kept on the concurrent list of the Central Government, oppose any devolution of additional rights and powers to the federated units and hobnob directly with their counterparts in the Central Government in order that the Sikh aspirations for more power can be checked effectively. This makes Sikh politicians fret and fume and charge Punjabi Hindus as being "obstructionist counterweights", while the Hindus retort by calling them "oppressive", "boorish", and "communal". Such a state of affairs makes possible the sustenance of a bi-polar, high-tensional politics, in which the SAD and Hindu communal bodies, such as Rashtriya Swayamsewak Sangh (RSS) and Jana Sangh, feed each other's extremism. The misinterpretation or mal-implementation of liberal constitutional provisions, as already referred to earlier in this paper, will always be expected to engender strong Sikh reactions, but intra-community segmental realignments, frustrations arising from the loss of political power, clash of mutually-countervailing aspirations of selfish politicians, and failure to achieve the promised political stability and economic growth at government level, may also be twisted into extremist community posture. In the atmosphere where community-interest becomes the only idiom of political commerce and indiscriminate politicization of religion enjoys social approbation, it will be no wonder if the Sikh extremists mark their time to revive the call for a Sikh homeland on the plea of protecting Sikh culture. And from what we know of the history of instinctive Sikh responses to such situations the Sikhs may cede their reason to sentiment and throw their lot behind the extremists, preferring to side-track the awkward question of "what, after homeland?" In this context, the writer is reminded of the study of certain tribals, who had been taught drill by the British colonials for a full year, but it took the former only a split second to break all their disciplined formations and run helter-skelter, when they heard a country minstrel's voice from behind a sand dune, promising a musical recital of their forefathers' exploits.

The intimations of religious experience, the affirmation of a cultural value system, the preservation of a glorious historical tradition, and the continued assertion of an independent status have all come to be inextricably mixed up in the Sikh mind with unshorn hair. Whether a Sikh falls as a result of revolt against formalism or for the fun of fashion, it is regarded by the leaders of the community as a warning to the communal monolith and as a symptom of the crisis of identity. That is why the call of the *Panth*, the community, exercises even now, a great pull on the Sikh mind.

From the preceding account of Sikh responses to current affairs, it is clear that the onrush of secularism, with all its emphasis on materialism, privatization of religion, rationalism, science and technology has overtaken the Sikh community before its intellectuals have had time to formulate proper ideological answers to it. Presently, they are trying to maintain the community's image of compactness by undertaking ad hoc programmes, without coming into clash with the Indian Constitution. For example, the elite among the Sikhs are establishing in and out of their Punjabi-speaking State of the Punjab. English-medium public schools, in the fond hope of capturing all India competitive jobs and a bank with Sikh directors is accommodating qualified Sikh young men on its staff. But such programmes are in the nature of lollipops for a community, whose real need is a satisfactory existential adjustment with social reality in a way that its historical identity may remain intact.

NOTES AND REFERENCES

1. K.L., Gauba *Passive Voices*, Thacker & Co. Ltd., Bombay, 1973, p.58.
2. "...The Shah Commission ... has firstly arbitrarily truncated and reduced, as much as they could, the existing Punjabi region, and secondly, applied all principles of demarcation with a left-handed justice—made use of a principle where it could harm the Punjab and made use of a principle where it could harm the resultant territorial interests of

Haryana and Himachal Pradesh . . ." *Some Documents on the Demand for the Sikh Homeland,* All India Sikh Students Federation, Chandigarh, 1969, p. 33 hereafter cited as *Some Documents.*

3. K.L. Gauba, *op. cit.*, pp. 41-2, 361.

4.(*i*) "... A language is disowned because it has the misfortune, of being patronized by the Sikhs . . ." Ravel Singh, in the Foreword to *Punjabi Suba Demand,* Shiromani Gurdwara Prabandhak Committee, Amritsar, 1966.

4.(*ii*) "The Sikhs resent the stepmotherly treatment meted out to Punjabi language in the adjoining states of Delhi, Haryana, Himachal Pradesh, Jammu & Kashmir and Rajasthan . . ." Memorandum presented to Shrimati Indira Gandhi, the Prime Minister of India, New Delhi by the Chief Khalsa Diwan, Amritsar, on 14 July 1975, p.3.

4.(*iii*) See K.L. Gauba. *op. cit.*, p.363, for discriminatory treatment with Urdu.

5. Balwant Singh Ramuwalia, (President, All India Sikh Students Federation; now M.P.) *Punjab De Dhaun Utte Talwar* (Sword on the Neck of the Punjab), Shiromani Akali Dal, Amritsar, 1972, pp. 7-12.

6. Cf. the speech of Frank Anthony (Nominated Anglo-Indian) in the Lok Sabha, reproduced in K.L. Gauba, *op. cit.*, p.343.

7. "Apart from the legislature, the judiciary and the executive, there is another power in the State which is called, the Press, and allied means of these communications, such as Radio and Television. These are either state monopolies or virtual monopolies in the hands of members of the majority. There are not a few Sikhs who are sorely grieved at the treatment meted out to them in this quarter through misrepresentation as well as through suppression of news." *Some Documents, op. cit.*, p. 53.

8.(*i*) "Sikhs feel that they are not being trusted otherwise there was no reason why an exception should have been made in respect of formation of Punjabi Suba alone". *Punjabi Suba Demand,* The Shiromani Gurdwara Prabandhak Committee, Amritsar, 1966, p.4 of the initial unpaginated pages.

8.(*ii*) "Even the Deputy Prime Minister Sardar Patel suspected that most of the Muslims were disloyal to India . . ." Mohammad Ghouse, *Secularism, Society and Law in India,* Vikas Publishing House Pvt. Ltd., Delhi, 1973, p.8.

9. "... The most urgent problem of Indian nationalism today therefore is to Indianise or Hinduise such people and to develop in them national consciousness which may transcend their group consciousness as members of different religious communities. . . in short, they must adopt, Indian attitude, that national attitude towards their religion which must cease to colour their loyalties towards the mainsprings of Indian nationalism. All talk of separate Muslim or Christian or for that matter Sikh or Jain culture must stop. India is one country and it has but one culture." Balraj Madhok, *Indian Nationalism,* Bharati Sahitya Sadan, New Delhi, 1969, p. 96-7.

The works of V.D. Sāvarkar and Golwalkar may be consulted for more elaborate exposition of this point of view.
See also, *The Spokesman Weekly*, New Delhi, dated 15 May 1978, in which Hukam Singh, former Speaker of the (Indiān) Lok Sabha writes, "...The Policy of Indian Government since Independence whatever its complexion and whichever the cloak it has worn, has been to absorb and assimilate the Sikhs, and not to give any recognition by which these might further prolong their existence as a distinct community...."

10. The working Committee of Shiromani Akali Dal passed the following resolution in its meeting held on 20 July, 1966.
"... After having carefully viewed the findings, the reports and judgements of judicial and quasi-judicial Tribunals and Forums that have dealt with matters and cases involving important Sikh interests, COMES TO THE CONCLUSION that the entire judicial machinery and the judicial process of the Independent India, under influence of a certain section of Political Hindus, is prejudiced and has been perverted against the Sikh people in India in relation to their just and legal rights..." Quoted by S. Kapur Singh, in his speech made in the Lok Sabha on 6 September, 1966 reproduced in *Some Documents*, *op. cit.* pp. 33-4.
11. The formal Sikh greetings is *Wahiguru ji ka Khalsa Wahiguru ji ki Fateh*, i.e. The Khalsa belongs to God, God is the Victory.
12. Wilfred Cantwell Smith, *Modern Islam in India*, Lahore, pp. 189-90, quoted in *Secularism, Society and Law in India* p. 42, f.n. 32, See Also Hugh Tinker, *Foundations of Local-Self-Government in India, Pakistan and Burma*, Lalwani Publishing House, Bombay, 1967, pp. 41 and 49.
13. Hugh Tinker, *op. cit.* p 50.
14. "The worst feature of the Montford Reforms was the perpetuation of vested interests in religious communities..." Munshi, K.M., *Pilgrimage to Freedom*, Bhāratiya Vidya Bhawan, Bombay, 1967, p. 19.
15. A.B. Keith, *A Constitutional History of India*, Methuen & Co., Ltd., London, 1936, pp. 286-87.
16. "Modern Sikh History is centred round the Akali Party", Lord Birdwood in *A Continent Experiments*, quoted in Gulati, Kailash Chander, *The Akalis: Past and Present*, Ashajanak Publications, New Delhi, 1974, p 9. Reference may also be made to the New Policy Programme adopted by SAD at Anandpur on 16 and 17 October, 1973 in which it is claimed that SAD is the only forum for the expression of the corporate will of the Sikh community and fully entitled to represent it." Clause A (1) of the Manifesto in Punjabi, *Shiromani Akali Dal da Nawan Policy Programme*, published by Giani Ajmer Singh, Secretary. S.A.D. Amritsar, 1974, p. 3.
17. Dhanna Singh Gulshan, *Aaj Da Punjab Te Sikh Rajniti* (Punjabi), Dhaliwal Publishing House, Rampura Phul (Bhatinda), 1978, p. 34.
18 Gurnam Singh (Later Chief Minister, Punjab), *A Unilingual Punjabi State and the Sikh Unrest*, published by the author, 1960, p. 28, also

Kapur Singh, *Sāci Sakhi* (Punjabi), Raj Rup Prakashan, Jullundur, 1972, pp. 97-9. See also *Nawai Waqt*, Lahore, dated 16 December, 1968, reproduced on pp. 146-47, of *Sāci Sakhi*.

19. "... Mahatma Gandhi, Pandit Moti Lal Nehru and Pandit Jawahar Lal Nehru went to meet Baba Kharak Singh at his place .. and gave the Sikhs a solemn assurance that after India achieves political freedom, no Constitution shall be formed by the majority community unless it is freely acceptable to the Sikhs. This premise was then reduced into a formal policy resolution of All India Congress Commitee". Kapur Singh, *Four Speeches* (delivered in the ...Indian Parliament), The Sikh Cultural Centre, Calcutta, 1974, p. 9.
20. Referred to in the letter dated 5 July, 1960, to Prime Minister of India by Gurnam Singh, *op.cit.*, p. 39.
21. "... by some deliberate design or irresistible development of events, there pervades in the political atmosphere of India, an oppressive and stifling climate of dominant group opinion and governmental trend, in which it is forbidden to breathe unless in harmony with the wishes and prejudices of the communal majority. ." *ibid*, p. 38.
22. Kapur Singh, "Sikhism and Politics," *The Sikh Review*, Calcutta, August, 1971, p. 47.
23. "... in 1955, there was an agitation for this demand and twelve thousand Sikhs went to jail. Then in 1960, the movement continued for nearly eight months and 57,129 men and women went to jails ..." Arjun Singh Buddhiraja, *Two Talks between Sant Fateh Singh Ji and Shri Lal Bahadur Shashtri, the Prime Minister of India*, Akali Dal Delhi State, no date; p. 10.
24 The All World Panthic Convention of the Sikhs held on 10 January 1970 passed a bitter resolution which spoke of the Government of India's attitude of "great injustice, discrimination, oppression. zulam and violence" towards the Punjabis in general and the Sikhs in particular and complained that while creating the Punjabi Suba, it had resorted to "fraud, oppression and injustice of a low order and thus snatched from the Punjabi-speaking State, Chandigarh, Bhakra Complex and some Punjabi-speaking areas", Quoted in Ajit Singh Sarhari's, Punjabi Suba, U.C. Kapur & Sons, Delhi, 1970, p. 475.
25. "The unilingual Punjabi State was demanded by the Sikhs not because they considered any particular language as necessary for their spiritual survival or cultural viability but because they wanted to employ a fashionable political idiom to salvage their identity and to realise their destiny. . .", *Some Documents* p. 64. To be fair, however, to Sant Fateh Singh, the Dictator of Punjabi Suba Morcha he confined himself scrupulously to the linguistic parameters only.
26. *Abdul Yadan* the lectures of Sant Fateh Singh, President SAD and Dictator of Punjabi Suba Morcha, published by Sant Chanan Singh, Bagga Singh, Gurdwara Budha Jauhar, Ganga Nagar Rajasthan, 1962, are a good example of the powerful stimulus that is successfully created among the Sikhs through reference to their martyrs.

27. "... the process of disintegration of the collective soul of the Khalsa, set into motion by the Constitution Act 1950, with its overtones of secularism . , ." *Some Documents op. cit.* p. 71.
28. "... the corroding influences of ideologies that stalk this sacred land of the India in the guise of socialism, communism . . . " *ibid*, p. 71.
29. The following observation made by Kapur Singh, ex-M.P. in a speech made at the Annual Meeting of the All India Sikh Students Association at Chandigarh on 23 August, 1978 may be relevant in this connection : "In such a State (*i. e.* the proposed Sikh Homeland), we shall be able to ban public smoking in the interest of national health, and penalise apostasy, back-sliding and other forms of decay in human character, through legislative measure . . ." *ibid*, p.71
30. David Martin, *The Religious and the Secular*, Routledge & Kegan Paul, London, 1969.
31. Peter E. Glasner, *The Sociology of Secularisation*, Ambika Publications, New Delhi, 1977.
32. Benjamin A. Reist, "Church and State in America: A Theological Enquiry" in Robert Lee & E. Martin ed. *Religion and Social Conflict*, Oxford University Press, New York, 1964, p. 133.
33. "... To do away with poverty, hunger and shortages and to increase production of goods and wealth in order to bring about a just and good system. . ." (Translation from Punjabi), *Shiromani Akali Dal da Programme* (as adopted by SAD Working Committee at Anandpur on 16 and 17 October, 1973 and later passed by the General Body), published by Giani Ajmer Singh, Secretary, SAD Amritsar, 1974, p.3.

8

Breakdowns in Secular Situations

Ratna Naidu

THE IMPLICATIONS of the title of this paper notwithstanding I hasten to underline that the secular situation is an ideal construct in the minds of visionaries ; reality is ever fraught with the shadows of the sacred. The explanatory frameworks for the inexplicable impregnate human conduct in modern times as much as do scientifically reasoned ethics. That the unscientific explanatory frameworks are buried deep in the unconscious regions of the minds of men do not make them any less potent in activating irrational attitudes and motivations.

In multi-religious, multi-ethnic societies, where terms of exchange between communities is an important consideration, the purity of secular principles and motivations is an essential ingredient for good government. It is clear from the history of secular states that at best secularism has been an approximation. This paper will enquire into situations of breakdown of secularism.

When and how, do governments formed under avowedly secular contracts become trapped into religious concerns ? Further, how and why in such a governmental system do citizens get differential treatment based on their different religious nexus ? The following analysis can be conveniently divided into two: (1) The deliberate violation of secular contracts rationalized by the state in terms of the ethics of humanitarianism, and conversely, by religious leaders in terms of the ethics of religiosity ; and (2) The inadvertent violation of the secular philosophy by the majorities vis-a-vis the minorities because of the template of collective memories and myths which consciously or unconsciously guide action.

Secular philosophy provides a framework for the conduct of life based on the twin values of science and humanitarianism.

Science gives glimpses of utopias inherent in its infinite potential for material progress, and humanitarianism, that—"man is the measure of all things"—firmly anchors aspirations to the well-being of mankind here and now. Religiosity and religious phenomena or questions of life after death are part of a philosophy that neither denies nor recognizes the relevance of religious precepts (based as they are on non-observable deities and life after death) for the conduct of life. It is obvious, therefore, that there is no logical opposition between religion and secularism—they would seem to involve mutually exclusive systems of philosophy.

It follows that the citizen's contract with the secular state allows him religious freedom, and the right to have the conditions of his citizenship defined without reference to his religious affiliation. More fundamentally, since in the secular state the structure of religious authority and secular authority are separated, in theory any number of organized religions can flourish and propagate without let or hindrance from the state. However, when we look at the history of secularism and secular states, we find that the breakdown of these contracts between the citizen and the state have been more the rule than the exception.

Long before the clear conceptualization of the notion of a secular state, pressures of governance of more complex societies split separate the organizational and authority structure of religious and political institutions. But the value system of the two spheres continued to be the same even though the aims, objectives, method of operation, and spheres of influence of religion and political interests are different. While religion provides meaningful frames of reference which make possible the acceptance and the endurance of the vicissitudes of life and death, the endeavour of political authority is to evolve normative frames of reference which coerce individuals to the societal process, and therefore make society possible. These frames of references, as mentioned, could and for centuries did mesh. The social hierarchy sanctioned by religious authority was the normative pattern within which exchange of goods and services was regulated by political authority. Religious stoicism enabled the acceptance of disabilities, discrimination, and inequality generated by biological and social heredity and buttressed by particular systems of political economy.

It was the psychology of humanism and the methodology of science that so challenged the religious acceptance of fate as to drive a wedge between the religious and political frames of reference. Indeed, we are aware that in communist countries (as in the USSR) the political will generated by scientific humanism almost sought to wipe out religion from the societal process. But the religious experience which has evolved since the beginning of time and has shaped and shapes so much of human life, such as kinship, fads and foibles in food and drink, rituals, morals and manners, belief systems, ceremonial calendars, psychic disposition, and so on, did not collapse at the foundation (was it ever seriously expected?) by the fervour of scientific humanism even in communist countries.[1]

Elsewhere I have presented an analysis of religious experience in the sociological context. I would like to take the liberty of quoting at length a passage from that analysis to bring out two points, namely, that to the human condition religiosity is a functional imperative and that there are patterned ways in which this imperative interacts with other imperatives which are necessary to the societal process. I followed the theologian Friedrich Schleirermacher in defining the essence of the religious experience as "a feeling of absolute dependence".[2]

> ....Religion is seen as a mode of self-consciousness, whereby the individual is aware of his infinite creative potential, and of his ability to determine the course of events, but is at the same time grounded in 'absolute dependence' on the Holy. To put this in mundane terms, the individual is never infinitely free : nor at any moment is he conscious of being an absolute creator, . . . there is always a grid of constraints within which he operates.... Yet the extraordinary experience is the consciousness of confrontation with something which one cannot determine at all. In a narrow sense, one might say, this is the religious self-consciousness . . . . The 'feeling of absolute dependence' is not merely a psychic reaction of the individual in relation to the Absolute, but is rooted

> in the experiential matrix of relative dependencies and by implication relationships . . . .
>
> . . . Each religion depicts a certain image of the cosmic world involving both concepts of the world and of God. The conceptual imagery of religious language functions as a controlling mechanism both for absolute and relative dependencies, aiming always to secure world-consciousness and God-consciousness in a stable relationship.
>
> . . . With each new discovery in the world of science, each new theoretical formulation of the phenomenal world, resulting in the evolution of new ways of adapting to the environment, the relation between world-consciousness and God-consciousness receives a jolt. The reformation movements (such as the Protestant movements in the West, Buddhism in Asia) and new religious revelations and interpretations of the scriptures are very often attempts to restore equilibrium between God-consciousness and World-consciousness after the World has acquired new dimensions. After acquiring new dimensions, the World requires new ways of defining relationships between man and his environment, including his fellowmen.
>
> ...Religious symbols, then, encourage certain types of behaviour patterns and discourage others, restrain and guide motivations, and always ground these in the context of ultimate existential questions. Since religious values indicate the kind of cosmic world a society prefers to imagine, they have considerable psychological hold over the members of the society even if religious forces do not have a direct impact but are filtered through cultural values.... .[3]

The conceptualization of ther eligious experience as outlined above, was presented in the context of an earlier work, but it would seem still satisfactory for the purposes of my exposition here.

The analysis also indicates how religion and politics may interact, so that the belief system, and following from it, the coercive norms and values from one sphere infiltrate the values and norms of another sphere. Religious dispositions and ecclesiastical authority may vigorously challenge political will where it feels it dictates against its sense of religiosity. Since, as we have seen, religion has to conceptually tie the world of the Gods to life on earth, the sense of religiosity (experienced mundanely through propitiating sacrifices, reverential rituals, and so on) could be violated at numerous points where pressuers of change taking place in other spheres bear down on the crust of these traditions. Conversely, the political will of the people has sanctioned inroads into the affairs of religious organizations by governmental fiat, as and when they violate humanitarian principles. These cross-pressures have resulted in several types of relationship between the church and the State in the course of the evolution of Western democracies. Among these the two predominant historical types[4] are (1) recoginition of a state religion which is then subsidized and accorded a pre-eminent position, and also influenced and controlled by the state in various ways, as in England ; and (2) the jurisdictional type (as in Holland) where the different religions are given equal status, recognition and support by political authority.

The ex-colonial newly constituted nations, attempted to leap-frog into modernity by a more rigorous separation of religion and politics by constitutionally declaring themselves secular states. But only the developed among the newly constituted nations such as the United States of America, could in their circumstances of open frontiers, buoyant economy, and expanding productivity try to remain faithful to their constitutions.

In the circumstances of forced draft industrialization which is taking place in most of the states of Asia and Africa, the political will of the modernizing elite is often in conflict with the religious authorities for their reactionary role in society. In the communist countries where the political elite's commitment to economic development and modernization is total and unequivocal, religion is definitely considered a liability.

The conflict between religion and politics in the context of state sponsored development can be in terms of routine practicalities of performance. Richard Pipes's analysis[5] of the interference of the Soviet State in religious rituals of the Muslim population brings this out. Clearly, the fasting required of the faithful during the entire 28 days of the month of Ramzan may affect their performance at work. As a result the Ramzan fast is severely repressed by State authorities. Another important Muslim ritual, the five daily prayers require stoppage of work which in the Soviet system amounts to "economic sabotage". Further, Friday, the day for communal prayer is a regular working day in the USSR. Thus religious experience which requires elaborate rituals which affect one's performance at work is a direct challenge to the efficient functioning of the communist political economy with its emphasis on the relentless drive for increased production for the welfare of the masses. Yet, the ruthless suppression of these rituals so crucial to the Muslim religious experience, surely involves the breaking of the secular contract, which guarantees "free practice of religious rites"[6] in the USSR.

The conflict between politics and religion also arises where the values of the one are incompatible with the values of the other. For instance, political will generated by scientific humanism put pressure on world religions for the reinterpretation of specific meanings of different types of social organizations which coercively bind individuals to society. Thus in India there has been tremendous pressure on religious leaders to derecognize the scriptural sanctity of the caste system and for this purpose to reinterpret relevant texts. Predictably, there has been resistance on this issue from the more conservative among the religious leaders such as the Sankaracharya of Puri whose public utterances justifying the practice of untouchability on the basis of Hindu texts caused countrywide controversy.[7] It is significant that there was presure from the public on the Government to take action against the Sankaracharya since his utterances thereatened to violate constitutional safeguards against casteism.

One may, in this fashion, identify the areas where the secular contract (the separation of the affairs of the state and that of religion) is vulnerable to assault. Typically these are the areas where religion interlocks with other functionl subsystems of society. The educational institutions, for instance, are an area of conflict because here values are learnt and transmitted through generations. While religious traditions provide the fundamental framework of values, political will also generates a set of values—those which give direction in the conduct of the affairs of the state. To the degree that these latter values are incompatible with the values of one or the other religion, religious groups may encounter opposition from the state in running their own school system. Similarly, interference from the state may be encountered by religious groups on the question of the appropriate use of their corporate wealth. Indeed, these are typical areas where the State has come into conflict with particular religious groups both in India and the USSR.[8]

As is evident, the breakdown in the secular situation seems more evident today in the aggression emanating from the State. However, one cannot underestimate the powerful role played by religious lobbies in the affairs of the State, especially in the less authoritarian political systems, and also if religion happens to be a powerful force in the body politic. Turkey is a good example of the latter.[9] An extraordinary process of secularization was initiated there as early as in 1924. As is well known Islamic laws were discarded in preference for a civil code, religious instruction were purged from schools, and the Imams lost official support in terms of pecuniary and other benefits. The trivial, but in many respects a fundamental, insignia of the secular State are the symbols which accompany the ceremonial activities of the State. All rites with religious significance are excluded from such ceremonies. The oath on public occasions is taken on a man's honour and not in the name of God. By 1928, the Turk had stopped taking the oath in the name of Allah and was taking it on his own honour.[10] But Islam which is woven deep into Turkish peasant society surfaced back into the affairs of the State within two decades. By the early fifties, the process of desecularization had started and today Turkish secularity is of the same twilight variety as in most places in the world.

The role played by religious lobbies in political policy making in the United States—certainly a country of secular reputation—is well known. Most of the denominations of the Protestant Church, the Roman Catholic Church (whose political arm is the National Catholic Welfare Conference), the Jewish Synagogue, and others, maintain offices in Washington D.C., for the avowed purpose of shaping policy at the national and international level.[11] Thus, it would seem that even in a country like the USA which undoubtedly cherishes secular principles, the shadows of the sacred find release in the affairs of the State through institutional channels.

There is finally the more subtle method by which the sacred myths of religion operate to break down the secular situation. This is through its hold over the unconscious regions of the minds of men. There is always a residue of religious symbolism perhaps filtered in the form of cultural values which remain dormant in the minds of apparently the most non-religious of men. These certainly bias action in one direction rather than another.

The inadvertent violation of the secular philosophy by the majority vis-a-vis the minorities takes place most often due to biased images which one religious group has of another. This stereotypical imagery forms part of the collective memory of communities. This imagery is lethal to the pluralist-secularist philosophy precisely because it operates almost at a preconscious level.[12] In multi-religious societies, a ritualistic claim to secularism can camouflage a great deal of discrimination against minority religious groups.

The majority religious groups having a common cultural heritage dominate administration and government, both in terms of numbers and in terms of positions in the upper echelons of the governmental and political hierarchy. In times and countries of stress and scarcity, who gets what and how, whether punishment or reward, is certainly determined by one's religious and ethnic nexus. For, the rule of law is always cushioned by powers of discretion and controls are inevitably welded to the convenience of the power elite. The discretionary edges of judgements, decisions, allocations, and so on, are tilted in favour of the familiar, the known, and the loved. The outgroups, the minorities, and the stranger have to bear the brunt of their "strangeness" vis-a-vis the dominant cultural group in the State.

Elsewhere I have pleaded for research and training,[13] almost psycho-analytic in orientation which may enable those who confront situations involving a number of religious and or ethnic groups (the administrator, the teacher, the law enforcement personnel) to guard against patterns of instinctual behaviour which is inherent to their identitive and affiliative condition. In the absence of such enlightened thinking and policies, secularization in societies of scarcities such as the USSR and India may merely steamroller processes such as that of Russification[14] and Indianization.[15]

Religiosity, the necessity for a feeling ultimately of "absolute dependence", in one form or another, is a functional imperative to the human condition. Realistic recognition of this would enable the secular state to apply humanitarian principles also to questions of religion. The state could, for instance, co-opt religious leaders of different faiths to the decision-making process and continuously dialogue with them to impress upon them the necessity to evolve meanings from the ancient scriptures which would give support to the moral pillars of modern governments. Likewise, the secular pluralist State must safeguard against the in-built persecutive tendencies of the dominant religious groups vis-a-vis the minorities. For as we know, even political leaders imbued with scientific humanism and cosmopolitanism are prisoners of the concepts and imagery which are their cultural heritage, and which in turn are tied to the faith of their forefathers. A benevolent State would protect its religious minorities from the administrative prejudices which emanate from such imagery.

NOTES AND REFERENCES

1. Non-Soviet writers mention continuing religious practice and faith and the articulation of the felt need for faith in the USSR. See for instance Robert C. Tucker, "Religious Revival in Russia", in Alex Inkeless and Kert Geiger (eds), *Soviet Society : A Book of Readings*, Boston, Houghton Mifflin Co., 1961. Reprint d from "Party and Church in the Soviet Union —— Travel Notes" *The Russian Review*, Vol. 18 (1959), pp. 285-93. There is an excellent account also in Hendrick Smith, *The Russians*, New York, Ballantine Books. 1976 pp. 557-86.
2. Friedrich Schleirermacher, *On Religion : Speeches to its Cultural Despisers*, trans. John Oman, New York, Harper Torch Books, 1958 ; and *The Christian Faith*, trans. H. R. Mackintosh and J. S. Stewart, New York, Harper Torch Books, 1963.
3. Ratna Dutta, *Values in Models of Modernization*, Delhi, Viaks, 1971, pp. 65-6 ; jointly published with Schenkman, Cambridge, Mass, 1971.
4. A convenient summary of these types is available in Ved Prakash

Luthera, *The Concept of the Secular State and India*, Delhi, Oxford University Press, 1964.

5. Richard Pipes, "Assimilation and the Muslims : A Case Study" in Inkeles and Geiger (eds.), *Soviet Society : A Book of Readings*, *op. cit.*, pp. 588-607. Reprinted from Muslims of Soviet Central Asia : Trends and Prospects", *The Middle East Journal*, Vol. 9 (1955), pp. 147-62 and 293-308.
6. This is the fifth point made in the Decree of the Council of People's Commissars, 23 January 1918 on the separation of Church and State (reprinted in N. Struve *Christians in Contemporary Russia*, London, 1967, pp. 378-79). However, one may note that the sixth point in the same decree, says that "no one may defect from the fulfilment of his public obligations by reason of his religious views". Muslims would of course deny that the Ramzan fast detracts them from fulfilling their work obligations.
7. Most newspaper reported (in 1970) the Sankaracharya's views and the controversy which followed. See also, Balbir Singh *Foundation of Indian Philosophy*, Delhi, Orient Longman, 1971, p. 263.
8. For an account of State encroachment into administration of temple endowments in India and relevant legislation, as also other facets of state regulation of religion in India, see Donald Eugene Smith *India as a Secular State*, Princeton, Princeton University Press, 1963 ; also Luthera, *The Concept of the Secular State and India*, *op cit.* pp. 115-33. There is a large body of literature on regulation of religion in the USSR of which the following could be mentioned : Vladimir Grovski (ed), *Church and the State Behind the Iron Curtain*, New York, Friedrich A. Praeger Inc., 1955; John S. Curtis, *The Russian Church and the Soviet State, 1917-1950*, Boston, Little Brown & Co., 1953; R. Conquest (ed.), *Religion in the USSR*, London, Bodley Head, 1968; W. Kolarz, *Religion in the Soviet Union*, London, Macmillan, 1962; David Land, *Politics and Society in the USSR*, London, Weidenfield and Nicolson, 1970; and Inkeles and Geiger (eds.), *op. cit.* This list is possibly biased since it does not take into account Soviet source materials.
9. See, Eleanor Bisbee, *The New Turks*, Philadelphia, University of Pennsylvania Press, 1951; H.A. Rees, "Secularism and Islam in Turkish Politics" in *Current History*, Vol. 32, 1957; Luthera, *op. cit.*, pp. 53-7.
10. This extent of secularization was astonishing in a State which was not even multi-religious and need not have worried about the sentiments of other religious groups in its ceremonial moments.
11. See Leo Pfeffer, *Church, State and Freedom*, Boston, The Beacon Press, 1953; Anson Phelps Stokes, *Church and State in the United States*, 3 vols, New York, Harper and Brothers, 1950.
12. For further analysis and elaborations of these points, see my book *The Communal Edge to Plural Societies; India and Malaysia*, Delhi, Vikas Publication (in press).
13. *Ibid*,

14. Russification refers to the process of increasing political, cultural, demographic and economic domination of the Russians over other ethnic and religious groups in the Soviet Union. The Russians who constitute the cultural majority in the Soviet Union and traditionally Slavonic, adhere to the Russian Orthodox Church, speak the Russian language, and by their numerical preponderance control the political and governmental machinery. Among the minority religious groups who feel most threatened by the political and cultural dominance of the Russians are the Jews and Muslims. On Russification see, Richard Pipes, "Reflections on the Nationality Problem in the Soviet Union" in Nathan Glazer and Daniel P. Moynihan (eds.), *Ethnicity Theory and Experience*, Cambridge, Harvard University Press, 1975, pp. 454-65; Joseph L. Nogee (ed.) *Man, State, and Society in the Soviet Union*, London, The Pall Mall Press, 1972 ; "The National Minorities", pp. 500-43; Inkeles and Geiger (eds.), *op. cit.*, pp. 584-88; and Lane, *op. cit.*, pp. 447-49. On Russophilism see Smith, *The Russians*, *op. cit.*, pp. 557-86.
15. The term Indianization refers to the slogan raised by Professor Balraj Madhok and some of his followers in the erstwhile Jana Sangh that the Muslims should be Indianized. Muslims interpret this as being forced to accept the cultural dominance of the Hindi-Hindu majorities who dominate political and economic life in India.

PART TWO

SOVIET CONTRIBUTORS

9

Religion as a Social Phenomenon

I.A. Krivelev

The problem dealt with in the present paper has a number of new aspects, of which the following are discussed below : (1) The individual and the social content of religious ideology ; (2) the influence of religion upon social development; (3) the church as a social institution based on religious ideology ; and (4) the social role of religion at the present time. It goes without saying that within the scope of one report these questions can be discussed only briefly.

Throughout the history of pre-Marxist and modern non-Marxist treatment of religion one of the approaches has been to regard religious ideology as a sum total of individual experience, though at different stages of that history and with different scholars this approach has had the different forms and colours. Religion as a "sense of absolute dependence" (F. Schleyermaher), as a product of "I and God" relationship (S. Kierkegaard), meditation of the "philosophizing savage" (E. Taylor, G. Spenser), the subconscious and the related activities of "I" and "Super-I" (S. Freud and neo-Freudians), the psychological burden and dramatic inward experiences of a personality left alone in the world (existentialism—K. Jaspers, M. Heidegger, and G. Marcelle), the "religious experience" of the individual (pragmatism, especially that of W. James), and the individual's "meetings" with God (modern Protestantism—K. Bart, neo-*hassidism*—M. Buber)—for all the difference of their initial philosophical stands and of the scientific, social and ideological value of these theories, all of them treat religion as a purely personal phenomenon.

Such an approach distorts the actual essence of religion. The key to understanding the peculiarities and content of individual consciousness lies in the social environment, in which a given individual lives, with its distinct system of social relations, level and character of material and spiritual culture, and generally accepted views and ideas. The consciousness of an individual is not a spontaneous and closed within itself product of his own self but a social phenomenon. Both by its origin and by its content it is intimately imbued and interacts with the consciousness of other individuals who constitute a social group, a class, and a society. It is quite natural therefore that the modern psychological theory does not confine the sphere of its investigations to individual consciousness only, 'social psychology being the most essential of its parts. Being systematized and formulated in doctrinal, logical, and consistent form, the content of social psychology constitutes ideology, the social nature of which is obvious.

Almost as soon as a person is born the process of his "socialization" begions, leading him to assimilate all that is accessible for him in the mass of material and spiritual values of the society in which he lives. This assimilation is not a passive process, for the individual is, so to say, an atom of this society and his activities form part of its life.

This is the principal basis for Marxism's negative attitude to the Robinson Crusoe-like reasoning, that is, when a person, his consciousness in particular, is considered "within himself and itself" and out of touch with the life of society. The rational part of the concept of collective ideas put forward by E. Durkheim and L. Levy-Bruhl had been known to Marxism as the theory of social consciousness long before their works were published.

If these ideas are applied to the religious life of an individual —and there is no reason whatsoever not to do so—then we have to infer that his religious feelings and the so-called religious experience are bound up with the social group psychology and not with the narrowly understood individual psychology, and, if the problem is to be considered at a still higher level, with religious ideology.

Documents, which contain dogmatic principles of any religious teaching, are not products of individual ideologists. While recognizing the role of those men who are believed to have nursed their respective religions, be it Christ (if he really existed), Mohammed or Buddha, we are aware that their preachings were not to remain a voice in the wilderness only, but were based and fed on the urgent emotional experience and aspirations of the people at large and corresponded to the turn of mind of the day. Any religious teaching that eventually took root was in this sense a social product.

Prior to becoming a more or less hardened dogma, such new teachings had for some time—in some instances for centuries—been the subject of struggle between different social and church groups. Sometimes this struggle concentrated around rather subtle nuances in certain religious formulae. It would be naive to believe that, for example, long conflicts between different church camps literally over the Greek iota, that is over the question whether the Greek word, denoting comparative merits of Son God in relation to Father God in Christianity, should be spelt with this letter, were only due to the ardent desire to find the final and infallible truth in the matter. Different theological attitudes were in fact nothing else but symbols and "the Colours" of different social and political groupings, that is, of the embodiments of state and political power. This is one more proof to the social basis of religious ideological formulae.

To believe in the truth of the dogmatic tenets established by the Church authorities is compulsory for the believer. It is true that under different historical conditions the extent of this compulsion is different. There was a time in the history of different religions when the believer's disagreement with a letter of dogma entailed relentless persecution. Today the demand to believe in the truth of dogmatic tenets of the church is not so unconditional, the church winking at considerable differences in the interpretation of the doctrine—not only among the rank-and-file but also among the clergy and noted theologicians. The content of religious faith has, of late, become far more individualized than in the past. Non-confessional religiosity, understood to mean that man is not bound by any single religion and does not belong to any church but believes in certain religious truths, mostly rather vague, such as God, the world soul, a supernatural source of moral imperatives, etc., has become rather widespread. Even so, religious views are not solely the product of individual consciousness, being largely evoked by reading, intercourse with other people holding similar views, and the mass media. Hence, the above phenomena of modern "individualization" of religious views and experiences are not at variance with our thesis about the social nature of religion.

The stress on the individual or, conversely, social roots of religious consciousness is essential in dealing with the problem of the origin of religion. The positivists of the evolutionary trend, whose typical representative in the last century was E. Taylor, proceeded in this question from the assumption of the individual thinking of the "philosophizing savage", which raised before him the questions concerning the nature and origin of the surrounding world phenomena. His level of thinking and factual ignorance in these matters led him to fantastic inferences, and so he developed religious ideas about spirits and souls and later—about gods, angels and devils. There is also a seemingly opposite answer to the problem of the origin of religion, based in fact on the same individualistic assumptions. I am referring to the theory of deception which was known far back in ancient times and roused a broad response in the Age of Enlightenment in France. According to this theory religion was born when "the first fraud met the first fool" and deceived him. In this light, religion appears to be not a social product but a product imposed on society by malevolent individuals. Neither of these variants of the individualistic theory has any scientific foundation.

The concept of the "philosophizing savage" regards primitive man as a thoughtful individual who sets himself and solves "eternal problems" which essentially have nothing to do with his everyday life. Ethnographical and archaeological findings show, however, that primitive man's consciousness is closely tied up with his material and productive activities. And the conditions and nature of these activities are by no means specific for each individual, being common for such collectives as gens and tribes and for the groups of people that compose them.

The consciousness and thinking of primitive men included, in the first place, themes relating to the conditions of their life and work, which were precisely the things fantastically reflected in their consciousness. These themes were social in content and their religious and fantastic reflection was also engendered by, and belonged to social rather than to exclusively individual consciousness.

The theory of the origin of religion, according to which one man, driven by self-interest, inspired other people with religious illusions, does not hold water either from the general theoretical viewpoint or in the light of ethnographical and historical facts. Religion was the result of collective self-deception and not the deception of many by one. Thus, religion is a social phenomenon by its origin as well.

Moreover, religion has a paramount social importance. Since its inception, it has had substantial influence over every aspect of life in society, especially over the development of spiritual culture. Whether this influence has been, as its advocates claim, progressive and stimulating or, conversely, retarding and hampering is another question which deserves special comprehensive and concrete research in various fields and aspects of culture at different stages of its development and of the class struggle.

Since it came into being, religion as a social phenomenon could not but play an important role in the life of society at every stage of its history. We are referring here to the role of both religious ideology and religious institutions.

Religious ideology does not always have a direct and definite influence on human behaviour and thereby on social development. The behaviour of social classes and groups as well as that of individuals depends on the circumstances of life and their position under these circumstances. When real class, group and individual interests are at variance with the existing ideology, the latter practically ceases to be a guide to action though it is still preached in sermons and pious exhortations which are not translated into reality. There are many examples of how the the same people and social groups, while sparing no efforts in preaching certain religious ideological views, live a life which is, in its very principles, directly opposite to these views. It should be noted that in the history of religion this is a rule rather than an exception.

The paradox, it is true, is mitigated by the fact that the documents formulating the fundamental tenets of some religious ideology or another contain as a rule mutually contradictory principles relating to man's individual or social behaviour : alongside with the prohibition of murder one can find numerous instructions as to when, whom and what to kill for it is not only advisable but necessary to kill ; alongside with the prohibition of adultery, stories of absolute fornication scenes are told from the lives of some most reverend characters whom religion recognizes as righteous and even holy.

US Presidents as a rule show their Christian piety and adherence to the tenets of the Gospel. But this did not prevent them from killing hundreds of thousands of innocent people in Vietnam. Truman, a devout Baptist, started the devilish use of the atom bomb. And Baptists are specially noted for their zeal in preaching the gospel ideology of brotherly love and the Decalogue of the Old Testament which prohibits murder! But then, it is easy for them to refer to those passages in the Old Testament which directly order genocide in respect of the ancient peoples of Palestine and even to those in the New Testament where the preaching of love for men alternates with threats, damnations, and promises of eternal hell.

The "many-sided" character of religious ideology makes it possible for it to play a contradictory role in the history of society. But whenever its meaning comes into open conflict with life and its demands, it sinks into the background and life passes it by.

This question is especially important when seen against the interests and aims of social life and struggle. If the adherents of those religions which recognize divine providence and a Supreme Being's systematic concern about the good of mankind were in the least consistent, they would have to give up every effort to change the social order in the interests of man and humanity. The fatalism manifest in most religions would have to doom their adherents to quietism, indifference, and inaction in social life and class struggle. Even nowadays one may occasionally notice this motif in Christian preaching disseminated by the modern mass media : mankind's deliverance from all social and other evils and calamities cannot be brought about until the second Advent of the Saviour, so the efforts of all political parties, governments and any other social force of today to bring about a radical change for the better in the destiny of mankind are futile and pointless. Yet, despite this, clerical organizations never cease active interference in social struggle and, to justify it, resort to some "convincing" quotations from the Holy Scripture and the Holy Legend.

This results in a very contradictory role which was played and is being played by religious ideology in the history of social, namely, class struggle. This is especially true of those periods in the history of society when non-religious forms of ideology were practically non-existent. At that time, the interests of the oppressors and the oppressed and of the conflicting social forces in general found their expression in different though equally religious ideologies. In medieval Europe, for example, heretical doctrines were ideological expression and an embodiment of the corresponding social movements directed against the existing feudal system, the latter being sanctified by the orthodox Catholic doctrine. Does it mean then that religious ideology as such can be considered neutral to social progress and capable of expressing the interests of the exploiters and the exploited, of the progressive and the reactionary sections of society? It it were so, the entire problem would be reduced to whether the given religion is reactionary or progressive.

We do not share this view. Religion as a whole does not lead people to improve the social order in the interests of the working and exploited majority and to change society in a revolutionary way but to preserve the *status quo* in the hope that it will be changed for the better through the interf rence of forces from beyond. Religion blinds people to the scientific recognition of the forces and phenomena of nature and society and leads to blind belief in its dogmatic postulates which are on the whole contrary to this cognition. There are, of course differences in the form and degree both with regard to different religions and to one and the same religion at different stages of its history. but in general the above evaluation remains, in our view, correct for religion, as an ideology, as a whole.

The fact that progressive social-revolutionary movements often assumed religious form and took on religious slogans does not contradict the above characteristic of religion. What was progressive in all those cases was the social content of the movement, its religious form only showing its immaturity and the dimness of its social and political make-up. The religious-ideological form of the movement was the source of its weakness rather than force.

The role of religion in social development should not of course, be considered from its political side only. The influence of religious and church institutions and of religious ideology itself extends to all spheres of social and individual life. The general development of material and spiritual culture, particularly of natural and social sciences, the history of art, the evolution of morality and morals, the development of forms of social and family life—all these aspects of the life of society have always been influenced by religion. And if we disengage ourselves from those separate stages and marginal aspects of development, which do not bear on its essence, it should be admitted that throughout and everywhere in the course of history religion has been a kind of slag in the "production process" of social life.

While the social basis of religion as an ideology can be established by theoretical analysis, then the whole point about the church as an institution is easy to see and does not need special argumentation.

In the course of historical practice the church acquired, as a rule, additional features and functions which bore only an indirect, if any, relation to religion. Formally, the church united people solely on the basis of their common religious faith, served their religious needs, and ensured their salvation in the other world. But its functions also had a more "earthly", perfectly practical and vital meaning. The people united by the church paid for its religious services with material values and the church became a wealthy land, castle, factory, bank, and railway owner, a leading partner in major joint stock and holding companies. In the Middle Ages, the Catholic Church in Europe possessed one-third of all cultivated land.

The economic power of church organizations today is also very great. The available data show that the funds of all the religious organizations in the USA amount to 79.5 billion of which the Catholic Church has 44.5 billion and the Jewish religious communities about 7 billion dollars. The budget of the Baptist organization alone, headed by Billy Gray, is estimated at 15 million dollars. As regards the Catholic Church as a whole, its financial resources are expressed in figures comparable to the national property of some major capitalist countries. One might ask : What does it all have to do with religion? The answer is that the question of church property has a direct bearing on the problem dealt with in this report.

Since the funds possessed by the church are put into industrial and commercial rotation, they produce new dividends, so that the church continues to grow rich, in this case owing to factors that bear no relation to religion. But religious sources such as charges for religious rites, donations, and soon continue to make substantial contribution to its income. Moreover, in some countries, like the FRG, for example, special church taxes are imposed on the citizens who formally belong to certain religious communities. In a number of countries, especially where the church is not separated from the state, the latter finances it through special provisions in its budget in which case, the church is financed precisely as a religious organization having definite ideological functions. Part of the church funds are used for religious purposes such as the publication of sermons and apologetic literature and running special educational institutions that train clergymen, missionaries and preachers. Finally, the upkeep of the clergy itself involves spendings directly associated with religion because it is the clergy who serve the religious needs of the believers by performing religious rites and acting as mediators between people and supernatural forces. In short, the economic power and activities of the church express one of the aspects of religion's social character.

The economic power of the church helps to support the other spheres of its power and influence. It is all the more important for the church that its practical authority has always been based, among other things, on the ideological factor, namely on the belief of the believers that the church is the sole possessor of absolute truth and that any disagreement with it means heresy fraught with the danger of eternal damnation of the human soul.

At different stages of their history churches played an important political role. There were also theocratic states in which power formally was in the hands of none other than God himself, which is what the very term "theocracy" means. There are a few naive people, however, who do not understand that the term "hierocracy", that is, the power of the clergy and of the church hierarchy, would be more appropriate here. This definition can be rightfully applied to the Arab caliphates of the Middle Ages, to the State of the Holy Altar and to the State of the Dalai Lama in Tibet. In all of these cases, the existing social system did not, however, mean anything unearthly or spiritual. It was an earthly class and political institution which displayed its religious origin only in its form.

The church has always expressed definite class interests and played a definite role in social life and in every form of class struggle. Without going into history we can substantiate this thesis with present-day facts. Some time ago Turkish sultans in the capacity of Caliphs claimed to be at the head of the pan-Islam world movement which pursued the perfectly secular aims of the exploiter classes of the Near East rather than religious ones. If we consider the past few decades in the history of West European states, the social and political activity of the Catholic church is particularly striking. It finds its organizational expression in the existence and functioning of political parties, which call themselves Christian Democratic, trade unions, directly associated with the church, and various "enlightening" organizations and association which are directly or indirectly dependent on the church. Clericalism as a religiously tinted political movement, directed by church organizations, is a real phenomenon of the present day.

Churches have never been indifferent to topical problems of their contemporary societies. The famous pronouncements ascribed to Christ by the evangelists : "My kingdom is not of this world" has been repeatedly and convincingly disproved in the course of the history of Christianity. Christian churches of all denominations have always interfered in the affairs of "this world", striving in all cases to make their views on any matter prevail. A vivid example is provided by the declared views of the Vatican on the main social problem of today—the attitude to capitalism and socialism.

Even at the end of the last century the Vatican began to come up with encyclicals and other official documents on this problem. Beginning with the famous *Rerum Novarum* (1891) these documents have been offering a church solution to the struggle between labour and capital—a solution which provides for the unchanged preservation of the basis of the capitalist system. In the course of decades, as the historical inevitability of the replacement of capitalism by socialism becomes increasingly more evident, emphasis in the Vatican documents has shifted : direct denunciation of socialism is disappearing, while notes of certain sympathy, though rather vague, for the interests of the oppressed, both in the capitalist world and in countries that were, until recently, under colonial rule, are becoming stronger. But the church, of course, by no means approves of the active forms of struggle against the existing society, which are called for and organized by the most progressive forces of today. Be it as it may, it should be emphasized that from the point of view of the problem at hand, the church is an active social force—a fact which is in full accord with all its traditions and which will apparently continue to characterize it as long as it exists as a social institution which provides an organizational framework for religion as a form of social consciousness.

The most topical of all problems connected with religion is the problem of the role of religion as a social phenomenon today, at the present stage of social, political, and cultural development.

Church organizations of different religions and denominations are very active in the purely political sphere. In countries where the church is formally separated from the state there seems to be no room left for it to be directly involved in the political struggle. But this is practically the case only in socialist countries where this separation is consistently ensured and where churches exist precisely as religious organizations whose business is to serve the religious needs of believers. In capitalist countries, however, religious ideology continues to hold an important place in political life. One can note in this connection, the religious oath taken in the courts of law or when assuming certain offices, for example, a Bible oath taken by the US President at his inauguration. In the armed forces there are as a rule chaplains of different denominations; formally, their functions are to serve the religious needs of the believers—soldiers and officers, while in practice they are a component part of the apparatus for military and ideological indoctrination of personnel in the spirit dictated by the interests of the State. The teaching of religion at State schools is also an element of the mechanism for the systematic upkeep and cultivation of religion which exists and is carefully preserved in capitalist countries.

Churches in capitalist countries are carrying out systematic political activities, whose religious-clerical colouring today is not so bright as it was a few decades ago when some clerical political parties were headed by priests or bishops (one will recall the Centre party in Germany and its head Reverend Kaas). In some cases, the connection of a party with the church interests and aspirations may not even be expressed in its name (Austrian People's Party, for example), but in others the name of the party often expresses its actual or ostentatious connection with religious ideology and the church: the Christian Democratic Party in Italy, the Christian Democratic Union in West Germany. The names of some Eastern countries expose their ties with Islam. But Israel, for example, which is not called a Judaic state, gives much room and broad rights to the Rabbinate within the structure of its organs and state functions.

The involvement of churches in political and social movements is expressed not only in the activities of political parties but also in those of clerical trade-unions, youth and women organizations, student unions, farmers' associations, cooperatives, and the like. Through them churches seek to extend their influence to every section of society but, in the first place, among the working people, attempting to lend their practical social needs a religious meaning and to keep these groups under control. They often fail to achieve these ends because the people, united by clerical organizations, often begin, in the course of the struggle for their real class interests to see in its true light the essence of the religious form which is given to them in the ideology preached by these organizations. The latter develop "leftist" trends within themselves which start disobeying the church leaders in matters related not only to practical action but to ideology also. It is not infrequent that there appear social organizations of the left and democratie trends, which, though independent of the church, have some religious colour in form and even in content. In some cases, the church winks at these organizations ; in others, it tries to put obstacles to their development or even prohibits them. Thus, in France in 1951, under the pressure of the church the Union of Progressive Christians, set up in 1947, ceased to exist and in 1955 *Quinzaine*, a Catholic journal of the left trend, was suppressed owing to the interference of the church. While being unable to arrest the process of radicalization of their mass organizations, churches make every effort to hinder this process and to keep these organizations on the traditional road of religious and social conservatism.

A study of the nature of the social and political views preached by religion is essential to understand its social role today. The impact of this propaganda is greater than that of the ordinary political propaganda because, in this case, certain views and slogans are put forward as God-pleasing, soul-saving and pious. In this context, the content of the political propaganda that is being carried on by church organizations is of special interest.

The general picture looks very variegated. There are church groups and schools of theology holding left views and actively advocating the ideals of peace, democracy, and social progress. The names of some of these modern Christian schools of theology are self-expressive : theology of hope, theology of revolution, etc. Not that these names are true to fact but the very tendency which they indicate is significant. As regards the social and political view of the official church bodies in major modern confessions, they deserve a special mention.

A short time ago (1959) the Vatican prohibited Catholics on pain of excommunication to cooperate with communists and vote for them in parliamentary elections. Soon, however, these tactical principles were changed. Despite the efforts of the right-wingers, the documents of the Second Ecumenical Council contained no formulas, previously considered indispensable, condemning communism and atheism and proclaiming the system of private property to be "sensible" and God pleasing. Encyclicals on social and political matters, published by Paul VI after the Council (*Pacem in Terris*, *Populorum Progressio*, etc.) indicate a certain, perhaps only outward, shift of the Papacy to the left. The documents no longer mention the need to defend private ownership as the basis of social life, and it even recognizes as positive certain modern progressive-democratic tendencies and movements. Appeals for peace among nations and the condemnation of racism and even of colonial oppression are rather categorical. There is no doubt that such changes in the social and political attitudes of the Papacy are due to the pressures of the time, to the world-wide successes won by socialism, and to the continuous growth of the democratic and progressive forces rather than to the inward evolution of this church institution. To maintain their old attitudes under these conditions would mean for the Papacy running the risk of losing very important positions in modern society.

Even the World Council of Christian Churches, which leads the ecumenical movement, can afford to make very "left" gestures and even actions. It publicly denounces racism and colonialism and occasionally allocates funds to support anti-racial movements. If one recalls that the World Council is composed of the representatives of the churches from some socialist, and a great number of capitalist countries, then it becomes clear that appropriate political actions are agreed upon within it not without internal struggle ; it should be mentioned, however, that in some cases certain churches of capitalist countries, for example, the Evangelical Church of the FRG, are initiators of such actions.

All this, however, does not mean that modern churches have come over to the side of progressive and socialist forces. The Vatican and other major church institutions continue to make, though not frequent, anti-communist and anti-Soviet statements. In some cases, the tendency and character of these statements are determined by tactical considerations and by desire to preserve the "balance" between the principal conflicting forces of today. The main point, however, is that the social and cultural progress of society is inevitably linked with complete secularization of every field of its material and spiritual life, with the spread of atheism and withering away of religion and, consequently, with the inevitable end that all the churches must come to. They are doing everything in their power to resist this inevitable process, resorting to concessions, disguised, and attempts to dig in on intermediate positions.

The social stand of churches is not always aimed at adjusting to the progressive processes going on in the world. There are church institutions whose activities are directly aimed to support reactionary phenomena of the present day. The Rabbinate in Israel and in many other capitalist countries, especially in the USA, is doing everything in its power for the ideological and even material support of Zionism and Israel's aggressive policy. The leaders of Christian churches in some African countries that are still fighting for liberation from the colonial yoke pursue a double-faced policy, playing into the hands of die-hards of imperialism and racialism, like Jan Smith. It should however, be noted that some Christian clergymen in South Africa hold progressive anti-racist views. Yet, the problem lies not in the views and activities of certain individuals but in the fundamental essence of the important social phenomenon represented by religion and institutions related to it.

Referring to those stages of the historical process when progressive social movements often found a religious ideological expression, V.I. Lenin wrote: "There was a time in history when ...the struggle of democracy and the proletariat assumed the form of struggle of one religious idea against another. But this time is long gone by."[1] Today the class interests of the democratic layers of society and the interests of the progressive forces of social development find expression not in the mystic and symbolic religious form but in adequate slogans, which represent the interests of the forces of progress, and in precise and substantiated demands. Their religious disguise and the attempts to prove their validity by appealing to Christ or Mohammed, Moses or Buddha can only obscure in the minds of the struggling masses the clearness of purpose and the means to achieve it.

This does not mean that the revolutionary-democratic forces of today refuse to cooperate with those groups and sections of the working people which, while advocating progressive changes are guided by religious slogans and influenced, in certain measure by religious ideology. Peace, democracy, and social progress, the replacement of the outgoing capitalist system by the socialist system—in the struggle to achieve these aims, atheistic working people form a united front with such believers.

REFERENCE

1. V.I. Lenin. *Works*, Vol. 48, p. 232 (Russian edition).

10

Religion and Religions From the Historical-Ethnographic Viewpoint

S.A. Tokarev

Scientific writings on religion often debate the question as to the main element in religion. Is it beliefs, ideas of the god or gods, or, religious moods and sentiments, religious rites, the cult or religious morality, religious-social organization, religious communes, the church, or, denominations?

The answer to this question most often is that the main thing in religion is the belief in the supernatural, in gods, spirits, demons, devils, black magic, and the like, the rest in religion being derivative and secondary.[1]

How far correct is this solution of the question?

Of course, the content of religious ideas, belief in various supernatural beings and phenomena comprise a very important component of the complicated entity which we call "religion". But is it first in importance?

Let us have a closer look at the matter.

Anyone dealing with ethnographic or other descriptions of the beliefs of any people cannot fail to notice the extreme diffusion, ambiguity, and often contradictory nature of these beliefs. With respect to one and the same nation one investigator describes these beliefs in one way and some other investigator in a totally different way (depending on the choice of the informer and other causes). Let us take at random two or three examples out of hundreds.

Totemic beliefs of the tribes of Central Australia have been described more than once and by well trained investigators, such as B. Spencer, Fr. Gillen, Carl and Thomas Strehlows, and others, and still the content of these beliefs remains unclear: Are totemic images of ancestors men or animals, or both? Are sacred *churinga* the "spiritual part" of the ancestor or the "second body" of man? Is *Altjira* a god in heaven or ancient mythical times? And so on.

In the hunting cults of the Siberian peoples a prominent role is played by the worship of the "masters" of nature, the *taiga*, and animals. But what is the meaning of these "masters"? Are they spirits, patrons of animals, particular natural phenomena or these natural phenomena themselves (*taiga*, mountains, the sea, and the like) which serve as objects of worship? If they are spirits, do they bear any relation to the images of ancestors, to shaman spirits?[2]

What are the notorious "fetishes" of the peoples of West Africa? Are they worshipped material objects to which supernatural properties are attributed? Or are they spirits of other imaginary beings reposing in these objects or tied with them in one way or another? Debates over this have for a long time been going on in science.

It is no wonder that with this indefiniteness of the objects of religious worship and slurred nature of the very content of beliefs each field ethnographer, describing these beliefs, willingly or unwillingly tried to fit them into the framework of his habitual concepts, whether these concepts are taken from the arsenal of theological terminology (god, demon, devil, soul, etc.) or from scientific terminology (fetish, totem, spirit, mana, etc.). It is not surprising that the same beliefs (of one and the same nation) figure in scientific literature as ethnographic or magic (pre-animistic) conceptions, depending on the theoretical views of the author.

Critical verification of the literary descriptions of the beliefs of different peoples led Paul Radin, one of the eminent American ethnographers, to a bold but well founded conclusion : in general, the overwhelming majority of beliefs described by ethnographers among peoples of different countries belong not to the people in question, not to the mass of the population, but only to a small stratum of shamans, priests and other "religious thinkers"; they are not only custodians and connoisseurs of beliefs (in most cases ethnographers obtained their information from them), but also creators of these beliefs ; the common people, that is, the overwhelming majority of "believers", do not know these beliefs and do not particularly care about them, except, perhaps, in moments of some catastrophes ; it suffices them to perform the established rites, to make sacrifices.[3]

If we turn to a large stage of the history of religion—religions of the ancient states of Egypt, Mesopotamia, India, classical antiquity, and so on, it would not be difficult to see that though the information available to us about the content of religious ideas, images of gods and other supernatural beings is at times fuller and more reliable owing to religious texts and iconography, much still remains mere guesswork. The space of this report does not allow greater detail here, but any student of the ancient world knows how scanty, patchy, and at times contradictory is our information about the images of gods of the ancient East and even classical antiquity and how complicated is the question of their origin.

Lastly, as regards even the modern big ("world") religions—Buddhism, Christianity, and Islam—here too we find the same picture. First of all, we must not think that the content of the dogmas of these religions is universally known. Not at all. They are known to professional theologians and a few "secular" specialists. A vast mass of believers, for example, Christians, have a very hazy idea of the content of the Christian doctrine. It may be said that the majority of believers do not know it at all. This is proved by the results of special religious-sociological surveys carried out in the USA. Thus, the 1954 Gallup poll established that though 96 per cent of those polled regard themselves as Christians, 60 per cent of them could not give the names of the Divine Trinity ; 65 per cent did not know who delivered the Sermon on the Mount and 79 per cent failed to give the name of a single prophet of the Old Testament. According to another survey, 53 per cent of the polled do not know the names of four Evangelists.[4]

Still more important is another fact. Just as in national-state religions, here too we discover that the content of the teaching of three world religions differs rather significantly. These differences are particularly striking in the case of Buddhism and Islam where the contrast reaches its extreme (in this respect Christianity occupies an intermediate position as it were). Islam preaches faith in one deity (Allah) and Buddhism recognizes an indefinite multitude of deities of various ranks; Islam preaches unconditional and passive submission to god and Buddhism originally professed complete disregard of god's and man's independent road to salvation and later on it began to rely on living deified men and various magic actions; in Islam we see faith in one irreversible historical process consummated with the Last Judgement and in Buddhism infinite cycles of world periods guided consecutively by various deities; Islam preaches the idea of personal salvation of the immortal human soul and Buddhism negates personal immortality and preaches the teaching of eternally disintegrating and combining dharms. . . .[5]

Just as in relation of national-state religions, here too the sharp contrasts observed in no way prevent us from uniting Buddhism, Christianity and Islam into one category, one type—a type of "world religions".

The foregoing gives a sufficient explanation of the extreme divergences in scientific literature concerning the classification of religious phenomena and periodization of the history of religion (Hegel, Comte, Lubbock, Frobenius, Achelis, Parrish, and many others). Some of these authors tried to stretch the point and build a periodization of religion according to the succession of worshipped objects and others did this according to types of human attitudes to the deity.[6] The latest attempts of this kind—the classification of religions by Erich Fromm (authoritarian and humanistic religions)[7] or by Arnold Toynbee (progressist and cyclical systems)[8]— are of some interest but do not solve the problem.

On the other hand, the Marxist theory of society and the general course of its historical development already contains a sufficiently firm basis for construing a stricter and more objective history of religion. From the Marxist standpoint, religion is a *social* phenomenon, being one of the forms of *social consciousness.* In other words, it is one of the forms of "ideological" relations between people. This leads to the following definition of religion : it is not so much man's attitude towards god (gods) as the *relation of people to one another--in connection* with their ideas of god (gods).

For there is not and never has been one universal human religion. Each people has its own religion, its own rites, its own faith. It is not for nothing that in people's everyday life—for instance, among Russians—man's confession was in the past always taken as a sign (even as a synonym) of his ethnic origin. Of a man of other nationality it was usually asked what faith he professed.

And not only in everyday life, in common parlance, but also in scientific usage, in modern ethnographic science it is accepted to treat confession as one of stable ethnic traits, at times even the most important of them distinguishing a given (ethnic-confessional) group from other, neighbouring or kindred groups. Iezids are fire-worshipping Kurds ; Parsees are fire-worshipping Indians ; Sikhs are of a Hinduist-Moslem syncretistic religion ; Copts are Egyptian Christians ; Hemshins are Armenian Moslems ; Bosnians are Yugoslav Moslems. Even though these definitions are inaccurate and there is no full coincidence of the ethnic and confessional group of a man, all the same, for national statistics, for practical political-administrative measures and in the delimitation of state and administrative boundaries the religion of people is taken into consideration. It often appears as an important and at times the most important qualifier. And the content of religion, its theologian-dogmatic aspect is of small concern to anyone in such cases.

It can be said that in the scientific cognition of religion and its history the most important thing is not the study of the names of gods or spirits or mythological accounts of them, not the description of rituals, even though they may be most detailed, not even the dogmatic content of a religion—the most important thing is to make a historical study of the *social function* of a particular religion (and, in general, any religion) as one of the social traits distinguishing one group of people from another.

In this sense religion is not an exception among other social phenomena. On the contrary, like any other phenomenon of culture, both material and spiritual, it performs a crucial social function of *uniting* and consolidating a definite group of people in one way or another and thereby setting it *in opposition* to all other groups.

This dual or, rather, intrinsically two-fold role—as a factor of *integration* and *segregation* at one and the same time—is specific to all elements of culture without any exception. Religion is one of them. And perhaps it more obviously and explicitly performs and has always performed this role.[9]

The history of religion is a history of how various relations took shape between people in the course of social development and how these relations were projected into the ideological sphere, the sphere of religious ideas.

This also the principle to be used in scientific periodization of the history of religion the main contours of which correspond to the general division of history into particular periods.[10]

The earliest period in the history of religion embraces *tribal* or, more precisely, *clan-tribal* cults. For all the diversity of details, their essential features, as can be seen from extensive ethnographic material, are similar among peoples of all parts of the world. And, most important, the same is their social aspect. One of the most ancient cult forms—the funeral cult—expresses the idea of care for the deceased member of the community and the symbolism of the reintegration of a group (community,) which suffered this loss. Totemism is another most ancient form of cult expressive of the solidarity of a clan symbolized by the totem, rites, and myths about totemic ancestors. Witchcraft (evil sorcery) is an expression of vague realization (or feeling of inter-tribal strife and enmity. The cult of the all-tribal god is the limit of the consciously realized social integration attainable under a communal-clan system.

In all these forms of belief which are well known to ethnographers we see a combined manifestation of the forces of intra-clan and intra-tribal integration and inter-tribal (inter-clan) segregation. It is not for nothing that all totemic rites, ceremonies of age-based initiations, secret unions growing out of them, are always accompanied by forms of strict secrecy backed up with a death penalty for the breach of the secret. Apparently, even the most primitive forms of religious beliefs had never been a common asset even for members of one tribe and one clan.

Corresponding to the epoch of early class (slave, early feudal) societies are "national" and "state" religions. They are diverse but uniform in their scheme. The merging and generalization of clan-tribal cults gives rise to all-national or all-state pantheon. Integration embraces large masses of people and extensive territories. Ancient tribal patron gods of Egypt's "nomus" (Horus, Khnum, Hator, Ptah, Osiris, etc.) become the objects of national worship. Ancient patron gods of Greek *polises* make up the Olympian pantheon. Here and there the head of a pantheon assumes the image of the strongest most powerful, and even sole god. This happened with Jahwe of the Jews. But parallel to this and to a much greater extent grows the force of segregation.

At the early stages religion appears, properly speaking, not as a factor of segregation but as its indicator. Inter-tribal wars characteristic of the epoch of transition from the pre-class to early class system—conquests, inter-tribal associations with concomitant early forms of dependence (tribute payment, slavery, clientele, etc.)—all were engendered not by religion but by material causes. However, these forms of inter-tribal antagonisms are realized as a struggle of cults, the triumph of some gods over others, theological subordination and hierarchy of gods. Princely worshippers of Horus united the whole of Egypt placing their god above all others. Later on supremacy in Egypt's pantheon passed in the process of succession of dynasties and capitals of the state to Ptah, Atum (Ra) and Amon. In Mesopotamia the struggle of town communes was reflected in the alternate prominence of Enlil, Ninurta, Marduk, Assur. The formation of a vast monarchy of the Persian Achemenides signified the triumph of their national god Ahura-Mazda over all other gods.

But up to the end of the ancient world, to the late ancient epoch, nowhere did the cult community acquire independent significance. It was not separated from ethnic community. Egypt's gods were united in a common pentheon but remained Egyptian gods : their cult did not overstep Egypt's boundaries for a definite period of time. Even the formation of large multi-national did not lead to the mixing-up of cults. A victor people did not impose its gods on conquered peoples.

Even Persian kings, who worshipped Ahura-Mazda and made this cult obligatory among Persians proper, did not not spread it among dozens of conquered people, grievously permitting them to continue worshipping their national gods. Only in the Hellenistic and Roman epoch, owing to intensive and ever broader ethnic reshuffling, a sort of international cult began to take shape ; some of the particularly popular local national gods began to go beyond their former narrow ethnic framework of worship, acquiring followers far beyond their homeland. This happened to Amon of Thebe, Serapis, Isis, Kybele, and Mitra. This was the first step towards the formation of "world-religions" a third great epoch in the history of religions of which more will be said further on.

National gods were the embodiment of the forces of segregation and mutual repulsion of those ethnic (national) groups or states which were their worshippers. But this mutual repulsion contained many hues and shades—from peaceful, if isolated, co-existence to irreconcilable mutual sanguinary destruction. An extreme degree of fanatical exclusiveness was reached by the cult of Israeli Jahwers : in the epoch of the conquest of Palestine Jahwe enjoined his worshippers to destroy mercilessly, to the last man, the population of conquered towns who worshipped their local deities (the Bible calls them "abominations"). Later on, in the epoch of comparatively peaceful neighbourhood of the Israelis and Canaenans Jahwe again enjoined his "chosen" people to maintain full isolation from them, especially in marriages and a strict national-religious endogamy was introduced : "and the need of Israel separated themselves from strangers" (Nehemiah, 9, 2).

The same closed system is characteristic of the Indian castes (*jati*) with the only difference that here each caste represents a closed endogamic group.

The mutual isolation of national-religious organisms (peoples and states) had also another and highly important aspect : this mutual isolation created the fiction of internal solidarity of each of these organisms, that is, obscured in a way internal social contradictions. By opposing Egyptians to all non-Egyptians, Romans to all non-Romans, national religions befudged the class consciousness of the masses, which, of course, fully accorded with the interests of powers that be.

Compared with this crucial function of national-religions—to serve as an indicator and factor of international segregation and, thereby, to play into the hands of the dominant social stratum of each particular people—the content of religious beliefs seems to be their less important aspect. These religions could be monotheistic (Judaism), dualistic (Zoroastrianism) or polytheistic (the majority of ancient religions); they could be oriented towards life on earth (Confucianism, Judaism, antique cults) or life in the other world (Egypt); they could have rich mythology (Greeks) or almost none of it (Romans); they could be impregnated with mysticism (Hinduism) or be profoundly hostile to it (Confucianism and Roman)—all the same, the main social function of national religions did not change on account of this.

The next, the third epoch in the history of religions begins with a peculiar historical paradox. It is an epoch of what is known as world (supra-national) religions. The paradox consists in the fact that these religions—Buddhism, Christianity and Islam—arose as an attempt to overcome all segregation radically and fundamentally. Universal integration was preached. They denied ethnic, cultural, and political differences. "For there is no difference between the Jew and the Greek; for the same Lord over all is rich unto all that call upon him," Apostle Paul wrote (Romans 10, 12). In Christ's realm "there is neither Greek nor Jew," he wrote, "circumcision nor uncircumcision, Barbarian, Scythian, bond nor free, but Christ is all, and in all" (Coloss., 3, 11).

The preaching of Shakya-muni Buddha was likewise addressed to all people without distinction as to caste and ethnic group. The universalism of the Moslem religion was expressed in the non-recognition of national or other divisions among people except the division into "believers" and "pagans". The very fact of the incredibly rapid expansion of Mohammed's doctrine in Asia, Africa and partly in Europe testified to some great force of integration. This new and widely integrating force brought into life as a sort of its own antithesis a still more powerful and sharp segregation. Buddhist monk "disciples" were sharply differentiated from the laymen, from everything mundane. In Christianity this assumed still sharper forms. Jesus who preached non-differentiation of Greeks and Jews frankly admitted, even emphasized that he brought to earth "not peace but sword" (Matthew 10, 34). With a touch of cynicism he even demanded of his followers that they should "hate . . . their father, and mother, and wife, and children, and brethren, and sisters . . ." (Luke 14, 26). He demanded that all "believers", "brethren" dissociate themselves from "pagans". In Islam the opposition of "believers", and "pagans" reached its extreme when they were required to wage merciless war against the "pagans".

Soon another segregation began. New religions did not remain united. From the first steps the Christian church split into a multitude of sects, "heresies" and local churches the struggle between which dragged on for centuries flaring up now and again and assuming severe, bloody forms. Rivalling churches and sects anathematized each other again and again. In Islam the struggle between sects (Sunnites, Shiites, etc.) was no less fierce. In Buddhism the struggle of sects did not lead to mass bloodshed, but at times reached a high pitch of tension.

Successive schisms and fragmentation of the Christian Church (churches) led at times to an unexpected result—the restoration of a system of national religions to a certain extent. Thus, the monophysite "heresy", condemned at the Chalkidon Council in the year 451, became the national church of the Armenians (and also Abyssinians). Presbyterianism became the national church of the Scots and the Anglican Church took hold among the English. Maronitism became the church of Christians in Lebanon.

It would be very naive to think that at the basis of these divisions, schisms, and conflicts lay dogmatic differences—different interpretation of theological truths. That Armenians, Copts and Abyssinians separated from other Christians because they were convinced about the unitary (and not dual) nature of

Christ ; that the Russians, Rumanians, Serbs, Bulgarians and Greeks do not recognize the authority of the Pope because they are confident that the Holy Spirit emanates only from the Father and by no means from Father and Son, and so on. The overwhelming majority of common believers are even ignorant of these theological subtleties. Theologians themselves know about them, but their main concern is church subordination and not dogmatic disputes. Armenian hierarchs dissociated themselves from "Chalkidon" diophysites because they did not want to submit to the Byzantine patriarch and strove to have their independent church. The Eastern orthodox hierarchs split from the Western church because they did not want to submit to the Roman Pope (nor could they, even if they wanted, for they were subordinated to the Byzantine emperor).

We could cite also examples of church schisms when there were no dogmatic divergences at all. The most vivid example is provided by the Russian "old believers" who stubbornly, from the 17th century up to our days refuse to have anything to do with "Nikonians" from whom, however, they do not differ in any dogmatic details but merely in ritual trifles like the spelling of the name "Isus-Iisus" (Jesus), double or triple "alleluia"; and the manner of making the sign of the cross during prayers ; but for these insignificant differences people were ready to go into exile and to accept death and burned themselves and others. Fanatics among old believers sincerely regarded the whole world opposed to them as "the kingdom of the Antichrist".

The forces of segregation operate in world religions, just as in national religions, not only in the peripheral zone—between churches, confessions, and sects—but also within these communities. There is no equality within them : the clergy and the flock ; numerous gradations among the clergy : deans and archdeans, priests and archpriests, bishops, archbishops, metropolitan bishops, exarchs, patriarchs ; monks and laymen and, within monks, novices, lower and middle ranks, archimandrites, and so on. This is just within the framework of the Orthodox Church. The Catholic Church is no less motley hierarchically. Among Protestants hierarchy is more simple but no less clearly expressed. The mess of "laymen" is not homogeneous either : women cannot be priests ; a woman cannot enter the altar ; rich men making a big contribution to a monastery or church enjoy privileges.

In a word, "fraternity" within the church community is rather relative. Even nominally each layman must take care only of his own salvation or, at most, of the salvation of members of his family. In the New Testament literature (Apostle Paul) the believers are given the vile advice that they should obtain the salvation of their own souls at the cost of destroying the souls of their kin. In the message to Romans Apostle Paul says : "Dearly beloved, avenge not yourselves, but rather give place unto wrath. . . ." —"Therefore if thine enemy hunger, feed him ; if he thirst, give him drink ; for so doing thou shalt heap coals of fire on his head." (Romans 12, 19-20). Fine mercy, indeed ! There you have the love of neighbour !

And it is hardly needed to say that in world religions, just as in national religions, the fiction of the religious community of people of the same faith only covers up and conceals the sharpest class antagonisms, creating the illusion of the community of the spiritual interests of the rulers and the ruled. "The idea of God" Lenin said, "has always tied the oppressed classes hand and foot with faith in the divinity of the oppressors".[11]

And so, religious morality is essentially egoistic. It is egoistic because it replaces and mediates relations between people with the attitude of each individual towards God. The Gospel enjoins to love God more than one's "neighbours" (*i. e.*, men). Asked about the most important commandment in the law, Jesus replies : "Thou shalt love thy God with all thy heart, and with all thy soul, and all thy mind. This is the first and great commandment. And the second is like unto it, thou shalt love thy neighbour as thyself" (Matthew 22. 36-39 ; id , Mark 12, 30-31; Luke, 10, 27). We have just seen how the love of "neighbours" was interpreted—by such authorities at that as Apostle Paul! Consequently, from the religious (Christian in this case) standpoint, if love of man comes in conflict with love of God, the former must be sacrificed in favour of the latter. This logically leads to the justification of religious wars, crusades, church Inquisition, persecution of "heretics" and atheists. The value of human life is denied in the name of the absolute duty of man towards God. Destroy heretics! Destroy pagans! Destroy the enemies of God!

This naturally gives rise to the question: why is it that in religion the balance of forces of integration and segregation is so drastically disturbed? Why is it that religion, which is even usually cast in the role of unifier of people in society, one of the strongest unifiers at that, turns out to be in practice a force which disunites people rather than unites? Why do the forces of segregation prevail in it?

We do not need to go far, it seems, to find the answer. Man, suppressed by the elements of nature and, to a still greater extent, by social oppression and social anarchy, naturally strives to deliver himself from both. But how can it be done? He may either try to escape from the power of these elements and this oppression, mitigating and propitiating them or to overcome these forces, remake hostile elements, both natural and social. The former path is religion; but escape from the world evil is also an escape from the suffering brethren: save just one's own soul! The latter path is the path of the unification of people for joint struggle against the world evil. This is the path of socialism and communism.

This is why religion, contrary to all attempts of "God-seekers" and "God-builders", is radically and basically opposed to socialism and communism.

The great materialist thinker Spinoza coined this aphorism: "If Peter tells us something about Paul, we learn more about Peter than Paul." This is a very profound aphorism through it must not be taken too literally and turned into an absolute truth.

Could it not be applied to the study of religion? I think, it could.

Great sculptors of ancient Greece—Phidias, Polykleitos, Praxiteles and Leohar—left for us beautiful sculptural images of Zeus, Apollo and other Olympian gods. But from them we learn not about these gods, but about the creators of these statues, about the high artistic culture of classic Greece.

Homer's poems the *Iliad* and *Odyssey* tell about the same Olympian gods. But from these poems we learn more about Homer (and other poets of the time), about the great Homeric epic poetry than about the gods of Olympus.

Andrei Rublyov painted the image of the Holy Virgin and many other icons. But from them we learn more about the artistic genius of Rublyov and his cultural milieu than about the Holy Virgin and saints.

Theologians of medieval Europe left a multitude of rather profound writings about the properties of the deity and various doctrines of the Christian dogmaticism. But from these works we learn not about God and his qualities, but about the flexibility of the human intellect and those social and cultural conditions under which this intellect was directed towards examination of purely imaginary subjects.

The Gospels and other New Testament literature set forth many details about Jesus Christ, his life and doctrine. But from them we learn not about Jesus Christ (we do not even know exactly whether he existed at all), but about the social and ideological struggle in the setting of which these works were written.

In short, from Spinoza's aphorism we get one more confirmation that the main task of the historian of religion is not penetration into the essence of the images of religious fantasy, their similarities and distinctions, but the study of the social and cultural environment and concrete historical conditions in which these images were created, of the alignment of people, their unification or, conversely, dissociation which was reflected in the creation of religious ideas.

NOTES AND REFERENCES

1. See, for instance, I.A. Kryvelyov, "Ob osnovnom opredelya yuschem priznake religii" (On the Main Determining Feature of Religion). In the book: *Voprosy istorii religii i ateizma* (Questions of the Religion and Atheism), 4, Moscow, 1956.

2. See, for example, L.Y.Sternberg, Pervobytnaya religiya v svete etnograffi (Primitive Religion in the Light of Ethnography), Leningrad, 1936, p. 31 ; V.G. Bogoraz, Chukchi, II, Religion, Leningrad, 1939, p. 4, 11.
3. P. Radin, *Primitive Religion,* New York, 1937 (1957).
4. See, W. Herberg, Protestant, Catholic, Jew. An Essay in *American Religious Sociology,* New York, 1956, pp. 14, 236. See, also Y.A. Levada, *Sotsialnoya priroda religii* (Social Nature of Religion). Moscow, 1965, p. 198.
5. S.A. Tokarev, "Problemy periodizatsii istorii religii" (Problems of the Periodisation of the History of Religion) in the book: *Voprosy nauchnogo ateizma* (Questions of Scientific Atheism), Issue 20, Moscow, 1976, p. 80.
6. See, S.A. Tokarev, *Ranniye formy religii i ikh razvitiye* (Early Forms of Religion and Their Development), Moscow, 1964, pp. 6-10.
7. E. Fromm, *Psychoanalysis and Religion,* New York, 1967, pp. 34-7 and others.
8. A. Toynbee, *An Historian's Approach to Religion.* Oxford (USA), 1956, pp. 10-13, and others.
9. See S.A. Tokarev, Razgranichitelniye i obyedinitelniye funktsii kultury (Segregating and Integrating Functions of Culture) (Reports for the Ninth Congress of Anthropological and Entological Sciences, Chicago, 1973), Moscow, 1973.
10. S.A. Tokarev, *Problemy periodizatsii.*
11. V.I. Lenin, *Collected Works,* Engl. Edition, Moscow, Progress Publishers, Vol. 35, p. 129.

11

Creative Role of the Scientific and Materialist Atheistic Weltanschauung in Moulding a New Type of Man

P.K. Kurochkin

THE VICTORY of the scientific-materialist weltanschauung in the social consciousness of the Soviet people is one of the important achievements of socialism.

As Comrade L.I. Brezhnev, General Secretary of the OPSU Central Committee, noted in his Report of the CPSU Central Committee to the 25th Party Congress, present-day Soviet society "is a society with a crisis-free steadily growing economy, mature socialist relations and genuine freedom. It is a society governed by the scientific materialist world outlook. It is a society of firm confidence in the future, of radiant communist prospects."[1] In this society, as the new Constitution of the USSR states, the creative ability, of the new system and the advantages of the socialist way of life are becoming increasingly evident, and the working people are more and more widely enjoying the fruits of their great revolutionary gains.

The rule of the scientific and materialist weltanschauung is based on profound changes in the political, economic, social and cultural spheres of the life of society. The objective foundation of this phenomenon can be achieved by the building of a mature socialist society, the successes of the scientific and technological revolution, the increasing social homogeneity of Soviet society, the levelling of the social and cultural standards of the country's nations and nationalities, and by the assumption by all sections of the population of the ideological and political positions of the working class. The versatile and purposeful ideological, theoretical, and educational activities of the

Communist Party have become a launching pad for an unprecedented rise in the Soviet Union's cultural and ideological development.

The scientific and materialist weltanschauung is based on the foundation of all the philosophical, natural scientific and social scientific, political, moral, and aesthetic views and convictions, which express the interests and ideals of the working class. The mastering of the scientific world outlook—the dominant element of the spiritual make-up of the Soviet people—helps in taking an active part in life and in solving pressing problems in the development of socialist society.

The scientific and materialist weltanschauung is inseparably linked with atheistic convictions. The atheism of the Marxists, according to V.I. Lenin, is a "direct and inevitable deduction from dialectical materialism".[2] The idea of the close relationship between the materialist and atheistic views, that was characteristic of the progressive social thought of the past, has been turned by Marxism-Leninism into an important feature of communist ideology. The notions, widespread in Western literature, about so called political atheism being allegedly conditioned by only tactical considerations of the communists distort the real state of affairs.

Being a component part of Marxist social science, the theory of scientific atheism has two aspects, the first consists in the scientific criticism of religion ; and the second one in the study of the positive and creative role of atheism and of the atheistic appreciation of the world for the development of the cultural and spiritual life of society. The theory of scientific atheism studies the regularities of the historical replacement of religion by the scientific weltanchauung in the course of the revolutionary transition of society from capitalism to socialism and communism. Scientific atheism is based on a wide range of philosophical, sociological, social and psychological, historical and other investigations ; while the process of atheistic education is inseparable from the total complex of tasks of communist upbringing.

These two (*i.e.* the critical and positive) aspects have been characteristic of Soviet social science from the very beginning. The critical aspect prevailed in the early decades of the atheistic movement in the USSR, although at that time, too, the new attitude of the masses to atheism, born of revolutionary practice, was also an object of active scientific studies. The advance of Soviet society and the gradual liberation of public and private life from religion were concurrent with the intensification of studies in the positive and creative content of the scientific and materialist atheistic understanding of the world. These studies were, to a large extent, preconditioned by the success of the scientific criticism of religion. It should be acknowledged, at the same time, that the creative functions of this world outlook were and are not being demonstrated fast enough and that much less has been done in this field than in the sphere of critical analysis of religious ideology and morality.

The society dominated by the scientific weltanschauung gives priority to revealing the constructive and life-guiding role of atheistic views on contemporary science and culture. The time has come to show the breadth and depth of the positive role of atheism. We shall comprehensively reveal the wealth of the scientific weltanschauung and socialist humanism.

What are the reasons for this correction in the theory and practice of scientific atheism?

Firstly, socialism not only eliminates the social conditions that give rise to the need for religious and other illusions, but also shapes in the broad masses a new social demand for the scientific and materialist atheistic world outlook. This demand stems from the very essence of socialist system which can progress only through the conscientious realization of objective social regularities and conscious and active participation of the broad masses of people in running all spheres of the life of society. Socialist democracy, the further expansion and deepening of which are reflected in the new Constitution of the USSR, and the guarantee of the freedom of conscience are important conditions of the free choice of the scientific materialist atheistic stand adapted by most citizens in our country and rule out the possibility of a political confrontation between different groups of the population on the grounds of their attitudes to religion and atheism. It is essential that the new social demand for the scientific and materialist atheistic weltanschauung should mean more than mere freedom from religious views alone. The building of communism requires from every member of society to develop his personality and spiritual wealth.

Secondly, the scientific and materialist atheistic weltanschauung must be reproduced (in an expanded and more profound form) in every new generation of socialist society. This historically new and difficult task requires a considerable improvement in atheistic education activities, which should be comprehensive in character and different in their approach to different groups and sections of the population, the majority of which are not religious today. Concentrating their activity on the religious part of the population and on improving the knowledge, conviction, and vigour of the atheists, the researchers, sponsors, and propagators of scientific atheism consider it their main task to steadily reduce the reproduction of religiosity and to progressively inculcate atheism in the new generations in socialist society. This is the mainline to a society completely free of religion.

Thirdly, there is an external aspect to the problem. The positive effect of scientific atheism is important for rallying world-wide forces in their struggle against imperialism and militarism and for the unity of believers and non-believers in achieving their common goals.

Increased attention to revealing the creative role of the scientific world outlook does not lower the importance of studying religion itself. Soviet social science has long-standing traditions of criticizing the religious ideology, and this criticism is closely connected with the practical demands of educational activities. Recent years have seen thorough studies of the specific features of religion as a social phenomenon, the peculiarities of the struggle between the scientific-materialist and religious-idealist world outlook in the epoch of the scientific and technological revolution, the evolution of the church, the church in present day conditions, the psychology of religion, the role of religion and the church in the historical process, and so on. Moreover, the pressing problems of the study of religion are best seen through the prism of the "positive alternative" to religion.

The major task facing the researchers, sponsors and propagators of scientific atheism is that of showing what a person who departs from religion gets. This is an important factor in the spiritual life of socialist society and for a comprehensive and harmonious development of a man's personality. Consolidation thereof increases man's spiritual world and organically combines with humanism and collectivism. It also has a great effect on the development of the intellectual life in socialist society.

The rapidly growing part played by science and intellectual activities in boosting the productive forces, changing living conditions, and in educating people is an extremely important factor today. Present day science has launched a mighty and successful offensive against all vestiges of the past, winning from them one position after another. In its turn, the scientific and materialistic atheistic weltanschauung has a positive effect on the progress of knowledge.

Consolidation of the dialectical and materialistic atheistic weltanschauung stimulates man's intellectual development and spiritual renovation. It goes without saying that believers as a whole are not opposed to scientific knowledge. According to sociological studies, most believers today respect science and positively assess its achievements since from their own experience they know about its beneficial effects on the improvement of working and living conditions and on the rise in material and cultural standards. The consistent inculcation of scientific knowledge in believers and hesitant persons is an important potential, furthering the development of the scientific world outlook.

The enrichment of the non-believers' intellectual world can be illustrated by the rise in educational standards. Field research in the Voronezh Region by Professor M.K. Teplyakov shows that of the people who are no longer religious on the one hand, and people who have retained religious convictions on the other, 16.7 and 0.1 per cent, respectively, have incomplete or complete higher education, 22.7 and 0.9 per cent secondary education, 12.8 and 5 per cent a seven year education, 12 and 18.8 per cent primary education, and 9.7 and 66.8 per cent are almost illiterate.[3] So, the gap in education between the non-believers and believers is rather wide.

Although science plays a decisive part in establishing atheistic views, the dissemination of the irrefutable truth alone is insufficient in shaping a scientific weltanschauung. It is a well-known fact that there are still very knowledgeable people who hold religious and idealist positions. The scientific and materialist world outlook is not only an explanatory position, but also a new attitude to the world and an expression of the socialist way of life.

The *moral value* of the scientific and materialist atheistic weltanschauung is a theme which deeply concerns life today.

The advocates of the religious-idealist outlook did and do allege that religion is the treasure-house of the highest moral values and the only force which can ennoble people and keep them from evil deeds. Science and practice, however, refute the beneficial effect of religious beliefs on the progress of morality and at the same time testify to the high moral potential of the scientific weltanschauung. Considering God to be the creator of morality, religion distorts its relation with the interests of people when it appears as something imposed on them from the outside and alien to them, and therefore, often leads to hypocrisy and a discrepancy between words and deeds and between what must be done and what is actually done. Materialism and atheism state that man is the creator of morality, dispel religious mystification, and show morality as a natural product of the life of society and a form of its culture.

History confirms the idea of many thinkers of the past who foresaw that a society of atheists would be more respectable, more humane, and happier than a society built on religious principles. At present, most Soviet people are atheists and non-believers and at the same time have high moral standards. Even most believers (who explain their religiosity mostly by moral motives), are not guided in their behaviour by religious teachings and do not rigidly associate their plans for the present and the future with the achievement of "heavenly bliss". Socialist reality inculcates in believers a new attitude to life and a realistic understanding of their interests and duties.

Theologians, churchmen, and secular advocates of religion have repeatedly alleged that the absence of faith means people will do whatever they like. Battista Mondin, Dean of the Philosophy Department of the Catholic University in Rome, where an institute for atheistic studies has recently been set up, says that without God, everything is egoism, arbitrary rule and violence. Therefore, atheism rules out humanism, but involves barbarism, rules out freedom but involves oppression, and rules out truth, but involves obscurantism.[4]

As can be seen, departure from religion, materialism, and atheism were and are depicted as immorality, dehumanism, and collapse of the moral and democratic principles of life. But is it not a collapse of morality when it rests on the fear of posthumous punishment or illusions of a bliss in the world to come rather than on man's civic consciousness, his understanding of the social meaning of moral demands, and his conscience? Can one enrich his moral potential if he only thinks about a ticket to heaven rather than about his happiness on earth? Genuine morality must rest not on religious illusions, but on the real interests of all classes of people, as well as on the struggle for real happiness on earth. It is not accidental, therefore, that the society, which is ruled by the scientific and materialist atheistic world outlook, and which came into being and is developing on the basis of the conscientious activities of the masses, has done more in historically short period to improve man's morality than any other society did during the whole period of its existence.

At the dawn of human history, religion "merged" with morality. Today we are witnessing mankind's transition from the age-old "alliance" between religion and morality to the organic unity of morality, materialism, and atheism. At the highest stages of social development, *i.e.*, in conditions of mature communism, morality will be completely free from religious-idealist influence. Religious belief, as well as the morality of the exploiting classes, is of a transient character and will perish as society progresses whereas scientific atheism, closely related to communist morality will steadily develop and strengthen.

What is the emotional life of a man free from religious sentiments ? There are situations in which people sincerely denying the religious and idealist picture of the world are not sure about whether religion can help in solving the "accursed problems" of life : consolation for sufferings and overcoming of the fear of death. To win the broad masses, religion and the church have deeply penetrated into a man's emotional psyche. According to a sociological study conducted in the Ukraine, one-fifth of the believers polled consider religion to be mainly a consolation for difficulties and adversities.

For centuries now, religious and church propaganda have treated materialism and atheism as a "disease of the soul" (this expression was first used by Plato) and as something detrimental and incompatible with normal life psychology. Meanwhile, it is precisely religion and religious sentiments which paralyse emotional development of a personality, narrow his various interests and demands, and undermine man's will to better the conditions of his existence on earth.

Having achieved considerable success in the psychology of religion, we must pay more attention to the psychology of atheism and to the people's emotional world free of religious illusions, with history providing abundant material on this urgent problem for thought and generalizations. Considering the representatives of materialism and atheism of the past (Epicurus, Diderot, Holbach, Chernyshevsky, etc.), it can be said that their sincere kindness, loftiness, boldness of thought and noble deeds were not just exclusive features of their personalities ; but a logical result of their conscientious materialist stand. Born of socialism, the rich emotional life of the Soviet people, free from the fear of the morrow and for their place in life, which is characteristic of capitalism and which is damaging to the psyche, is very much due to the victory of materialism and atheism and to the progress of science, education and culture.

The emotional world of people free from religion is inseparable from their weltanschauung. It is shaped on approaches to the formation of a scientific world outlook and makes up the psychological basis of the latter. The victory of the scientific weltanschauung consolidates the new psychology and provides it with a broad ideological support and a firm weltanschauung basis. The unity and interdependence of the scientific world outlook and emotions, free from the belief in God, enhance people's convictions and increases their social activity.

Way back in the seventeenth century, when people were dominated by religion, a French thinker Pierre Bayle expressed confidence in the emergence of an "atheistic society" in the future. Socialism is paving the way to a society free from religious illusions. The rule of the scientific and materialist atheistic weltanschauung in the USSR refutes the thesis about religion's immanence to the historical process and the "eternal religiosity" of the Russian soul.

It is noteworthy that people are becoming increasingly conscious that religion and the church have no prospects. According to a study in the Penza Region, 49.1 per cent of the workers polled said that religion would wither away, and 7.2 per cent assumed that religious beliefs would possibly continue in the future. The numbers of people constantly raising their skills were 70.4 and 3.7 per cent, respectively.[5] Hence, our contemporaries regard religion as a historical anachronism.

The complete victory of the scientific and materialist atheistic weltanschauung is an irreversible historical process, an important social regularity, and a result of the drastic changes in all spheres of social life of society and varied educational activities of the Communist Party.

REFERENCES

1. Report of the CPSU Central Committee and the Immediate Tasks of the Party in Home and Foreign Policy, Moscow, 1976, p. 103.
2. V.I. Lenin, *Coll. Works*, Vol. 15, p. 405.
3. M.K. Teplyakov. *Problemy ateisticheskogo vospitaniya v praktike partiynoj raboty* (Problems of Atheistic Education in Practical Activities of the Party), Voronezh, 1972, pp. 134-35.
4. *L'Observatore Romano*, 16 February 1977.
5. E.M. Baykov. *Religiya i Dikhovnyj Mir Chelòveka* (Religion and Man's Spiritual World), Safansk, 1972, pp. 100, 117.

12

Russian Folk Free-thought in the Thirteenth to Nineteenth Centuries

A.I. Klibanov

THE HISTORY of Russian folk free-thought has not been studied to any appreciable extent. But it should be recalled that it cannot be divorced from the history of Russian spiritual culture, consisting of the struggles of ideas that reflect the class struggle and of the mass social protest against the dictatorship of the Church that served the exploiter classes in word and deed because, after all, it is an inalienable part thereof. The significance of folk free-thought cannot be equated, however, only with that of the instructive and brilliant page it represents in the histories of culture and social thought in Russia and other countries for no matter how deeply into antiquity its origins may go, it is yet a potent factor of spiritual emancipation of people still labouring under the influence of religious beliefs. The everlasting (not in the sense, of course, of being constantly identical to itself) quality of folk free-thought lies in the fact that the emancipation of people from religious beliefs is a historically determined process. If we come down to the level of each individual, such emancipation will also be a *process* or, in other words, a consistent succession of states, a change of phases of his mental development, as a result of which the given individual forms his atheistic conviction.

After the victory of the Great October Socialist Revolution in Russia, the outlook of the wide masses of the population has undergone a transformation—a mass departure from religion and an even larger departure from the hitherto reigning State Orthodox Church. Thus, upheavals in the history of ideological development of society may not at all exclude acts of mass breakaways from the religious, but they are necessarily a product of historical development. It is not without its ideological prerequisites either, which are developed and accumulated by previous generations. The fact which remains true, irrespective of whether the one breaking away from religion realizes it or not, is that he does so because his outlook is closely bound up with the cultural traditions, those of folk free-thought in particular.

We regard folk free-thought as a historically determined stage, marking the ascent of immediate producers to their spiritual freedom. Social consciousness is a derivative of social being which implies that ideology may transcend the bounds of existing socio-economic relations or that consciousness may lag behind the development of its social base. We can obtain a better understanding of views held by modern believers only if we exercise a historical approach to the process of emancipation of the wide masses from religion and look upon it as a "stage-by-stage" phenomenon. F. Engels wrote in his time, that "the movement of the proletariat necessarily passes through different stages of development ; at every stage one section of people lags behind and does not join in the further advance."[1] This is all the more true of peasant movements and especially of the religious form of consciousness which is deeply rooted in all spheres of material production and social status of peasants. Though the solution of the agrarian question provided for by the Great October Socialist Revolution was more radical in significance than any bourgeois revolution has been able to offer, the greatest persistence was shown by religious beliefs in the countryside. This does not mean, however, that they remained unaffected at all by the great historical transformations which took place in the country. The Great October Revolution attracted to atheism a great number of peasants who actively participated in the Revolution and the Civil War and provided an outlet for the centuries old anti-clericalism which shook the edifice of the Russian Orthodox Church to its very foundations. It should be noted, however, that various religious sects persecuted under Tsarism took advantage of this wave of peasant ideological activity and enlarged their following. A concrete historical picture which provides an idea of the extent of the peasant anti-clerical movement at the beginning of this century, its ideological content, and lastly, of the areas of agreement between the peasant anti-clericalism and proletarian atheism can be found in the following monograph written by L.I. Emeliakh : *Anti-Clerical Peasant Movement in the Period of the First Russian Revolution* (Moscow-Leningrad, 1965) ; and *The Historical Prerequisites for Overcoming Religion in the Soviet Village* (Leningrad, 1975). The above mentioned works go a long way in promoting better understanding of the historical traditions and ideological prerequisites of mass atheism in the USSR. The problem of disseminating atheism among workers in pre-October Revolution Russia proved to be considerably less complicated. During its entire history, the Russian proletariat showed, at best, a modest response to religion, it proved impervious not only to the exhortations of the State Church but also of the "purified" and "refined" religions represented by all manner of sectarian ideologists. This is convincingly shown in the book by M.M. Persits, *The Atheism of the Russian Worker* (Moscow, 1965) written on the basis of extensive and representative material.

The domain of knowledge of interest to us is considered in the above mentioned books within a period of time which, though replete with epoch-making events, is rather late in history. The history of Russian folk free-thought is an object which calls for a special and systematic study. In practice, it rather frequently happens that free-thought and atheism are approached only as subjective factors helping to overcome religious prejudices. The approach is, no doubt, quite correct, but not adequate, because, apart from that, free-thought and atheism also signify perception and comprehension of, and the practical attitude to reality. Scientific atheism is a product of history as such and not only that of philosophical and historical thought. Scientific atheism incorporates the processes of its own establishment and development in their "skimmed" form.

Our sociologists who for a number of years have been discussing the criteria to be used for classifying population by "levels" of belief and unbelief, perhaps, ignore this theoretical and practical promise inherent in visualizing atheism as a product of history and not only as a tool for enlightenment and education. By putting the "tape" of history of scientific atheism in reverse and thus identifying its earlier stages and their relationship, we shall be able to apprehend the characteristics of various categories of believers in terms of their historical content and to see that it is not merely the composition of views, the signs of overcoming them by people of various faiths (for example, Orthodox, Catholic, Islamic, Buddhist, and Judaic) the sign which, incidentally, may not be different in each case, that make the above mentioned "levels" different from each other. The "levels" will reveal themselves as systems formations, which are definitely (socio-historically) determined. They will exihibit their *own* (consistent for each respective period of time) *logic* and not only naivete, ignorance, narrow-mindedness, etc. Knowledge of this logic makes it possible to converse in a common language with the one who "vacillates" or who is an agent of deistic, pantheistic or other, views which signify a departure from traditional religion, to comprehend the pattern of thinking on the part of the interlocutor and to be heard by him, in your turn. Otherwise, it is different to visualize how else the mutual understanding between two people of whom one is an agent of scientific and atheistic convictions and knowledge while the other "vacillates" between belief and unbelief or represents some or other stage of free-thinking, can be arrived at. But it stands to reason that what we have in mind here is a dialogue either with the "vacillating" or those unbelievers who are only embarking on the road of breaking away from religion or with believers in whom it may be possible "to awaken... an intelligent attitude towards religious questions and an intelligent criticism of religion".[2] Indeed, the saying "All's well that ends well" is fully applicable to the question under discussion.

It is probable, however, that in using various methods of concrete inquiry into the "levels" of belief and unbelief, a sociologist has each time to deal with the individual consciousness only of his *contemporaries*. And if this is so, can the consideration of historical development of atheism in the reverse order be justified ? But, on the other hand, this objection could be just as valid also in the case of a researcher operating the "time machine" and thus effecting direct contacts with believers who lived many centuries ago. Elaboration of a system of criteria and classification based on the principles of historism, and determinism, can be made possible only if we abstract ourselves from the given concrete individual, from all that goes to make up his singleness because personality "in general" does not exist, it is necessarily a product of history, though not always its contemporary history, and though its development as a product of the given historical reality may not be complete yet.

In studying the phenomenology of mind, Engels saw a scientific achievement in that its great author "laboured to discover and demonstrate" in "historical subdivisions" of the spiritual culture of mankind "the pervading thread of development".[3] We, in our turn, are interested in historical subdivisions pervaded by the threat of development, that of folk free-thought, in particular. And, in studying the modern forms of outlook of believers, it is highly important for us to know within which "historical subdivisions" they lag behind, in order to determine the point from which to follow this thread further. And what is most important is that each personality and not only a social group or class is an agent of a definite "historical subdivision" of spiritual culture regardless of its will and consciousness, though a personality can also act according to its will and consciousness. Engels wrote that the phenomenology of mind might be called "a parallel of the embryology and palaentology of the mind, a development of individual consciousness through its different stages, set in the form of an abbreviated reproduction of the stages through which the consciousness of man has passed in the course of history".[4] An abbreviated reproduction of the preceding stages of development in the individual consciousness through which the human consciousness has passed may be, by force of some or other objective or subjective circumstances, social and individual conditions incomplete, broken, and truncated. In the same way, formation of social consciousness of some or other class or social group may stop without having exhausted its potential for theoretical development. Within which "historical subdivision" has the development stopped ? Lenin wrote that "it would be biggest and most grievious mistake a Marxist could make to think that the millions of the people (especially the peasants and artisans), who have been condemned by all modern society to darkness, ignorance and superstition, can extricate themselves from this darkness only along the straight line of a purely Marxist education".[5] Lenin also cautioned against insulting the feelings of believers and wrote : "The keen, vivacious and talented writings of the old eighteenth-century atheists wittily and openly attacked the prevailing clericalism and will very often prove a thousand times more suitable for arousing people from their religious torpor than the dull and dry paraphrases of Marxism, almost completely unillustrated by skilfully selected facts, which predominate in our literature and which (it is no use hiding the fact) frequently distort Marxism."[6] It should be pointed out that the keenness, vivacity, and talent of atheistic writings were never an insult to the feelings of believers—they were akin to folk free-thinking.

The atheism of contemporary times owes a great deal to folk free-thought, which found its expression in various folklore genres, and in them predominantly, though, at the same time, theoretical expression as exemplified by the existing writing monuments of folk art was not strange to it either. In terms of both a repertory of ideas and the mode of their expression, folk free-thought—is an original source. This is clearly shown in Western Europe in the book by M.M. Bakhtin *The Art of Francois Rabelais and the Folk Culture of the Medieval Times* (Moscow, 1965), which received a wide acclaim. The medieval folk free-thought was not, and could not be, anti-religious but it was beyond any doubt anti-Christian, and especially anti-Church. This was a critique of Christianity, its ecclesiastical organization and its hierarchy from the positions of folk beliefs. The critique was distinguished by spontaneous and materialist approach to the mental grasp of the surrounding reality, alien to the renunciations and abstractions, characteristic of the Christian doctrine and morals. Contrary to the "vertical rhythm" of medieval Christianity, the folk culture had a "horizontal rhythm", was down-to-earth, tended to simple truths and rules tested and retested by practical experience. This culture was full of life—assertive, boisterous, uproarious, public, and festive—in complete contrast to the Christian advocacy of ascetism and seclusion and Christianity's ideological values. This was the kind of culture capable of nourishing the atheism of the present times—keen, vivacious, and talented. Among the producers and consumers of the folk culture with its pagan free thinking we often encounter representatives of the clergy, more so, the lower rung church hierarchy. This can, probably, be explained by the fact that the lower clergy had their own accounts to settle with higher spiritual and temporal feudals and that their conceptions, morals, and tastes were closer to those of the simple folk and, was for long, no more than only tinged with Christianity. This was understood and vividly expressed by R. Roland in whose writings the Brevesque's *curé*, Chamaille is, in fact, the self-same Colas Breugnon but only wearing a frock. Let us recall the scene in which the tipsy company of Colas, his friend Payard and *curé* Chamaille perform "several variations on long-robed lords, sandal-wearing hypocrites, corpulent prelates and sponging monks". And, as it should be expected, "the best and the most brilliant improvizations of songs were offered, in that instance, by Chamaille."[7]

Russian parallels to the phenomena of folk culture studied by Bakhtin are to be found in the books by A.A. Belkin *The Russian Skomorokhs* (*Mountebanks*) (Moscow, 1975) and D.S. Likhachev and A.M. Panchenko *The World of Amusement in the Ancient Russia* (Leningrad, 1976). Our interest in these parallels is prompted by the study of the unity of historical ways of establishing and developing folk culture, and of the specific features of the Russian folk culture. The inadequacy of scientific elaboration of the former puts it in the foreground. It should be noted that the very question of the Russian folk culture of amusement in Russia was raised in our pre-revolutionary historiography approximately in the middle of the 19th century. Profound and promising views regarding the folk culture of amusement were already put forward by the progressive scientist, I.E. Zabelin (1820-1908), who was also an outstanding erudite. He pointed to a "special element of gaiety" that existed in the Russian society before Peter the Great and traced its development during his reign and afterwards. The element of gaiety in the pre-Peter Russian society had, according to Zabelin, neither a "higher purpose and higher idea" a "pure ideal" nor a "pure ideal ahead" and was distinguished for its negativism. "In reality," wrote Zabelin, "it was a naive, unconscious or, in part even a scoffing mockery of life which expressed only another extreme of its profound and extensive negation which had for centuries underlain its spiritual development."[8] By negation ("...the centuries-old negation on which our spiritual and ethical culture grew"[9]) Zabelin meant negation of Western culture, the European forms of life, lifestyles, and morals which were themselves subjected to it "by force of the immutable laws of vital succession". The transformations made by Peter the Great were, according to Zabelin, also the "negation of a negation".[10] The Soviet researcher V.P. Andrianova-Perets sternly comments on the thesis of Zabelin, "though an owner of a richest, for his time, collection of satirical texts, I.E. Zabelin, failed, however, to discern in them anything except 'a special element of gaiety'."[11] Later researchers did not give their predecessor any attention which would be worth mentioning regarding the problem of the "culture of amusement". However, Zabelin was evidently right in characterizing the "element of gaiety" as being naive and even unconscious. In the latter case it would be quite appropriate to cite the words of Marx about Greek mythology as being the "unconsciously artistic elaboration of nature."[12] Marx considered Greek mythology as a product of folk fantasy and extended the concept of the "unconsciously artistic elaboration" to nature and society.[13]

Without considering the question of whether the Russian folk "element of gaiety" was indeed "unconscious" and "naive" we wish to recall, nevertheless, that creativity of this kind did take place. And one can well agree that the "element of gaiety" in ancient Russia could do without the "pure ideal ahead". Its "ideal" lay in an idealized pre-feudal past in contradistinction to the dominant culture and the dominant class generally. The ideal was behind rather than ahead but even this was enough to cause dismay among the temporal and spiritual feudals and bring persecutions upon the culture this ideal served to express unconsciously or otherwise. The widespread notion of the double nature of the "element of gaiety", sacred and profane all at once, is strongly in need of a further analysis. It is true, within some limits, the Church tended to connive at the motives of profanity in folk culture. Much the same attitude of connivance was, in fact, adopted by the Church with regard to the phenomenon of double faith for here the Church was up in arms against it, there it adjusted the Christian mythology and cult to pagan beliefs. But all through its history the Church was never able to cope either with the "element of gaiety" or double faith—all that remained for it to do was to put a good face to the matter.

The folk "element of gaiety" which arose in ancient Russia (it also had its prehistory) has many analogies in the West European "culture of amusement" and is a significant phenomenon in the history of folk free-thought. It can be characterized within a broad framework of medieval culture with all its patterns and categories.[14] Here we have the "historical subdivision" to which, in our view, Russian pagan free-thought belongs. (Criticism of the feudal Church by the population adhering to folk beliefs can hardly be visualized in the form of the famous "dispute" between Bishop Stephen and the Magician Pam, described in the 14th century by the Russian writer Epiphanius the Wise. In this work, Bishop Stephan who puts Pam to shame is depicted, in effect, as a master of wizardry of a higher class than Pam.) While the people's beliefs faded in the course of centuries and could not be called as such any longer, the "element of gaiety" remained and provided support for the folk opposition against the Church. Such persistence of folk free-thought in its folklore genres can be explained by the growth of hatred towards the Church and the clergy on the part of people. But not only by this. The sharp breaking up of the patriarchal village took place only after the reform of 1861 while the complete elimination of the vestiges of the medieval times was effected in the course of the Great October Socialist Revolution. The folk beliefs that still persisted represented the "historical subdivision" of the spiritual culture which owed its existence and long persistence to the patriarchal village, that is, a historically definite type of mental production giving rise to the given products of spiritual culture.

The legacy of the Russian folk free-thought is vast, indeed. Among the researchers who were engaged in its collection, we find such outstanding scientists as V.I. Dal, A.N. Afanasiev, I.A. Khudyakov, and P.V. Kireyevsky. A brilliant contribution has been made into the treasure-store of the Russian folk free-thought and into their study on the basis of the Marxist-Leninist methodology by Soviet researchers.[15] One can hardly find a folklore genre which is unaffected by the free-thought motives and plots. Fairy tale, epic, song, proverb, saying, they all exhibit the anti-clerical ideas and the people's protest against the Church. None of the good or bad features of the latter was left unnoticed by folk free-thought. The Church's ideas about the other world, its subservience to the dominant social classes, its cupidity and the role of the clergy as exploiters, customs of monastery life, church ceremonies and cult rituals, icon worshipping, and so on, were all subjected to criticism, castigation, and derision. The stories brought to life by folk free-thought show a surprising persistence and vitality. For example, "The Story of a Reveller", which while figuring already in the list of stories for the 17th century was written, probably, earlier and expressed, in the words of Adrianova-Perets, "doubt in recognized Church authorities",[16] not only lived to our day but occupies a fitting place in the anti-religious propaganda. The newest text of the story entitled "How a Drunkard Got Into Paradise" was carried by a non-believer newspaper (25 August 1940) which had a mass circulation. This is not the only example. It points to the fact that this is an independent field of scientific inquiry.

We wish to conclude the above views on folk free-thought, of which the "element of gaiety" constitutes a most graphic feature in the words of an eminent Russian scientist, E.V. Anichkov : " . . . where the primordial folk poesy has not disappeared, it is in our country. The efforts to eradicate it have not been successful. Masses of Skomorokhs roam the Russia for many long years ; no weddings or festivals took place without old songs, revelries and dances. The poesy lived on and developed to make up a whole library of many dozens of volumes when in the 19th century a search for all this would begin in backwoods areas, out-of-the-way corners and remote places, and when the texts of songs and their tunes would be recorded from the horse's mouth. Their store would turn out to be indeed, inexhaustible. The Church would not give in entirely. It would remain unbending. Secular disport and secular art would never cease to be reputed diabolic . . . And strange, indeed should look this struggle in which victory was to be won not by those who 'however, emerged victorious, beyond any doubt' ".[17]

Its history can be traced back centuries though it is "younger" than free-thought which developed in the channel of folklore consiousness. Between the various ways of development of folk free-thought there are distinctions but also meeting points of mutual influences. Folk philosophical free-thought belongs, in our view, to a "historical subdivision" which is different from that we spoke of above. We have in mind the historical process of isolation of the individual. As Marx wrote, "man isolates as an individual only as a result of historical process".[18] And again Marx wrote, "...ancient social organisms of production are, as compared with bourgeois society, extremely simple and transparent. But they are founded either on immature development of man individually, who has not yet severed the umbilical cord that unites him with his fellowmen in a primitive tribal community, or upon direct relations of subjection."[19] The folklore expression of folk free-thought corresponds to "simple" and "transparent" socio-production relations, that is, pre-capitalist relations. The objective prerequisite of the Renaissance which laid open the inner world of man and proclaimed his intrinsic value as an individual had been the breaking up of the centuries-old relations of personal dependence of man and their replacement by his material dependence—the impersonal power of capital. This was the basis for the progress in man's isolation and freeing him from the obligations his identification with a blood-related territorial, professional, caste, or estate group had imposed on him. The ability of the individual to act independently from some or other smaller social group, or rather from a number of various social groups, each of which demanded that he should abide by the general canons, rules, and traditions for the given group, as was the case in the medieval times, thus impelled him to rely only on the forces that resided in his own self. This was a step forward from man's immaturity as an individual to the assertion of his individuality. But the individual's intrinsic forces were unilaterally expropriated from him by his material dependence, by the power of capital, and the economic coercion which exhausted his spiritual and physical strength. The masters of the late Renaisance, Shakespeare among them, could already see that their brightest dreams were dashed and, it seemed, irreversibly so against the realities to which people were becoming slaves. Marx wrote : "Personal dependence based on material dependence, such as second large form of universal exchange of matter, universal relations, all-round requirements and universal potentials". And again : "The free individuality based on universal development of individuals and on turning their collective, social productivity into their social wealth, such is the third stage. The second stage creates conditions for the third one."[20]

The folk philosophical free-thought is a product of individual ideologists—who, as a rule, came from peasant backgrounds. They made their greatest theoretical achievements in the 18th and 19th centuries. In Russia, the capitalist mode of production emerged only after the 1860s. But the beginnings of the philosophical free-thought in the urban milieu go back to the epoch of feudalism, at the boundary between the 13th-14th centuries. It remained a monopoly of democratic circles and the urban lower classes almost till the last third of the 17th century when the spread of free-thinking views imbued with religious relationism began among peasants (not rarely by peasants themselves). The ideologists of folk philosophical free-thought at the "urban" stage of its elaboration and development included the lower clergy, artisans, serfs, and urban plebeian elements, generally. For reasons of space our review of this most interesting field of folk ideological creativity can be only cursory. The earliest extant example of folk free-thought is *A Word About False Teachers* which dates back to between 1274 and 1312. Its author who, however, did not disclose his name, evidently belonged to the lowest ranks of the church hierarchy. The main theses propounded in this work are the following : (1) The clergy is ignorant, remiss, and venal. They conceal from the people true teaching and harbour hatred for those who teach the truth. (2) A person may not necessarily be ordained to qualify as a teacher of people, and such a person may come from amidst ordinary people. (3) The sacred books (Bible) should not remain a monopoly of the clergy. They are the common heritage of the people and should be studied without the mediation of priests (who are false teachers) but in response to the prompting of the "holy spirit" residing in man and constituting the source of reason and inspiration. The advocacy of "book learning" can be carried not only in temples but everywhere and before all. It is generally conjectured that the author of *A Word About False Teachers* came from Novgorod or Pskov.

The heresy movements which took place in the 14th, 15th centuries in the country's largest centres—Moscow, Novgorod, Pskov, Tver, and Rostov propounded bold theses regarding sovereignty (self-power) of man, his mind, and soul, and rejected from these positions the institute of the Church and its orthodoxy as authoritarian which enslaved man spiritually, through idolatry, interpreted as the worshipping of icons, tabernacles and orthodox relics in general. The Church teaching about resurrection from the dead was questioned as contradictory to commonsense. This was recorded in the sources about the heresy of the Strigolniks (the meaning of the word is not now known) at the end of the 14th and the beginning of the 15th century, and that of Judaizers at the end of the 15th and the beginning of the 16th century (the Church accused the heretics of being converts to Judaism). In the variety of trends which arose in the midst of the people and opposed the reigning Church, two cardinal ideas connected with one another can be highlighted. Firstly, the assertion of man, the idea which crystallized at the beginning of the 17th century and is best expressed by an anonymous author, who was probably a low ranking civil servant: "In creating man, God bestowed self-power on him and ordained him to be his own master and not a slave". Secondly, the view of the Universe as an eternal entity, which owes its existence to itself (or "self-being" in the parlance of the 16th century). Representatives of the Church only took issue with this idea (it was preached and substantiated by heretic Feodosy Kosoy in the middle of the 16th century) but they could not think of the "self-being" concept other than in terms of God. The arguments put forward by Feodosy Kosoy are not known. Indirect data indicate the possibility of Kosoy's borrowing from Greek thinkers. The names and ideas of Parmenides, Thales, Democritus and Diogen were well known already in the 13th century in translations made from Medieval encyclopaedias.

Monk Zinovy debated with Kosoy's followers: "Who else but God can be capable of creating all the grandeur of the sky and the expanse, the space of the earth and sea, and whatever there is in them, who but God who is above all this? No, for such a lot of things to be without beginning and uncreated is impossible! If the sky and the earth, and water, and air, and the sun, and the stars, and whatever was in existence for a long time, before we and our fathers and our grandfathers were born, is, indeed, without beginning and uncreated, then all these are Gods : the sky, the earth, and the sea, and the stars—since they are without beginning."

We can now dwell on how the ideas concerning "self-being" of nature and "self-power" of man fared among the free-thinkers in Russian cities and towns. At the very beginning of the 17th century, a well known Russian essayist, Pososhkov, echoed Zinovy's criticism : "Some of you (free-thinkers—A.K.) say and not only say but insist that there is no God, that the world exists of itself and has no creator nor owner but that we are of ourselves, and are in possession of the whole world. . . ". Zinovy also employed against Feodosy Kosoy the accusation that the latter did not believe in God which was no more, however, than a polemic device. Feodosy Kosoy did believe in God but not the one we learn about from the teaching of the Church. In his outlook, belief in God and his materialistic conjectures about eternity and the uncreatedness of the universe lived side by side. The free-thinkers with whom Pososhkov debated could hardly be atheists, either. Here again we have a polemic device. But in the period from the middle of the 16th century till the beginning of the 18th century, the conceptions and arguments of the folk free-thinkers underwent some changes. Now, they could do without the authority of ancient philosophers. Judging by Pososhkov's works, they relied on the teaching of Copernicus. That the Russian society was familiar with the Copernican ideas can be confirmed on the basis of the facts relating to the 1680s.

In the peasant milieu, criticism of the Church's teachings from the "commonsense" positions could be traced to the last third of the 17th century. The peasant religious free-thinkers who had identical approaches to life and belief and their common opposition to the Church rallied in circles, where they elaborated the criteria of "spirit" and "truth" and on this basis, not only revised the teaching of the Church but formulated rules for behaviour and the concept of "conscience" (at the end of the 17th century and the beginning of the 18th century) as the supreme regulatory principle. These socio-ethical concepts were developing during the entire subsequent history of peasant free-thought. The ideas of "self-power" of man and "self-being" of nature were also adopted by the peasant free-thinkers but only in a modified form. A characteristic example of the former can be provided by the formula elaborated by the peasants who founded the movement of "Spiritual Christians" in the 1760s : "The sky and the earth meet in man and nowhere else on the earth" ! As for more general views of the world, the Spiritual Christians believed that God, Nature, and Man were links of the same chain of being in which God appears as "Wisdom". When a well-known German researcher of agrarian relations Hakstausen familiarized himself with the writings of the Spiritual Christians, he thus summed up his impressions : "It would be interesting to draw a parallel between the teaching of these simple Russian peasants and our ancient philosophers, like Yakov Boehme, on the one hand, and our young Hegelians, like Strauss, Feuerbach and Bauer, on the other. So many contrasts, similar places and analogies" !

The peasant liberation movement in Russia which brought about the downfall of serfdom (the Reform of 1861) continued to develop in the post-Reform years and produced a galaxy of folk free-thinkers. In 1830, a peasant Fyodor Podshivalov who was an ardent advocate of reconstructing society on the principles of Truth, put forward a thesis that man was born for freedom, free labour, and happiness and not for slavery and anguish. These views on the universe were pantheistic and he rejected the Christian teaching with its advocacy of humility and patience as necessary only for landlords. In the middle of the 19th century, a peasant Ivan Grigoriev propounded an original teaching centred on the concept of man as a measure of all being. In the 1870s a peasant Timofei Bondarev started his preaching. He was one of the most profound folk thinkers whose language was vivid and arguments deep and polemic. L.N. Tolstoy maintained correspondence with him. Bondarev taught that inhabited worlds were many. Though he did not identify God with Nature, he, however, drew them together and regarded bread as having a divine importance, as a source of life which would be produced by each man with his own labour. The categorical imperative of labour is the main element in Bondarev's teaching. He was engaged in polemics with Tolstoy because the great writer championed "non-resistance to evil" and believed in the power of Christian love through which according to him accord, fraternity, and equality could come to reign in the world.

Sometimes folk free-thought came close to atheism. But be it the Serf Feodosy Kosoy, who preached in the middle of the 16th century, or the doctor Dmitry Tveretinov, at the beginning of the 18th century, or the peasant Timofei Bondarev, at the end of the 19th century, the Church qualified the teaching of all of them as atheistic. But a clarification is needed here. The study of the main factors of the history of free-thought and atheism in Russia in the 18th and 19th centuries demonstrates that the atheism then in the process of establishment and development was bourgeois in nature. We wish to emphasize, in the first place, that a great contribution was made to the history of free-thought and atheism by the representatives of the Russian Enlightenment in the second half of the 18th century and by the Russian revolutionary democrats (at an incomparably higher philosophical and scientific level). A certain role in the elaboration of anti-clerical, deistic, and even atheistic views (as was also the case in West European countries) was also played by individual authors from the aristocratic circles for example, Duke D.P. Gorchakov (1758-1824).

Folk free-thinkers were purveyors of the "cogitative material" which was elaborated and enriched by the representatives from among the nobility and the democratic intelligentsia. But the folk thinkers were also able to themselves elaborate and enrich the feelings, sentiments, and views of the working population which was against the Church. As far as circumstances permitted, they tried to increase their knowledge. The ability to grasp reality theoretically was not a privilege of the dominant classes. We know about the withering criticism levelled by Marx and Engels against Thomas Carlyle who proclaimed that the oppressed classes were "dumb" and "their speech was inarticulate."[21] Thus, at a theoretical level accessible to them the folk free-thinkers inscribed brilliant and meaningful pages into the history of free-thought and atheism.

Even in England, a country advanced economically, such free-thought promoted the formation of a mature atheistic thought, though at first tinged with deism and pantheism and, then, in the course of time, directly materialistic. A theoretically principled importance had a generalization made by Engels in his resumé on Guizot's work entitled "Why the English Revolution was Successful". Engels wrote : "...Guizot tends to forget that the free-thinking he is so appalled by was imported into France form nowhere else but England. Locke was its father while Shaftesbury and Bolingbroke gave it the ingenious form which was later to be so brilliantly developed in France. Thus, we are coming to an interesting conclusion that the same free-thinking which according to Guizot, caused the failure of the French Revolution was a most important product of the English Revolution which was religious in nature."[22] In principle, with all the specificity of free-thought and atheism in Russia where some survivals of feudalism (the reigning Orthodox Church was one of them) persisted until the October Revolution, the history of Russian free-thinking and atheism reveals the same pattern of ideological development.

We do not claim, of course, to have the complete picture of Russian free-thought presented in this paper. There is much in this field that remains to be studied. The facts concerning folk free-thought as a phenomenon of the spiritual life of the people, which can be traced back to the 13th century and which had been showing signs of stability during the following centuries and the latter's characteristics, are here of a most general nature. The stability of the phenomenon lies in the depth of its roots, in the fact that it arose as a result of the class oppression and represented a protest against it on the part of the exploited and disfranchised masses. We show that folk free-thought was in the process of development but, either in its folklore, or its philosophical form, it stopped short of scientific materialism and atheism—it remained free-thought. This is quite legitimate. In the very nature of the class which came out as the creator and agent of free-thought, there were, among other things, also its limits of theoretical development. Even in its most popular forms, that is, folklore, free-thought failed to reach the millions of peasants who, as it was demonstrated by the First Russian Revolution, were in the grip of patriarchal traditions, under the ideological influence of backward conceptions, supersitions, and lastly, under the influence of the Orthodox Church.

However, the socio-historical importance of folk free-thought is not determined by the fact that it was not of an all-embracing nature but that it was a symptom of a profound ideological ferment in the masses. It produced ideological values and it would be fallacious to belittle them, for folk free-thought turned out to be a promising phenomenon in the sense that it was one of the ideological prerequisites for overcoming religion in the Soviet village. The potential of the centuries-old history of the Russian folk free-thought has found its realization in the new socio-economic and cultural conditions created by the Great October Socialist Revolution.

REFERENCES

1. See "Engels "To Rebel", London. 20 June 1873", in *Karl Marx and Friedrich Engels Correspondence, 1846-1895*, Martin Lawrence Ltd., London, 1934, p. 327.
2. V.I. Lenin, *Selected Works*, in three volumes, V. 3, Progress Publishers, Moscow, 1975, p. 602.
3. F. Engels, "Ludwig Feuerbach and the End of Classical German Philosophy", in *Karl Marx and Frederich Engels, Selected Works*, Progress Publishers, Moscow, 1970, p. 590.
4. F. Engels, *ibid.*
5. V.I. Lenin, *Selected Works*, in three volumes, V. 3, Progress Publishers, Moscow, 1975, p. 601.
6. V.I. Lenin. *ibid.*
7. R. Rolland, *Colas Breugnon.* Collected in fourteen volumes, V. 7, p. 51, (in Russian).
8. I. Zabelin, *Home Life of the Russian Tsars*, Part 2, Moscow, 1915, p. 268 (in Russian).
9. *Ibid.*
10. *Ibid*, p. 268-69.
11. Adrianova-Peters, *At the Fountainhead of Russian Satire of the 17th Century*, Moscow, 1977, p. 108-9, (in Russian).
12. Karl Marx, *A Contribution to the Critique of Political Economy*, Chicago, Charles H. Kerr and Company, 1904, p. 311.
13. *Ibid.*
14. A.Ya. Gurevich, *The Categories of the Medieval Culture*, Moscow, 1972, and also by the same author *On the History of the Grotesque. The 'High and Low' in the Medieval Latin Literature*, Izvestia of the Academy of Sciences of the USSR. The Literature and Language Series, V. XXXIV, No. 4, Moscow, 1975 (in Russian).

15. See *The Russian Folk Poesy Against Religion and Church*, Moscow-Leningrad, 1961, and *The Russian Literature in the Struggle against Religion*, Moscow, 1963.
16. V.P. Adrianova-Perets. *At the Fountainhead of the Russian Satire. The Russian Democratic Satire of the 17th Century*, Moscow, 1977, p. 126.
17. E.V. Anichkov, *Paganism and Ancient Russia*, St. Petersburg, 1914, p. 187.
18. K. Marx and F. Engels, *Works*, V. 46, part I, p. 486, (in Russian).
19. Karl Marx, *Capital* V. I, Progress Publishers, Moscow, 1965, p. 79.
20. K. Marx and F. Engels, *Works*, V. 46, part I, p. 100-1, (in Russian).
21. K. Marx and F. Engels, *Works*, V. 7, p. 268-69, (in Russian).
22. *Ibid.*, p. 220.

13

Constitution of the USSR and Problems of Freedom of Conscience

A. Okulov

WITHIN THE general topic of our Symposium I would like, in my short report, to characterize at least in a general way the principles of freedom of conscience which have found a profound scientific substantiation in the new USSR Constitution adopted in October 1977.

The new Constitution appears before us not only as a major political document which sums up the 60-year experience of the Soviet state, but also as a document reflecting the invariable orientation of our Party on the further deepening and development of socialist democracy. The new Constitution proclaims rights encompassing the very essentials of the life of the Soviet citizen –the right to work, to rest and leisure, to health protection, to social security, to education, to enjoy cultural benefits, to freedom of scientific, technical and artistic creative work, and equal rights of citizens in all fields of economic, cultural, social and political life. "Reading our new Constitution", Comrade L. I. Brezhnev noted in his report, "people will see more clearly what extensive and varied rights and freedoms are enjoyed by the citizens of a socialist society. In the provisions of the Constitution the world will see a state which sets itself the aim of the continued growth of the well-being and culture of the entire people, of all its classes and groups without exception, and which is actively working towards the attainment of this aim".

The principles of the socialist state in its attitude to religion have also found substantiation in the new Constitution of the USSR. The guarantees of freedom of conscience contained in

Lenin's decree "On the Separation of the Church from the State and the School from the Church", and in the three previous Soviet Constitutions, are not only retained in it but they are treated more thoroughly and intensively and take into account the tremendous changes that have taken place in our society over the past 40 years after the adoption of the 1936 Constitution of the USSR. The new Constitution (Articie 34) states: "Citizens of the USSR are equal before the law, without distinction of origin, social or property status, race or nationality, sex, education, language, attitude to religion, type and nature of occupation, domicile, or other status. The equality of citizens of the USSR is guaranteed in all fields of economic, political, social, and cultural life." Article 52 says: "Citizens of the USSR are guaranteed freedom of conscience, that is, the right to profess or not to profess any religion, and to conduct religious worship or atheistic propaganda. Incitement of hostility or hatred on religious grounds is prohibited."

"In the USSR, the church is separated from the State, and the school from the Church" (Article 52). It is known that history had repeatedly posed this question. But it was only the October Revolution that ensured the possibility of solving it in a practical manner: and it is only socialism that has settled it. Showing the qualitative distinction of the Soviet solution of the problem of freedoms, including the freedom of conscience, V.I. Lenin wrote: "A hundred and fifty and two hundred and fifty years ago the peoples were promised . . . that mankind would be rid of medieval privileges, of sex inequality, of state privileges for one religion or another (or "Religious ideas", "the Church" in general), and of national inequality. It was promised, but they did not keep their promises. They could not keep them, for they were hindered by their "respect" for the "sacred right of private property". Our proletarian revolution was not afflicted with this accursed "respect" for this thrice-accursed medievalism and for the "sacred right of private property."[1]

Rejecting religious ideology as anti-scientific, our party always regarded the questions of religion as subordinate to the major problems of the class struggle, revolutionary transformations to the tasks of rallying the masses for the attainment of common aims. Even in pre-revolutionary years V.I. Lenin taught that the attitude to religious ideology and to working believers should be clearly distinguished. He considered inadmissible the use of any coercion in these questions, constraint and restriction of freedom of conscience, and urged that workers and peasants, professing faith, should be treated in a friendly way, not to antagonize them with a contemptuous attitude to their religious and political prejudices, but to consistently, tactfully, and patiently make use of every act of the political and economic struggle—to enlighten, and draw them closer to the conscious proletariat through joint struggle.

At all the stages of building the new society the Communist Party has pursued a clear, flexible policy as regards religion and its institutions. It was always guided by V.I. Lenin's reminder that "We shall always preach the scientific world outlook ... but this does not mean in the least that the religious question ought to be advanced to first place, where it does not belong at all ; nor does it mean that we should allow the forces of the really revolutionary, economic and political struggle to be split on account of third-rate opinions or senseless ideas, rapidly losing all political importance, rapidly being swept out as rubbish by the very course of economic development."[2]

Freedom of conscience has always been a constitutional principle in the USSR. But it was not a matter of simply proclaiming it as a constituent part of political freedoms, but of drawing believers into the mainstream of social and political life of the socialist country, of involving various sections of the population in the building of a new world. Freedom of conscience in Lenin's interpretation and the union of believers and non-believers in the struggle for socialism presupposed and conditioned each other. The Communist Party had always proceeded from the premise that any violation of the principle of freedom of conscience may have an adverse effect on the unity of the working people in the struggle for socialism. The building of the new society in our country has become the concern of all the working people of the USSR. All nations and nationalities—and there are more than a hundred of them in the USSR—workers, peasants, the people's intelligentsia, communists and non-Party people, believers and non-believers—have worked and are working in full accord for its creation. It is the road traversed by us in this respect that has brought our country to the prevailing scientific materialistic and atheistic world outlook. It has been in many respects a difficult and an instructive road, and was of great historic importance.

"We were the first", L.I. Brezhnev said, "We had to break out of age-old backwardness. We had to surmount the enormous force of historical inertia and learn to live by new laws, by the laws of collectivism."[3]

It is known that prior to the Great October Revolution the road to education—the most essential element of culture—was a thorny one for the children of workers and peasants. Four out of every five children and teenagers could not go to school. Vladimir Ilyich Lenin wrote with bitterness that the peoples of Russia were literally robbed as regards education, light and knowledge.[4]

Almost three-fourths of the population of pre-revolutionary Russia between 9 and 49 years of age were illiterate. 60 men and 83 women in 100 could neither read nor write. Many peoples of the then outlying national areas of Tsarist Russia did not even have a written language of their own. Illiteracy among the peoples of the outlaying districts amounted from 97 to 98 per cent.

Today every third citizen of our country is a student : 126,100,000 people have higher or secondary (complete and incomplete) education. We have 162,000 general educational and secondary vocational schools attended by 48,000,000 students and staffed by almost 3,000,000 teachers. There are in our country 4,300 secondary technical and other secondary specialized educational establishments. During 1918-1976 they trained 21,600,000 specialists. More students are studying at the country's higher educational establishments than at their counterparts in all the capitalist countries of Europe taken together. In 1976 as compared with 1914 the output of specialists with higher education increased sixty-fold.

Citing these figures we can say with good reason that transformations of such magnitude, changes so fundamental in depth, and such a noble, humanitarian task have never yet been undertaken.

Speaking about the great historic experience of the breakaway of broad masses from religion in our country, one cannot but recall that Tsarist Russia was one of the most religious countries of the world. The church was the mighty mainstay of the Russian autocracy. All the aspects of man's spiritual life were in one way or another connected with the church or religion. It was precisely on the supposed insolubility of this edifice that the enemies of socialism relied. For instance, Seregei Bulgakov, a prominent religious leader, maintained that not a single civilization in history had yet been erected on an atheistic foundation, nor could it be erected.[5]

But the history of the development of our society scouted not only Bulgakov, but also many other prophets who maintained that man cannot assert himself without relying on divine interference.

In spite of all these assertions, atheism, which in past epochs was not widely practised, became in the Soviet epoch a mass occurrence actively facilitating the peoples' struggle for the new society. If we take a look at the factors and motives which brought millions of Soviet people to unbelief, then, of course, first of all, the main links in this process were: a radical improvement in the material and social conditions of life, the abolition of class and national oppression, development of public education, growth of literacy and the general culture of the population, the wealth and accessibility of spiritual culture and the involvement of all people in the practice of social activities. It can be said that the question of faith was decided in the course of the realization of the ideals brought by the Great October Revolution.

For pre-Marxist atheism the problem of the withering away of religion was seen as a problem of the triumph of knowledge. Paul Halback wrote that if ignorance of nature had given rise to gods, then cognition of it should destroy them. Didro assumed that if the development of enlightenment was not slowed down, religion would be done away within half a century.[6] The historic experience of our country has shown the correlation between the development of knowledge and the destinies of religion to be much more complicated. No matter how absurd and unfounded some religious conceptions may seem in the light of modern science, they can still play the role of a social force, since the social need in them is still preserved to some extent. Life has shown that no antitheses of pure reason were able to persuade some believers of the absurdity of their traditional ideas ; archaic and illusory ideas are still shared by many people. Only the withering away of the social need in gods or in some religious concepts makes them absurd. Religious systems of the past vanished not because they proved to be "excessively unreasonable", but as F. Engels noted, because their social basis was destroyed.[7] Neither did Engels belittle scientific knowledge in the struggle against religion. In his *Dialectics of Nature*, he very vividly describes the role of science in the struggle against religion. "One army unit after another lays down its arms, one fortress after another surrenders to the impact of science, until finally, the whole infinite region of nature is conquered by knowledge and there is no more room left in it for the creator."[8]

The October Revolution has shown that man's life having been liberated from every kind of social oppression, is naturally freed in all its aspects from religious ideas, customs and rituals. We have never considered scientific atheism simply as a negation of religion, but as a definite system of scientific-materialistic views of a positive nature, which help man understand the meaning of his existence, determine his position in society, assert his personal dignity, etc. Karl Marx said that atheism is the denial of god and asserts man's existence precisely by means of this denial.[9] The very problem of religious "alienation" in the theory and practice of Marxism appears first of all as a problem of overcoming alienation. To have this problem solved means to transform the world in a revolutionary way, to change social relations and thereby man himself. It is not so much explanatory work as the very mode of our life and the socialist reality that have helped to dethrone religion and undermine its power over the minds of millions of people.

This cannot be denied even by prominent religious leaders from abroad ; Julio Jirardi writes in his book *Marxism and Christianity* that the success of Marxism in the modern world is unquestionable and significant. Maxism attracts to the USSR the masses and the intelligentsia, the poor and the rich, peoples with ancient culture and young nations : it has active, convinced, ardent, and noble followers, heroes and martyrs. Jirardi sees this power of Marxism in the fact that being first of all a humanistic doctrine Marxism affirms the value of man and his dignity. Marxism detaches itself from the tragic atheism of the

Nietzschean and existential type. It intends to revive man's confidence in man : to convince man that life has a meaning and is worth living.[10]

Showing the humanistic character of atheistic work in our country, Rabindranath Tagore wrote after a trip to the USSR in 1930 in his *Letters on Russia* : "Soviet power has rescued its country from humiliation, freed it from the clutches of spiritual enslavement, the creator of which was the autocracy. Clergymen in different countries condemned it but I cannot condemn. Atheism is much better than religion. With all its weight the boulder of Tsarism, religion and oppression bore down on the shoulders of Russia ; having come here, one can see with one's own eyes what great possibilities have been created by the throwing off of this boulder."[11]

But it is common knowledge that in the contemporary bourgeois world there are to this day many malignant persons who do not stop spreading different fables about the status of the church and believers in the Soviet Union. The writings of such people as Fletcher, Kollarz, Venger, Struve, Bourdeux, Simon, and others are aimed at disparaging the great gains socialism has brought to the working people of the USSR. In the numerous works of these authors one can find such "sensational" assertions as : "In the USSR believers are unprecedentedly persecuted and oppressed." Piling up one false allegation after another, even such an important church dignitary as the Archbishop of Vienna, Cardinal F. Kunig, declared that a believer in the Soviet Union is barred from various professions, he allegedly has no access to universities, is denied participation in state affairs, and the like. All this is done to present in a distorted form our country in the eyes of believers in the West. For decades clerical propaganda kept the peoples of the West in complete ignorance of the great social and cultural transformations that took place in our country. The masses were told only lies about the Soviet Union. The political content of the clerical anti-Communism has degenerated into endless and tedious talk to the effect that Communism is bad. The poverty of ideas which are contrasted with the new society has become too obvious. "Now even the most rabid enemies of the Soviet Union", wrote the French authoress Simone Tary, "are unable to deny that every Soviet citizen is accorded the possibility of developing day after day everything of the best inherent in him, year after year he becomes more deserving of the noble title of man".[12]

The new world of socialism, having opened for each Soviet citizen a broad field of activities, gave him also the possibility to freely profess any religion or to be an atheist.

In its legislation on religion the Soviet state is guided by the Leninist principles of attitude towards religion and the church. It secures for all citizens full freedom to exercise any religious cult. To meet the believers' religious needs there are over 20,000 Orthodox churches, Catholic and Lutheran cathedrals, and churches, Jewish synagogues, Muslim mosques, Buddhist datsans, Evangelical Christian Baptists' and Seventh-Day Adventist prayer-houses, etc. For training their priests religious associations have six orthodox academies and seminaries, two Catholic seminaries, a Moslem theological academy and a madrasah, a Judaic Yeshiboth, as well as about 20 monasteries and nunneries. The religious organizations in the USSR extensively publish various religious literature. In recent years apart from the periodical editions : *Zhurnal Moskovskoj Patriarkhii* (The Journal of the Moscow Patriarchate), *Pravoslavnij Vestnik Ukrainy* (Orthodox Herald of the Ukraine), *Bratsky Vestnik* (Brotherly Herald), *Musulmane Sovetskogo Vostoka* (Moslems of the Soviet East), and others, they undertook several times mass printing of the Bible, the Koran, theological works, prayer-books, church calendars, and various other divine service publications. To all this we can add that for the satisfaction of the believers' religious needs the Soviet state has turned over to religious associations free of charge church buildings, which are public property, as well as objects of worship.

All this testifies to the fact that freedom of conscience in the USSR isnot a declaration, but a living reality. The new Constitution has again convincingly shown that only under socialism the notion of freedom, human rights, democracy, and social justice is filled with real content.

NOTES AND REFERENCES

1. V.I. Lenin, *Collected Works*, Vol. 44, pp. 146-47.

2. V.I. Lenin, *Socialism and Religion, Collected Works*, Vol. 12, p. 146.
3. L.I. Brezhnev, *The Great October Revolution and Human Progress*.
4. V.I. Lenin, *Collected Works*, Vol. 23, p. 127.
5. S. Bulgakov, *Dva grada* (Two Cities), Vol. 1 or 2, p. 48.
6. *Frantsuzskie prosvetiteli 18-go veka i religiya* (French enlighteners of the 18th century and religion), Moscow, 1960, p. 677.
7. K. Marx and F. Engels, *On Religion*, pp. 155-56 (Russ. ed.).
8. F. Engels, *Dialectics of Nature*, Moscow, 1952, p. 158 (Russ. ed.).
9. K. Marx and F. Engels, *From Early Works*, Moscow, 1965, p. 568. (Russ. ed.).
10. J. Jirardi, *Marxism and Christianity*, Moscow, 1967, p. 12 (Russ ed.).
11. Rabindranath Tagore, *His works in eight volumes*, Vol. 8, Moscow, 1957, p. 211.
12. *Foreign Literature*, 1976, No. 10, p. 229 (Russ. ed.).

14

Islam in Tsarist Russia

V.N. Basilov & G.M. Kerimov

BEGINNING FROM the mid-16th century, Islam came to be a factor of the Russian Empire's home policy after the army of Ivan the Terrible had defeated and brought about the fall of the Kazan and Astrakhan Khanates. Having annexed the new territories, the Tsarist government embarked on a distinct course of christianizing conversion of the Moslem population of the conquered states. The Tatar feudal nobility who were willing to convert to Christianity, were given equal rights with the Russian nobility and were even allotted land estates in the central areas of Russia. The government sanctioned missionary activities of the Orthodox clergy among the Tatars. During the reign of Fyodor, the son of Ivan IV, an *ukase* (a decree) was published to destroy Moslem mosques.

This attitude of the Tsarist government was mainly due to political considerations. Islam was the ideology of the conquered states and the Moslem clergy was a formidable force capable of inspiring anti-government movements. Tsarism thought it necessary to crush this force, and during the following two centuries stopped short of nothing in their zeal. In the reign of Elizabeth (1741-1761) the conversion of the Tatars was particularly forced and cruel. The new converts formed a separate group, called *kryasheny* (*i.e.* the christened).[1] On the whole, however, the forced conversion had failed to achieve the desired results, and the reign of Catherine II (1762-1796) saw an abrupt change in the government's attitude toward Islam. The Tsarist administration ceased its struggle against Islam and consistently tried to draw the Moslem clergy to its side in order to use it for ensuring and maintaining proper order and public tranquility among the Moslems of the Russian

Empire. This policy, not new to some other European states, was a success ; and thereon it was the master line of Tsarism in the Moslem populated regions.

Henceforward, the Tsarist administration turned its attention to the religious needs of the Moslems. A decree of 1829 set up a regulation for building mosques in compliance with the plan approved by the Tsar. A decree of 1833 ordered the Moslems of Russia to comply with every provision of their religion and strictly observe its dogma.[2] During the acquisition of the Caucasus the Tsarist authorities did not miss their chance to show to the Moslem population of the area their support to its religion. Thus, while on a visit to Shusha, General A.P. Ermolov publicly reprimanded Makhti-Kuli-Khan of Tatar for the poor state of mosque near his place and demanded a new mosque to be built to match the splendour of the palace by his next visit.[3] He also ordered some more mosques to be built in a number of settlements. General Chernyaev, who was appointed Governor of Tashkent, issued in 1865 a special document which ordered the population on pain of the usual penalties to observe strictly all the provisions of Islam.[4] And it was not a coincidence that in 1888 in Tashkent an Orthodox church and a newly built mosque of Hoja Akhrar were inaugurated almost simultaneously, for the authorities wanted to demonstrate to the Moslem population that they cared equally for both religions. It was with gratitude that on the occasion of the 25th anniversary of the seizure of Samarkand (1893) its Qadi noted that "The mosques, madrasahs (medrese) and our holy places in Samarkand, which had been utterly neglected under the Moslem rule, were repaired and trimmed as far as possible."[5]

The protection offered by the Tsarist government to Islam was largely due to the necessity to neutralize the influence that Turkey exercised over the Moslems on the territories that Russia had annexed. The influence was very great, as, for instance, is evidenced by the migration to Turkey of a large group of people from the Crimea and Northern Caucasus who had been frightened by stories told by the mullahs about the religious persecutions which would be experienced by the Moslems of Russia. Turkish emissaries sought and found sympathizers among the Moslems of the Volga area, too. The

Tsarist government was obliged to counter the enemy's propaganda with some steps that would demonstrate its tolerance. Moreover, experience had shown that it was not expedient to discriminate against Islam and that the Moslem clergy, was, in fact, quite willing to cooperate with the administration of the "white *padishah*".

Beginning with the reign of Catherine II the Islamic clergy was used to strengthen the foundations of the Russian Empire. A decree of 1785 ordered the sending of mullahs (who were, of course, "reliable and devoted people") to the Kazakh steppe to educate the Kazakhs "in the spirit of subordination ... to the royal family and to forestall disturbances". Some mosques were built in the places populated by the Kazakhs.[6] In many respects this decree was crucial to the destiny of Islam in Kazakhstan. A Kazakh scientist Ch. Valikhanov had every ground for his conclusion that Islam had taken root among the Kazakhs, who earlier had known this religion in a perfunctory manner only, due to the assistance of the Tsarist government.[7]

After the conquest of the Caucasus the Tsarist administration actively employed some representatives of the Moslem clergy to convince the population of the necessity to submit to Russia.[8] If the efforts of the local mullahs could promise no success the authorities used the services of ecclesiastics from some other areas. Thus, for instance, in 1836 the *mufti* of Kazan, Tajeddin-effendi, went to Daghestan on a mission to persuade the mountain peoples to give up their resistance to Russia and to kill or surrender their leader Shamil. After the failure of Tajeddin, who was generously renumerated, a Kazakh, Qadi Osman-effendi, known for his loyalty to the Tsar was sent to the Caucasus. In the aftermath of the Tsarist victory the Moslem clergy in Central Asia was eager to prove its devotion to the Russian administration. Thus, in 1875, a group of the Samarkand nobility headed by a *quadi* , and some of the clergy sent a congratulatory note to the Governor-General of the Turkestan area on the seizure of Kokand town. It read: "This news had brought us great joy. You are kindly requested hereby to convey our feelings of loyalty and our sincere gratitude to his Imperial Majesty, our White Tsar".[9]

In their sermons the Moslem clergy urged parishioners to abide by the existing order. For example in the "Sermon to the Trans-Caucasian Moslems" the *mufti* of the Trans-Caucasus Hussein-effendi Gaibov, who was awarded numerous Tsarist decorations and whom the officials of the Ministry of Interior described as being "faithfully devoted to the throne and the fatherland" wrote in 1890s : "My dear Moslem brothers : Let God make you happy in both worlds. I consider it my sacred duty to tell you and command everyone and everybody that subordination and obedience to the Tsars and existing authorities, be they Orthodox or not, Moslem or not, are obligatory... In view of the so abundant favours and graces of our august monarch, our Shariat duty makes us serve his imperial majesty with care and zeal ... If, and let it to be better not, something on our part comes against his royal will, then this will mean going against the Shariat itself and we shall thereupon rob ourselves of happiness in both worlds".[10]

The Moslem clergy in the Russian Empire was controlled through special agencies. After the acquisition of the Crimea there were established first the Tavrian and then, in 1788, the Orenburg "Moslem religious assemblies". It was stressed by the government that the Tsarist administration preserved the right "to supervise that only people reliably faithful and of good conduct are admitted to run religious offices of the Mohammedan law".[11] In 1872 there were set up two religious departments in the Trans-Caucasus, that is, the Shiite and the Sunni departments. The Moslem clergy were, in fact, regarded as state officers. When on a mission, mullahs were paid for their travelling and daily expenses. At the end of the 19th century the postal correspondences of the Moslem clergy were allowed at the public cost.

The Tsarist government favoured the Moslem clergy with considerable privileges. The status of the Moslem clergy was connected with the problem of the *waqf* property (*i.e.* the property of the ecclesiastics and their organizations). Despite the fact, that the Tsarist officers were successful in restricting the clergy's rights to the *waqf* property, this property was enjoyed by the clergy practically till the proclaiming of Soviet power.

The courts preserved the religious basis of the Tsarist state. Although Moslems were permitted to apply to the Russian courts, nevertheless the local population still adhered to the habit of making use of the *kazii* (*qadi*) and *biy* (people's) courts, which usually functioned on the basis of the Shariat.

While making use of the Moslem clergy as a body, to hold numerous followers of Islam in subordination, the Tsarist government considered it necessary at the same time to keep control over the clergy themselves. In 1890-1891 the Tsarist administration abolished elections for the *mufti's* post in Orenburg and Tavrida (Crimea) ; henceforth *muftis* were appointed by the Ministry of Interior. Orenburg's Islamic Ecclesiastic Assembly adopted a decision according to which "... parish mullahs were allowed to take short leaves, however, not more than a two week period ... without any special permit from the Police Board, they had, however, to report each leave of absence to the local Police".[12] The mention of the Police Board here is very typical. Even reproofs for not keeping the religious ceremonies on time were given through the Police Board.

It is necessary to point out that the Tsarist government did not aim at eradicating or curtailing Islam as a Creed. This can be seen from the fact that during the reign of Catherine II the Quran was printed for free circulation among the Kazakhs. In 1800 the Moslems of the Russian Empire were granted by a decree permission to print their own religious books. On the basis of this decree the Eastern Printing House was moved from St. Petersburg to Kazan. The capacity of this Printing House was considerable from the very first years of its existence.

It would be incorrect to identify the activity of the Orthodox missionaries with that of the government. The Orthodox missionaries tried to attract Moslems to Christianity and their actions caused embarrassment among the Moslem population (thus in the year of 1894 the Orenburg's *mufti* even considered it necessary to declare officially that "rumours" concerning the forcible conversion to Christianity of the Moslems as "absurd" and "senseless").[13] The specific interests of the Orthodox Church did not coincide with the government's orientation, the latter saw the problem of Islam in a much broader political context and, therefore, rejected the idea of Christening Muslims. The Orthodox missionaries in Kazakhstan and

Kirgizia neither enjoyed support of the local authorities nor constituted any serious institution ; and their activities proved utterly fruitless. In the Caucasus, where a considerable part of the population were Christians, the administration showed some signs of favouring the work of the Orthodox missionaries. The Moslem Religious Boards of the Trans-Caucasus were forbidden to interfere with the affairs of the Moslems who lived in the areas of Batumi, Kars, Daghestan, Black Sea Governorate, districts of Zakataly and Sukhumi ; these regions were allocated to the missionary activities of the Orthodox Church.[14] However, the history of the Georgian settlements in the Zakataly district show a negligible influence of the missionaries in the life of the district. The Georgian population of some villages, who had been forcibly converted to Islam, returned to Christianity, but due to the lack of further support from the Tsarist administration they later turned back to the Islamic creed.[15] In the Volga region the process of Islamization (and assimilation with Tatars) continued although on a minor scale in the 18th-19th centuries among Chuvash, Mordvinian, and Mari populations who were still under the influence of Christianity or adhered to their pagan creeds.

However, Islam was not an obedient instrument of control for the Tsarist administration. Islam remained an ideology that could be easily used by anti-government movements. Some part of the Moslem clergy stood in opposition to the government, for under the Tsarist administration it had lost its former political and social influence and benefits. Thus there was a strong clerical opposition in Central Asia. Under the 1886 statute the Tsarist government abolished large scale feudal landownership in the area, and allocated land to those who actually possessed it. Among the big feudal landlords thus deprived were many representatives of the clergy.[16] The colonial authorities took from the clergy those *waqfs* that had no grant documentation. From then on the Moslem institutions did not enjoy the State economic support. Although usually the Moslem clergy preferred to keep clear of the anti-government movements of the Moslem population, or even tried to persuade the people not to violate the order (thus during the Pugachev's uprising the clergy agitated against the "rebels"), in Central Asia the clergy was among those that inspired anti-government revolts. In Samarkand in 1868 the students of such big madrasahs as Tillakori and Shirdor were an active force in the uprising against the Russians.[17] At the head of the Andijan uprising (1898) was Dukchi-Ishan, who proclaimed slogans of *gazavat* and the return of power to the khans. A direct result of this was the decision taken by the colonial authorities to seriously study the status of religion and religious institutions in Turkestan. (We may add that those sections of the Moslem clergy that supported the feudal order, later on were very active in their struggle against Soviet power.) Some movements that were anti-government also took a religious form. An example of such a movement was the sect of *vais* that sprang up on the petty bourgeois basis. The founder of the sect, Bahauddin Vaisov, had a large number of followers, due to a political programme that rejected all civil law, payment of customs and taxes, the Tsarist court, service in the army, mosque visits, and for conducting religious rituals. The Moslem clergy and Tsarist administration were united in the struggle against this sect. Mullahs wrote false reports and the police crushed the religious house of the "society" in 1884. The founder of the sect was found by doctors to be mentally sick and sent to a psychiatric hospital, where he died in 1893. The Tsarist authorities continued persecuting members of this religious sect. For example, Vaisov's son, who carried on the work of his father, was twice deported to Siberia (in 1895-1906 and 1910-1917).[18]

The modernist movement in Islam, usually known in Russian literature as *djadidizm*, began to gather momentum in the second half of the 19th and the beginning of the 20th century. This developed in Russia in a similar way as it did in other Moslem countries. That is, as a result of contact with European capitalism, and European science and technology which gave a powerful impetus to the development of the movement aimed at overcoming medieval backwardness. This movement took on the form of religious modernization, as all activity in Islam was regulated by the Shariat and, therefore, change in it was considered as a religious problem. Since Russia was the most backward capitalist power, so the modernization ideas among the Moslems of Russia did not receive the same impetus as they did in Egypt, Turkey, and

India ; it was merely a weak echo of the reformist ideas expressed by Djamal-ad-din Afghani, Said Ahmed, or Sheikh Muhammed Abdo.

The reformist ideas of Moslem modernizers in Russia were mainly limited to educational reforms (the term *djadidism* being derived) *Usuli djadid*, a new method of teaching. The reorganization of schools was the first and basic problem of the renovation movement. The programme of the Tatar mullah, who was also a historian Sh.Mardjani (1818-1889) recommended the exclusion of old and useless textbooks of scholastic content from the Madrassah and the introduction of secular subjects and the Russian language. True, the possibility of introducing any innovation or reform was facilitated by the provision that everybody had a right to interpret and find an answer in the Quran to any religious question.[19] However, this provision could be realized only under appropriate conditions, lacking which it had no practical effect on the development of Moslem modernism in Russia.

Modernism was met with severe opposition primarily from the Muslim clergy (the so-called *kadimists*). The latter in their activity against the *djadids* reported them to the police, accusing them of anti-government and even socialist activities. The Tsarist government met the Moslem modernization movement guardedly and took steps aimed at promoting the cultural development of the Moslem population. Thus in Central Asia the authorities permitted during the last decade of the 19th century the running of new method schools, and Russian schools were also opened, facilitating the acquaintance of the local people with Russian culture. For this purpose excursions by rich Uzbeks to Russia were encouraged and the madrasah students and prominent Tashkent merchants were invited to gymnasiums where they were acquainted with the Russian education system.[20] The *Kirgizskaya stepnaya gazeta* (Kirgizian steppe newspaper) published texts in the Kazakh langúage[21] intended for the local population. But on the other hand, Tzarist administration was extremely disturbed and frightened by the political aspact of *djadidism*.

The ideas of modernism took hold of various social strata of the Moslem population ; however, its main social force was the national bourgeosie. It was widespread in Tataria where there was already a well-developed bourgeoisie, which, having lost the benefits it derived from the role of mediator between the Central Asian market and Russian capitalism after the annexation of Central Asia was obliged to withstand the competition of Russian capital in less favourable conditions. Protectionist aims of the bourgeoisie terminated in the ideology of nationalism, and the movement's direct dependence on the interests of the bourgeoisie, therefore, gave it a nationalist orientation. The nationalist orientation of the *djadidism* in Russia took the shape of pan-Turkism or pan-Islamism, implying cultural development and rapprochement of all Turkic (Moslem) peoples of the country. As to its political aspirations, Tatar pan-Turkism saw as a rule its future within the framework of the Russian monarchy, although there were some circles in Central Asia who wished to separate from Russia. The government did not separate the educational problems of *djadidism* from the political views of the Moslem bourgeoisie. And, in fact, it was not always easy to separate one from the other, for often the rearing grounds of pan-Islamic and pan-Turkic ideas even in Tataria were big Moslem madrasahs (such as the Izhbob seminary) where the anti-Russian and anti-government propaganda was carried on.[22]

The government did not fear the principle of modernism itself. For example it gave protection, for political considerations, to the modernized Shiite sect of Babids who were persecuted in Iran ; and in 1901 the Tsarist authorities permitted the Babids to open a prayer house in Baku and later in Ashkhabad. What the government actually feared was the aim of the *djadids* to unify all Moslems of the country. Not understanding its inherent causes (even school reform was a common problem for all the Moslems of Russia). Tsarism saw pan-Turkism and pan-Islamism as linked primarily with Turkey's manoeuvres. Facing the formation in 1905 of a Moslem party "Ittifak", which considered as most important the "rapprochement of Moslems of all districts of Russia on the basis of social, cultural and political aspirations and problems of modern... life", the government could not but feel threatened by the great potential force of *djadidism*. For this reason even the new method schools were gradually considered undesirable by the Tsarist administration. After the Revolution of 1905 the old

Muslim school found supporters in the Russian state officials. This was due, as was pointed by V.V. Barthold, to the fear "of conveying to the natives rather too much information in their own languages and in doing so actually assisting the consolidation of native literature and local cultural peculiarities at the cost of hampering the Russification".[23] A deputy to the third State Duma, Maksudov, had every ground to upbraid the government with the fact that it systematically encroached on everything that was dear to a Moslem, it persecuted the Moslem school, literature, and language.[24] And in spite of all this the new method school survived especially in the pre-revolutionary years. There were ardent followers of the movement, who opened up schools at their own expense, without asking for permission from the authorities and it was impossible to step this process.[25]

It is characteristic of the pre-revolutionary years that the government began to use more enlightened measures against the undesirable aspirations of its Moslem population. In 1908 a journal *Moslem* began to be published in Paris, which toed the line of the Tsarist political secret police. This journal was even transported into Russia duty-free. In 1911 a newspaper *In the Moslem World* began to be published in St. Petersburg, which was, however, closed in 1912 due to its provocative character. The Ministry of Home Affairs recommended in 1912 the publication of a special journal, *Islam World*, enlisting for this purpose scientists and being directed against pan-Turkism and pan-Islamism.[26]

In evaluating the modernist movement of the Moslems of the Russian Empire, it is necessary to remember its multifarious character. Its educational activities undoubtedly were progressive ; its socio-political problems frankly reactionary. Although the programme of the "Ittifak" demanded the equality of the Moslem people at par with the Russians, and also demanded the freedom of press, unions, and religion, nevertheless the party acknowledged the state regime as a constitutional monarchy. The socio-political orientation of Moslem modernism is explained by A. Ageev and A. Khusein-zade, the publishers of the *Hayat*, a Baku newspaper with a pan-Turkish orientation : "In order to bring the world of Islam from the current stagnation we will have to fight against two forces : the leftists and the rightists. The rightists—conservatives who reject any innovation ... and by all possible means are trying to detain development of the people (whose creed is Islam). The leftists blindly copy our rivals (*i.e.* Europe) and throw themselves in the face of danger. In this way the rightists do not understand the clear spirit of Islam, and leftists consider that there is nothing in Islam that could help in the development of culture and evolution of society. They being unaware of the danger are spreading poisonous ideas of materialism, atheism and socialism ... There is no salvation outside Islam."[37] During the years of the revolution when the national proletariat including Moslems entered the path of resolute struggle against Tsarism, the obscure slogans of progress and freedom, together with the proclamation of brotherhood of all Moslem peoples, proclaimed by the *djadids* actually delayed the historical progress, distracting the Moslem masses from real and vital problems such as the overthrow of the exploiting order.

The information disclosed in the present paper makes it possible to draw up a picture of the peculiar state of Islam in the country, prior to the Soviet takeover. Due to the policy of the Tsarist government that gave the right of regulating the life of the Moslem population to the clergy, religion played a considerable role in the life of the Moslems and supported the feudal-partriarchal principles of the Middle Ages with the help of the Shariat. The historical problems of Moslem republics of Russia were overcome and their economic, political, social, and cultural transformation was brought about only with the advent of Soviet power.

NOTES AND REFERENCES

1. For more details see: Yu. G. Mukhametshin, *Tatarkriasheny* (The Tatar-Kriashens), Moscow, 1977.
2. L.I. Klimovich, *Islam v Tsarshoy Rossii* (Islam in Tsarist Russia). Moscow, 1936, pp. 24, 51-53.
3. N. Pogodin, Aleksey Petrovich Yermolov, Material dlia yego biografii. Za chaniya D.V. Davydova, othosiashchiyesia k periodu upravleniya Gruziyey Al. Peter. Yermolova. (A.P. Yermolov. Data for his biography. D.V. Davydov's remarks concerning the period of

A.P. Yermolov's governorship of Georgia). In: *Russkiy Vestnih*, 1863, V. 48, p. 360.
4. V.V. Barthold, Istoriya kulturnoy zhizni Turkestana (The History of the Cultural Life in Turkestan). In: *Sochineniya*, V. II, p. 1, Moscow, 1963, p. 351.
5. Cited from: L.I. Klimo vich, *op. cit.*, p. 37.
6. *Ibid.*, p. 21.
7. Ch. Ch. Valikhanov, O musulmanstve v stepi (On Islam in the steppes). In: *Izbranniye proizvedeniya* (*Selected Works*), Alma-Ata, 1958, pp. 187-95: see also: Alektorov A. Ye. Chem: kak my sposobstvuyem ukrepleniyu musulmanstva v Kirgizah (How we help Islam to become stronger among the Kirghiz).—In: *Materialy dlia izucheniya stariny, istorii i byta Kirgisov* (Materials for the study of history, olden times and way of life of the Kirghiz) issue 1, Orenburg, 1892.
8. A.V. Avksentiyev, *Islam na Severnom Kavkaze* (Islam in the Northern Caucasus). Staveropol, 1973, p. 39.
9. *Turkestanskiye vedomosti* (newspaper), 11 November 1875, No. 45.
10. Cited from: G.I. Mustafayev, Kriticheskiy analiz islamskoy ideologii v Azerbaidjane nachala XX veka (The critical analysis of the Moslem ideology in Azerbaidjan at the beginning of 20th century). Avtoreferat for doctorate thesis, Baku, p. 28.
11. Cited from: L.I. Klimovich, *op. cit.*, p. 22.
12. *Ibid.*, p. 54.
13. Sbornik tsirkuliarov i inyh rukovodiashchih rasporiazheniy po okrugu Orenburgskogo Megometanskogo Duhovnogo Sobraniya 1841-1901 gg. (Collection of orders and other directive instructions for the district of Orenburg Muslim Spiritual Assembly during the years 1841-1901). Ufa, 1902, p. 72.
14. G.I. Mustafayev, *Ideologiya islama v nachale XX veka V Azerbaidjane i yeyo kritika* (Ideology of Islam at the beginning of 20th century and its critical study). Baku, 1973, p. 58 (In Azerbaidjan language).
15. I.I. Datunashvili, Materialy k harakteristike sovremennogo sostoyaniya religioznosti v Belokanskom, Zakatalskom i Kahskom rayonah, Azerbaidjanskayg USSR). (Data for the study of the present day religious life in Belokan, Zakataly and Kah districts of Azerbaidjan SSR).—In: *Konkretniye issledovaniya sovremennych religioznych verovaniy* (The concrete studies of the contemporary religious beliefs). Moscow, 1967, p. 188.
16. O.A. Sukhareva, *Islam v Uzbekistane* (Islam in Uzbekistan), Tashkent, 1960. p. 71.
17. *Ibid.*
18. L.I. Klimovich, *op. cit.*, pp. 149-69.
19. A. Arsharuni and Gabidullin H., *Ocherki panislamizma i panturkizma v Rossii* (Essays on pan-Islamism and pan-Turkism in Russia), Moscow, 1931, p. 10.
20. O.A. Sukhareva, *op. cit.*, p. 72.

21. In the pre-revolutionary Russian literature the Kazakhs were referred to as the Kirgiz people.
22. A. Arsharuni and Gabidullin H., *op. cit.*, p. 25.
23. V.V. Bartold, *op. cit.*, p. 308; see also p. 313.
24. L.I. Klimovich, *op. cit*, pp. 233-67.
25. *Central Government Historical Archives of the USSR*, f. 821, op. 133, delo 450.
26. A. Arsharuni and Gabidullin, H., *op. cit.*, p. 31.
27. *Hayat* (newspaper), 1905, No. 1. (7 June): In brackets are the interpretation of the authors of this paper.

in Russia some Protestant sects of the Mennonites (at the close of the 18th century), Baptists (in the latter half of the 1860s), Evangelicals (in the 1870s), Adventists (in the 1880s), Pentecostals (in the opening decades of the 20th century) and others. Their proliferation was greatly helped by the missionaries from England, Germany, and the USA.

In the process of their evolution and class differentiation in pre-revolutionary Russia the Baptists, Evangelicals and others lost many of the inherent characteristics of sects and became specifically bourgeois churches. On the eve of the revolution there were over 200,000 Baptists, Evangelicals, and Adventists in this country.[3]

The Evangelical Christian Baptist Church took on its present form in 1944 through uniting the organizations of the Baptists and the Evangelical Christians. In 1945 and 1947 the Union of the Evangelical Christian Baptists was joined by some communities of the Pentecostals, that is, by the Christians of the Evangelical belief and the Apostolic Christians. In 1963, some of the Mennonites joined the Union too. According to the church administration, the organization of the Evangelical Christian Baptists number, at present, more than 500,000 members of many nationalities,[4] including Russian, Ukrainian, Byelorussian, German, Latvian, Estonian, Georgian, Armenian, and Ossetian believers. The Evangelical Christian Baptist, communities are to be found in many regions of the Russian Federation (RSFSR), the Ukraine, Moldavia, Latvia, Estonia, Kazakhstan and other republics of Central Asia, and elsewhere. The church is headed by the All-Union Council of the Evangelical Christian Baptists (AUCECB), whose printed organ is the *Bratski Vestnik* (the Brotherly Herald).

Outside the Union of the Evangelical Christian Baptists there are some Baptist and Evangelical Christian societies which function autonomously (the so-called "Free Baptists"). In the early sixties some of the Evangelical Christian Baptist bodies refused to recognize the AUCECB as their head and set up their own "spiritual centre", namely, the Council of Churches of the Evangelical Christian Baptists (ECB).

Adventism in the USSR is manifest in two main trends, that is, the Seventh Day Adventists and the Reformist Adventists. The Adventists do not have a single centre and their commu-

15

Islam in the USSR (1917-1945)

G.M. Kerimov

THE SEPARATION of the Church from the State after the victory of the Great October Socialist Revolution in our country could not help having its impact on the political stand of the Moslem religious organizations.

The evolution of the stand taken by Islam and the Moslem organizations in the Soviet Union with regard to the socialist State from 1917 to 1945 took place in three main stages : (1) a hostile attitude to the socialist order and support for the Moslem clergy by the *basmaches* (members of an anti-Soviet movement, *basmachestvo*, in Central Asia) and the counter-revolution (1917-1928): (2) loyalty to the socialist system (1928-1941) ; and (3) adaptation of Islam to the socialist way of life and an attempt to present the changes occurring in the country as the realization of age-old Moslem ideals (1941 and after). It is noteworthy that foreign specialists and theologians also recognize the above given stages in this evolution. They interpret the changes in the stand taken by the Moslem preisthood with regard to the socialist system as an ideological rapprochement and reconciliation of Islam and communism. Dr. Mohammad Shauki Fandjari, a modern Egyptian ideologist writes : " ...There are over 30 million Moslems living in Russia. The Bolshevik revolution took place in 1917 as a triumph of Marxism. Since that time Moslems have been through three stages in their attitude towards the revolution : the first stage was a stage of opposition and enmity towards the revolution because of the main differences. The second stage was one of mutual understanding and coincidence of views. The authorities in Russ ia were aware that they could only implant socialism in the Tatar and Caucasian regions by means of Islam.

Russian Moslem scholars understood that Islam approves of the following main aspects of Marxism: the struggle against imperialist exploitation, the elimination of reaction and feudalism, opposition to bribery and corruption and money-lending. The view that labour is the main source of wealth and the criterion of human dignity, and also the assertion of real equality and the participation of the people in governing the state, and so forth, all these most important aspects of Marxism, were known to Islam fourteen centuries ago. Then the third stage began, precisely a stage when Marxist socialist thought developed, during which socialism was enriched with Islamic thought, with Islamic ideas ...".[1]

There was no need to prove that socialism in the USSR was not subjected to the impact of Moslem ideas. This is clear to anyone who knows the history of the Soviet state.

We shall take up another aspect of the same question, that is, the universally known fact that Islam and Marxism represent different ideologies. But the Moslem organizations' enmity towards the Soviet system was not based on theoretical differences, for acknowledging these, the Soviet government guaranteed the Moslem freedom of religion. The conflict resulted from the Moslem clergy's support for the overthrown exploiter system, for counter-revolution, and from the use of Islam by the upper ranks of the priesthood as a political weapon against socialism. The Moslem clergy's change-over to a loyal stand was brought about by the adaptation of the Moslem priesthood to the new order, which had demonstrated its political stability and also its general superiority over the previous socio-economic system. In circumstances where socialism was victorious, anti-Soviet activity was pointless, not just because it was being firmly nipped by the organs of power; it would have cut off the clergy from the main mass of believers, who accepted the new system, which had abolished exploitation and brought the workers better living conditions and higher cultural standards.

One of the first measures taken by the Soviet government was abrogation of the Tsarist laws stating that religions were not equal. V.I. Lenin said that there should be no "ruling" belief or church and that all beliefs and all churches should be equal before the law.[2]

In an Appeal of the Soviet government "To All the Moslem Workers of Russia and the East", published on 3 December 1917, it was stated that :

> Henceforth your beliefs and customs, your national and cultural institutions are declared free and inviolable. Arrange your national way of life freely and unimpeded. You have the right to do so. You must know that your rights, like the rights of all the people of Russia, are protected by the power of the revolution, of its organs, and of the Soviets of workers', soldiers' and peasants' deputies.

The Bolshevik party's policy with regard to Islam was the outcome of fulfilling V.I. Lenin's recommendations that a thorough study should be made of Moslem needs. This is evidenced by the return to the Moslems of the "Holy Koran of Osman" by a special government decree of December 1917. (Before the annexation of Central Asia to Russia, this more than 1,000-year-old Arabic literary text had been kept in Samarkand. In 1869, on the instructions of the Tsarist authorities, it was taken to St. Petersburg and put in the safekeeping of the Imperial Public Library). The decree stated that on 1 December 1917, the Soviet of People's Commissars received an application from the Krai Moslem Congress of the Petrograd national area, expressing the aspiration of all Russian Moslems, that the "Holy Koran of Osman" should be returned to them. The Soviet of People's Commissars passed a resolution that the "Holy Koran of Osman" should be handed over to the Krai Moslem Congress forthwith. A copy of the resolution with instructions for its execution was immediately sent to A.V. Lunacharsky, the People's Commissar for Education.[3]

The leaders of the Communist Party and the Soviet government were well aware that effecting the socialist changes in the areas where Islam was traditionally practised would encounter serious difficulties. V. I. Lenin demanded that the difficulties involved in working among the Moslem population should be taken into account. At the VIII Party Congress in 1919, he asked what might be done with regard to such peoples as the Kirghiz, Uzbeks, Tadzhiks, and Turkmens, who were still under the influence of their mullahs. "In Russia, after long experience with the priests, the population had helped us to throw them out, but could we go to these peoples and say we would throw out their exploiters. We could not do that because they were completely subordinated to their mullahs. Here one should have to wait for the development of the given nation, for the proletariat to become differentiated from the bourgeois elements, which is inevitable."[4]

The first stage in the interaction between Soviet power and Islam was the most difficult. At that time most of the Moslem population retained its traditional way of life, when the priests played an important part in society. The number of Moslem priests as a percentage to laymen was several times higher than that of Orthodox priests. In the early years of Soviet power in Dagestan alone there were 40,000 ecclesiastics (sheikhs, imams, mullahs, cadis, mutallims, alims, and so on) per million of the population, that is, 4 per cent, while in Russia the Orthodox clergy did not even make up one-tenth of the population.[5] The Moslem priests were well acquainted with the life and psychology of the believers and were able to exercise spiritual influence over them. The mullahs always participated in festivals and various events in family and social life. The Islamic slogans about equality among the Moslems, the show of concern for the needs of the peasants on the part of the rich and clergy, and the giving of alms to the poor by the rich, concealed the actual social inequality.[6]

In describing the relations between the Soviet power and the Moslem clergy, it should be mentioned that some of the clergy did take up a loyal stand towards the socialist state immediately. Obviously, this circumstance is directly linked with dissimilar social positions among the Moslem priests. The lower and middle ranks of the priesthood came to enjoy a similar standard of living and way of life as the poor strata of the population. However, the main part of the Moslem clergy openly participated in anti-Soviet activities. They used the mosques as places to propagate anti-Soviet slogans and kindle anti-Soviet attitudes. During the Civil War, in the Northern Caucasus, counter-revolution waged a struggle against Soviet power along with the reactionary Moslem clergy, who supported Denikin. In his appeal to the peoples of the Caucasus, General Rudniev called upon them to fight against the Bolsheviks "for the sake of Islam".[7] In the name of the Moslems serving in Denikin's army, the White Guards appealed to the Moslems of the Caucasus. One of their appeals said : "Co-religionists, Moslems ! Who of you has not been subjected to persecution by the Bolsheviks ? Each of you who is capable of bearing arms should take to them. No other course is open to us, Moslems, if we are to save 25 million Moslems from the Bolshevik yoke. To arms ! May Allah be with us !"[8]

The Moslem priesthood also inspired the basmach movement which opposed the Soviet system in Central Asia. The following groups were represented among the basmaches : (*i*) the organizers of basmachestvo, the kurbashi, came from the nobility, and the priests acted as ideologists and propagandists in mobilizing forces and drawing the population into this anti-Soviet movement ; (*ii*) the *bais* (Turkic for the rich merchants, and other or the bourgeois elements provided the money, weapons, provisions, and fodder ; (*iii*) a considerable part of the peasantry, who being poverty-stricken and deceived by the priests and the *bais*, sided with the basmaches in the beginning".[9]

The basmach movement continually made use of Islamic slogans, and its leaders passed themselves off as the defenders of Islam and lawfulness. Here, for example, is a letter from Ibragim-bek, the leader of one of the basmach groups, to his accomplices : . . . "Get your forces together . . . carry out Moslem revenge in every kishlak which has betrayed our cause. Wherever peasants are found to pronounce the words "Shura-khukumat" (Soviet power) and help the Soviet authorities, kill them to a man and plunder their families and homes. Let this be made known to everyone who goes against the shariat, the prophets and the lawful sovereign, the emir".[10]

The reactionary Moslem priests, who called for the overthrow of Soviet power in Turkestan, betrayed Soviet activitists and sympathizers to the basmaches. However, time was against the basmaches and the reactionary Moslem clergy. The atrocities and outrages of the basmaches and counter-revolutionaries reached such extremes that even some of the most hostile to Soviet power mullahs, did not dare to justify their crimes. The advantages of socialism, which liberated millions of people from oppression and poverty and which provided the formerly landless peasants with land, facilitated further disintegration of the so-called integral Moslem society. Those peasants and lower ranks of the Moslem clergy, who had joined the basmaches, gradually stopped supporting counter-revolution. The left wing of the Moslem clergy, which convened its congress (*kurultai*) in 1924, recognized the Bukhara people's Republic as lawful from the point of view of the shariat. In the resolution it was stated that : "The Bukhara People's Soviet power is, to a large extent, just and kind and does not wish the blood of its brothers to be further spilled. And if our words, based on the Koran, do not reach the ears of recalcitrant, refractory basmaches, and if after that they do not lay down their arms, the above recalcitrants who disobey the will of God and the Sov(iet) government should be utterly destroyed with arms and the shariat will recognize their killing as lawful and sinless".[11] The defeat of the counter revolutionary groups in various areas of the country showed the fruitlessness of armed struggle against Soviet power. Moslem ecclesiastics frequently surrendered to the Soviet authorities of their own free will. Some of them found the lawfulness of the Soviet system justified in the statutes of the shariat. For instance one of these mullahs, Ishan Khodzha Domullo Dona-Khan, said : "Since Allah banished the emir for violating the laws of Allah and gave the people Soviet power, then the basmaches, who are fighting against Soviet power, are opposing the shariat."[12]

The Party and government organizations, which were engaged in effecting social and cultural changes among the the country's Moslem population, had to take into account the tremendous impact religion had on all sides of the Moslem's way of life. Suffice it to say, that even some of the local Soviet and party workers were not free of religious views. Thus, in Turkestan in the early years after the revolution many poor young people, who wished to defend the people's Soviet power, joined the Party. Many of them were illiterate. Having joined the Party, they still continued to keep in contact with the Mullahs, who were at that time the only literate people in the auls and kishlaks. In the kishlak of Turt-Kul in the Samarkand area, for example, the secretary of the Party cell, would ask the imam to read Party circulars to him and would take the imam's advice. In one of the village Party cells in Turkmenia the Party clerical work was dealt with by the aul's imam, since the secretary of the Party cell could neither read nor write.[13]

Taking into account the great religiosity of the population and the tremendous influence of Islam on the masses in the areas where Islam was traditionally practised, the Bolsheviks participated in the activities of several Moslem organizations. Thus, favourable conditions were created for explaining the goals and tasks of socialist construction to ordinary working class Moslems. For instance, the Moslem committees in Dagestan, which united representatives of the Moslem clergy and various anti-Soviet inclined groups, intensified propaganda among the population for the purpose of misconstruing Bolsheviks' policy. Therefore, some active communists from the indigenous population decided to join the Moslem committees. U. Buinakski and his comrades, D. Atayev, I. Aliyev, G. Saidov, and G. Dalgat carried on an extensive propaganda campaign among the working mountain-dwellers of Dagestan with regard to the re-elections to the Moslem committees. They campaigned everywhere, even in the mosques. "The shariat," wrote Ullubi Buinakski, "is needed by the exploiter classes and by the workers, but by each of them in different ways. Look, in front of us there is one and the same shariat banner, but there are two opposing trends : in Temir-khan-Shura clericals and beks use the shariat as camouflage to support and affirm the old society, while in Petrovsk true workers of the soil, the forces destined to destroy the old way of life, stand behind that same banner."[14]

The Bolsheviks' work to explain their cause to the people was organized in different ways. To facilitate the consolidation of Soviet power in the Northern Caucasus, an expeditionary detachment was formed in Astrakhan, mainly consisting of young people from Turkic-speaking nations. Soon after the detachment appeared in Dagestan, the people became firmly of the opinion that Moslems could be Bolsheviks, too, and that the various frightening rumours about the Bolsheviks were cock-and-bull stories.[15] This struck a palpable blow at the propaganda of the reactionary priests who intimidated mountaineers by telling them that "the Bolsheviks would destroy the Moslems and their belief". The communists and Soviet activists, who were representatives of the local population, also participated in the activities "of the Moslem trade-union organizaions". The Bolsheviks made the best use of the shariat, which is full of contradictory views, in explaining the tasks of the Soviet power to the people. "Through the shariat the beks justified their ownership of the land ... the shariat was also used among other arguments by the Dagestan socialists when they argued the necessity to confiscate the land from those same beks".[16]

It is commonly known that on the basis of Decree of the Soviet Government of 23 January 1918, on the separation of the church from the state, it was envisaged that the *waqf*, the property and lands of the Moslem organizations which together with religious taxes, made up their economic base, should be confiscated. It is interesting that the confiscation of the *waqf* lands called forth discontent not only among the priests, but also among certain groups of believers. The point was that a part of the taxes collected and of the incomes from the *waqf* was spent on such public necessities, as, for example, the construction of or repairs to public baths, bridges, roads, caravansarys, and the upkeep of madrasahs and mosques. During weddings or funerals the necessary articles (samovars, plates, cauldrons, carpets, and so on) for the ritual were loaned by mosques to people free of charge.

Thus, the *waqf* property allowed the clergy to convince the people that one task of the mosque was that of providing ordinary Moslems with material assistance. Besides, in nationalizing the *waqf* property, the necessary flexibility was not always observed, and certain mistakes were made in this matter. In some places there were cases where carpets, vessels, and other objects were taken from the mosque so that the ordinary religious rites could not be carried out, and this called forth the dissatisfaction of believers. The clergy and reactionary groups made use of this discontent for the purpose of propaganda against Soviet power. The Party and government quickly righted these mistakes. In 1922-1924 worship objects and decorations were returned to the mosques and in some places the *waqf* properties as well. At the same time, to supervise the priests and prevent abuse and appropriation of the *waqf* property, in many of the uyezds the Central Executive Committee of the Republic of Turkestan created collegiums consisting of activists, people's judges, and teachers.

The Party and government attentively took into consideration the traditions of the Moslems' customary way of life. Thus, the decree of the Central Executive Committee of Turkestan of 10 January 1921 announced : "The Central Executive Committee of the Turk republic, paying attention to the fact that the majority of the working masses in the Turk republic are members of the indigenous peoples of Turkestan, decrees that the resolution of the Krai Trade Union Conference of 29 November 1920, shall be put into effect as follows : the weekly day of rest compulsory for workers at every Soviet, public and private institution, enterprise and farm within the Turk republic shall be Friday."[17] Also the Moslem educational institutions, that is, maktebs and madrasas were allowed to function.

From 1924 to 1928 the Soviet government was faced with difficulties with regard to the Moslem priests' views on the gradual transition from the Arabic written language to the Latin alphabet. Many of the progressive thinkers of the Middle East spoke of the impracticabitity of the Arabic script in the case of the phonetic peculiarities of a number of languages. In the middle of the nineteenth century the well known Azerbaijan thinker and atheist M.F. Akhundov made a special trip to Iran and Turkey to explain to the rulers of those countries the need to reject the Arabic script since the difficulties involved in mastering it seriously hindered the spread of literacy. His mission was, however, unsuccessful. Only after the formation of a republic in Turkey was the Latin alphabet adopted on the orders of President Ataturk.

The Moslem clergy adamantly opposed the rejection of the Arabic script in the USSR. Playing on the Moslems' national feelings, the priests asserted that the thousand-year-old cultural heritage of the peoples who had recognized Islam in the past, would be consigned to oblivion. In 1928 the newspaper *Revolutsiya i Gorets* (Revolution and the Mountaineer) reported that the Chechen mullahs had gone on hunger strike as a sign of protest against introducing the Latin alphabet. The Moslem clergy described the education of Children on the basis of the new alphabet as an act of turning the Moslems' children into infidels (*kafirs*). The real reason for the ecclesiastics' irritation was that only they could read and write at that time. Teaching at the maktebs and madrasas was one of the Moslem priests' main sources of income. The appearance of new schools and a new written language deprived the ecclesiastics of their former source of well-being. The clergy spread the rumour that Russian language lessons had been introduced in Soviet schools for the purpose of Russianizing the Moslems, but they failed to mention that before the Revolution representatives of the propertied classes used to send their children to study in the big cities of Russia, so that they could serve in the Tsarist army and administration.

It is noteworthy that the prediction of the reactionary Moslem ideologists that the cultural and scientific heritage of the peoples of the Soviet East would be lost as a result of giving up Arabic script, was not justified. Many well-known works by medieval scholars and poets of central Asia, the Caucasus, and the Volga area were translated into both the national languages of various peoples and Russian, and this made these works available to a wider public. Now the peoples who practised Islam in the past are incomparably better acquainted with their cultural and scientific heritage than before the October Revolution.

The year 1928 may be considered a landmark, signifying the beginning of the second stage in the evolution of Islam in the USSR, when the Moslem clergy as a whole took up a loyal stand with regard to the government and to the Communist Party. There were obvious objective reasons for the priesthoods taking this stand. Firstly, by that time the priests had been deprived to a considerable extent of their role as a socially important force. All the State's activity in the sphere of public education with the change-over to instruction in the Latin (subsequently Russian) alphabet was managed without the mullahs. (It should be recalled that in the early years of Soviet power because of the lack of teachers some priests were permitted to work in the Soviet schools as teachers.) In 1928-29 the shariat courts were also abolished, the continuation of which had been a concession on the part of the State to an age-old Moslem tradition.

Secondly, the priests had to take into account the views of the ordinary believers, who from their own experience became more and more convinced that the changes being effected by the Party and government were aimed at improving the workers' living conditions. In the course of these transformations the foundations of the old way of life in which religion had found support, began to crack up. The liberation of women from the ancient patriarchal oppression was an especially important innovation in the Moslems' way of life. The legal equality of women legitimized by Soviet power, did not become virtual right away. Moslem women had to face serious difficulties in actually acquiring their freedom. The reactionary priests succeeded in persuading many Moslems that it was their duty to prevent their wives, sisters, and daughters from being drawn to the life of society and from studying in schools and higher educational institutions. In the early years of Soviet power women teachers and activists, who had given up wearing the *chadrah*, were sometimes killed, either on the incitement or with the direct participation of the mullahs. In Turkestan alone 2,500 women activists were murdered on the instigation of the clergy in 1926-27.[18] However, the process of women's liberation proved irreversible. The collectivization of agriculture which meant that women were needed to participate in social production, really accelerated this process.

With the victory of socialism in the Soviet Union, the ground fell away from under many Islamic institutions. One example of this is the tax system of Islam which was connected in the past with certain socio-economic conditions. Socialism abolished all forms of taxes and extortions sanctioned by Islam. With the victory of socialism there was no longer any need for the charitable activities of religious organizations. The State took it upon itself to care for those in need of help (the old and infirm, invalids and orphans).

After the abolition of the religious tax two forms of donation, the *zakyat al-fitr* and the *sadaka*, have continued till today. However, in the conditions of the socialist system they soon lost their former purpose. The *zakyat al-fitr* is the giving of alms to the poor upon the breaking of the Moslem fast. The *sadaka* is the giving of alms for any reason at any time ; but this term is also used in a different sense that is, sacrifice, usually in the form of a collective meal. As the well-being and cultural standards improved, believers began to consider it humiliating to receive any kind of alms, even if they had a fairly small income. The *zakyat al-fitr* has become assistance to the local mullahs, who collect these alms for themselves, usually in the form of wheat. *Sadaka*, as before, means sacrifice, but it has also acquired a completely different sense, that is, sacrifice for the sake of the mosque. Since the religious organizations and the mosques do not receive financial aid from the State, they are completely dependent on the contributions of believers. The salary that all officially registered priests receive from the Moslem authorities is allotted from the incomes of the mosques. Today, therefore, on the walls of the premises of Moslem organizations one may see special boxes with the inscription "sadaka", into which believers can put their contributions.

It is interesting to note that in a number of places the tradition of collecting *zakyat* did not die out immediately after the official abolition of the religious taxes. In their work the local Soviet organs came across cases where the *zakyat* collected was dealt with by the local authorities and spent on the needs of the population. For example, in 1924 in Kabarda, using the *zakyat* was used to acquire "a considerable number of tractors (80) and threshing-machines and increased assistance to the poor". These measures facilitated collectivization of agriculture.[19]

The economic, social, and cultural transformations in the country led to certain changes in the Moslems' world outlook, but even in the thirties most of the believers continued to retain the religious ideas and rites inherited from their ancestors. The believers were able to grasp the meaning of the social changes better than the weltanschauung principles of the new ideology.

The Second World War initiated a new stage in the evolution of Islam in the USSR characterized by the development of the restrained loyalty of the priest into active interest in the ideas and practical tasks of socialism and the attempt to take a greater part in the life of the country.

The Great Patriotic War was the most exacting test of the entire socialist system and of the friendship of the peoples of our multinational country. The Soviet Union came out of the war victorious and mightier than ever before. However, the war facilitated a certain revival of religion. Only a small part of the territory where Islam was traditionally practised, was occupied by the fascists, but all the peoples of the Soviet Union experienced the hardships of war. It was difficult to find a family, even in the regions most distant from the front, which did not have a member taking part in the war. The atheistic work became less intensive because many of the qualified workers had to leave for the front. The fact that the clergy took up a patriotic stand and appealed to believers to fight against fascism facilitated a revival of Islam and other religions during the war. In the mosques prayers and sermons were read for the swiftest possible victory of the Red Army. The population of the Soviet Union, including the Moslems, was well aware that the fascists enslaved and murdered believers and non-believers alike. Therefore, it was quite natural that the clergy supported the State. The war convincingly showed that the hopes of Nazi ideologists, that nationalistic movements would come into being among the Moslems in the Soviet Union, were based on a complete lack of understanding of the essence of the changes that had occurred in the consciousness of all strata of the population in the country during the years of socialist construction. The patriotic enthusiasm that was characteristic of Soviet people during the war, was just as typical of Moslems, too. Believers took into their homes refugees from the areas occupied by the fascists. They actively participated in collecting funds and worked indefatigably to bring the victory over the enemy nearer.

During the war the Communist Party and the Soviet government paid particular attention to the means of maintaining contact between the State and the religious associations. For this purpose the Council for the Affairs of the Russian Orthodox Church was created in 1943, and the Council for the Affairs of the Religions under the Council of Ministers was created in 1944. The latter was represented in the union and autonomous republics and in the krais and regions as well.

The structure of the Moslem organizations was also expanded. In addition to the ecclesiastical administration of the Moslems of the European part of the USSR and Siberia (in Ufa) three more independent Moslem ecclesiastical administrations were set up in 1944 for Central Asia and Kazakhstan (in Tashkent), Trans-Caucasus (in Baku), and Northern Caucasus (in Buinaksk). In two of these, Tashkent and Buinaksk (now Makhachkala), the administration was headed, as in Ufa, according to the tradition of Islam by the Sunnite branch, and in the third according to Shi'ite tradition, by Sheikh-ul-Islam. Since there were Sunnite communities in Azerbaijan and the other republics of Trans-Caucasus, they were represented in the Moslem ecclesiastical administration of Trans-Caucasus by a mufti who was the deputy to Sheikh-ul-Islam.

In the post-War years a decisive trend has become clearly manifest resulting in the development of Moslem ideas in the conditions of the Soviet Union : a striving to co-ordinate the social and cultural changes taking place in the USSR with the instructions and tasks set by Islam, to present the Soviet way of life as the realization of the ideals of Moslem dogma. This trend was evident even in the early years after the revolution when, as a result of the attentive attitude of the Soviet government to the specific way of life of the Moslems, the conviction became widespread among believers that the "ideals of communism and Islam were identical", that there were allegedly "no contradictions between communism and Islam". At that time the flexible Moslem theologians were already advancing the slogan of the "harmonious co-existence of Islam and the ideology of communism". Utilizing the popularity of the measures taken by the Soviet authorities, some mullahs told believers over and over again that "Islam and the shariat are the defenders of the poor and the opponents of profiteers".

In those years one even came across posters bearing the slogan "Proletarians of all countries, unite" in some mosques. The Kokand Moslem ecclesiastical administration decided to take part in the demonstration for the tenth anniversary of the October Revolution with its own poster bearing the words "Long live Soviet power, which has separated the church from politics.

However, the attempts of Moslems to find arguments in the Koran and the sunna, asserting the need for transformations being carried out by the Soviet system, were not sufficiently widespread in the twenties and thirties. Only in the forties did this trend gather strength and become an inalienable feature of the *weltaanschuung* of simple believers and was reflected in the teachings of the Moslem priests.

Despite a certain religious revival called forth by the hardships of war, the dying away of Islam, which began when the complex of social norms not compatible with the new system was discarded and further stimulated by the population's improved standards of culture, is continuing. In the immediate pre-war years this process was already noticeable in everyday life, for young people and the intelligentsia failed to observe many of the instructions of Islam. The spread of knowledge among the broad masses of the population, resulting from the cultural revolution, has brought about a considerable change in the world outlook of various groups of believers. The most obvious sign of the dying away of the religion in the Moslem areas was the spread of atheism among broad masses of people, which was formerly completely alien to the so-called "Moslem world".

NOTES AND REFERENCE

1. *At-Talia* Journal, N. 3, 1970, Cairo, pp. 91-2.
2. V.I. Lenin, *Complete Collected Works*, V. 7, p. 173.
3. M.M. Persists, The separation of the church from the state and school from the church in the USSR. M., 1958, p. 100.
4. V.I. Lenin, *Complete Collected Works*, v. 38, pp. 158-59.
5. N. Samursky, Dagestan, *Makhach-Kala*, 1935, pp. 126-27.
6. A. Bazarov, *Nekotoryje osobennosti i puti formirovanija ateisticheskogo mirovozzrenija tadzhikskogo dekhonstva*. Some features and ways of development of the Tajik dekhanstvo atheistic outlook. Dyushambe, 1971, p. 51.
7. A.V. Avksentjev, *Islam na Severnom Kavkaze*, Islam in the Northern Caucasus. Stavropol Publishing House, 1973, p. 61.
8. A. A. Davydov, *The Great October Socialist Revolution and the first years of struggle for the liberation of Moslem workers from religious superstitution*. Velikaja Oktjabraskaja sotsialisticheskaja revolutsija i pervyje etapy bor'by za osvobozhdenije trudjashchikhsja musulman ot religioznykh sueverij (Uchenyje zapiski Kabardino-Balkarskogo nauchnoissledovatelskogo Instituta, t. XIV) Nalchik, 1958, p. 30.
9. A. Bazarov, *op. cit.*, p. 66.
10. Tadzhikistan vo vtoroj pjatiletke, Tajikistan during the 2nd Five Year Plan fulfilment. M-Tashkent, OGIZ (SAOGIZ), 1933, p. 76.
11. *Bezboshnik*, 1928, N. 1, p. 74.

12. M.I. Irkaev, *Istorija grazhdanskoj vojny v Tadzhikistane,* The History of the Civil War in Tajikistan, Dyushambe, 1966 pp. 442-43.
13. A. Bazarov, *op. cit.*, p. 60.
14. M.Z, Magomedov. *Sotsializm i sud'by gortsev*. Socialism and fates of mountaineers. Makhach-Kala, 1976, p. 27-8; "Borba za vlast Sovetov v Dagestane". The struggle for the Soviet power in Daghestan. Makhach-Kala, 1957, p. 26.
15. M.Z. Magomedov, *op. cit.*, p. 40-1.
16. A. Takho-Gody. *Revolutsija i kontrrevolutsija v Dagestane.* Revolution and counter-revolution in Daghestan. Daggosizdat, 1927, p. 5.
17. V.P. Gidulyanov, *Otdelenije tserkvi ot gosudarstva.* The disestablishment of the Church. Edited by P.A. Krasikov. 3rd edition. M., 1926, pp. 61-2.
18. M.Z. Magomedov, *op. cit.*, p. 94.
19. A. Veshykov, *Put' k ateismu.* The Way to Atheism, 1965, p. 108.

16

Islam in the USSR (1946-1977)

A. V. Nurullaev

THE GREAT patriotic war that the Soviet people waged against the Nazi German invaders was a severe test for the socialist society. At the same time it was a turning point in strengthening the patriotic positions of the Moslem religious organizations and the clergy. The post-war period became a period when loyalty and even goodwill not only to the socialist state, but also to non-religious social ideals of the Soviet society were displayed by the Moslem religious organizations as their official position. On the other hand, this period became a period of intensive evolution which was happening to different sides of the Moslem religious complex, of more active influence that secular elements brought to bear upon it.

We will try to characterize the main features of this evolution. Conservatism and adherence to traditions are the typical features of all religions, including Islam. Fighting against everything new is an age-long tradition of Moslem theology. Inherent to Islam as to all other religions are "...determination and ability to legitimize any existing inreality and firmly established order of things".

Similar change occurred in the attitude of Islam to the socialist system, to the revolutionary socio-economic development. Till socialism was a theory "only", till it had not become a powerful real force during the revolution and in the first years after it, many Moslem religious organizations opposed it considering it to be a great evil which had ruined the order of things, established by Allah.

The clergy intimidated the Moslem with various doubtful stories ascribed to socialism. Part of the clergy directly participated in the struggle the counter-revolutionary and basmatch groups unleashed against the Soviet power.

However, many clergymen soon after the Revolution openly declared their recognition of the new system. In the twenties and thirties the Moslem clergy noted in their statements the progress that the country achieved in the provision of equal rights to the people of all nationalities and religions, in the development of economy and culture. At the same time the loyal Moslem clergy when speaking of socio-economic changes often gave contradictory appraisals and at times condemned the nationalization of land, factories and plants, criticized the measures to emancipate women and to improve public education as being hostile to Islam.

As to the general course of the loyal attitude towards the socialist state and the socialist system which dominated the Moslem religious organizations even during the pre-war period (despite the hopes cherished by the enemies of the country) it was further strengthened during the war. After the war, especially when a world socialist system came into existence, it became evident that socialism in the USSR gained a complete and final victory and therefore the loss by religion of its regulating functions in the main spheres of social life became irreversible. The Moslem organizations could not but take into consideration this historical reality.

Another factor which contributed to working out a new social and political position on the part of Moslem ideologists, and to the penetration of secular elements into the Moslem religious complex was the increased departure of the masses from religion.

Social and economic changes carried out in the country during the period of the Soviet power, the unprecedented development of culture, emancipation of women, separation of church from the state and school, ensuring freedom of conscience for the citizens and the complete equality of rights in all the spheres of public life irrespective of their attitude towards religion, caused a mass departure of population from religion. The latest sociological research conducted in some regions of traditional dissemination of Islam shows that this process still continues.

Information obtained during the selective polling lately conducted in four regions of the Uzbek SSR showed that under the influence of religion there are only 11.7 per cent workers,

29.4 per cent peasants, and 5.5 per cent civil servants.[1] In the Turkmen SSR (the Kunia-Urghensk district) 31.2 per cent of rural population, and in the town of Tashauze 11.3 per cent of the adult Turkmens, are under the influence of Islam.[2] The ratio between the non-religious, intermediate and religious groups in the Checheno-Ingush ASSR according to the authors is 5 : 2 : 3 respectively.[3]

In Kazan, the capital of the Tatar ASSR, 25.7 per cent of the polled adults called themselves believers, in the rural areas this figure amounted to 34.5 per cent.[4] In the Karakalpak ASSR among the polled adults in the rural areas there are 11.4 per cent of convinced believers, 14.4 per cent of traditional believers and 13.6 per cent of those who are undecided between religion and irreligion.[5]

Thus, the majority of the population has already drifted away from religion.

The great social and economic reforms in our country, and the cultural revolution *have changed the spiritual make-up of the citizens of the Soviet state who still remain under the influence of Islam.* Believers could not but be influenced by an unprecedented rise of people's culture, the broad propagation of scientific ideas among the masses aimed at showing the regularities of development of nature and society. A Moslem taking part in the construction of a new way of life, making his contribution not only to the material production but also to the management of society acquires the capability of seeing the social consequences of his activity, and learns to plan his personal life. He associates to a lessening degree his future and the future of the country with the action of supernatural forces.

In the recent decades due to the scientific and technical revolution, the strain and stress in man's life have increased, science and technology have found wider application in all branches of the national economy, a great progress has been made in the press, radio and television media and cinema. The volume of information received by the population for different spheres of technology, natural sciences, art and international affairs has grown sharply.

All these cannot but influence the world outlook of Moslems. The process of obliterating religious ideas from the minds of contemporary believers is now taking place. Many Koran ideas about the world, public relations in society, directions concerning the creation of family, the rights and duties of husbands and wives have become alien to the believers of the present time.

In the mind of believers religious notions exist together with the materialistic outlook. For many believers non-religious ideas occupy an important place. Now in their productive, social and cognizing activities they are guided by secular rather than by religious motives. Even in everyday life many people who consider themselves Moslems refuse to observe religious norms.

One of the signs showing the decreased influence of religion is the increase in the number of people who consider themselves believers and at the same time admit that religion has no influence on their lives or plays a secondary part. This is obvious from the results of recent studies. For example, according to a poll conducted in the Penza region, 23 per cent of the believers think that religion does not play any role in man's life.[6] According to a case study carried out in the Karakalpak ASSR less than 20 per cent of believers think that God is the Creator of the world, lords over the destinies of people and is the Absolute of the Universe. The rest of the polled Moslems either doubt that God rules over the world or admit that He does not exist at all.[7]

The Moslem ceremonies and holidays in the minds of believers gradually lose their religious content, some of the feasts are more often taken simply as traditions inherited from fathers and grandfathers. A considerable section of Moslems ignore even strictly obligatory Islam rites (*farz*). Thus the sociological research in the Daghestan and the Checheno-Ingush ASSR revealed that among those who consider themselves "devout Moslems" only 69 per cent recite the daily rosary (*namaz*). As to the moderate and traditional believers 55 per cent and 73 per cent of them respectively do not perform *namaz* at all and a considerable part of them (35 per cent and 23.5 per cent respectively) do not observe even the *kurban bajram*, the *mawlud* and other Moslem holidays.[8] Among the Moslems of Kazan there are slightly more than 40 per cent who perform *namaz* and not more than 60 per cent who had religious weddings.[9]

Many people who consider themselves believers do not believe in life after death, in the existence of Hell and Paradise. For example, the polling of 1,077 believers in the Daghestan ASSR who have no doubt about the existence of Allah showed, that 20 per cent of them do not believe in life after death and in unearthly requital, and 34 per cent of the Moslems up to 30 years old do not believe in unearthly requital.

These changes are indicative of the decay of religious conscience and cannot but influence the position of the clergy. Thus, Mufti Vali-zade Sharif, former Vice-Chairman of the Transcaucasian Moslem Board addressing clergymen noted, that in the changing world they could not follow all the shariah laws. He said *inter alia* : "It is high time for us to understand that many things in the shariah have become obsolete and more, they are repelling believers from religion." The Mufti assured his audience that discarding old-fashioned shariah laws, the clergy are neither sinning, nor acting against their religion, but on the contrary are strengthening its position.

During the years of the Soviet power the Moslem clergy have changed themselves. Many of them were born during the Soviet era and could not but feel the influence of the changes which were taking place. The formation of their world outlook was dominated by a new school. Many clergymen finished either primary or secondary schools during the Soviet regime. Among the contemporary clergy there are few people who have been dealing with religion all their lives. A considerable part of them have become professional ecclesiastics only recently. Previously these people were engaged in different branches of the national economy and contributed to the construction of the new society. Some clergymen who are in charge of conducting religious ceremonies in villages combine their religious duties with work in the national economy.

When we speak about the reasons which have inspired the Mohammedans to change their attitude towards the socialist system and the plans of constructing a communist society we cannot ignore one fact, that there is no celibacy in Islam, and in fact a great majority of Moslem theologians and clergymen have families. Relatives and children of clergymen are workers, doctors, scientists and their life and work are inseparably linked with the life of our society.

The Moslem clergy cannot but see the success of the Leninist national policy of the Soviet state aimed at ensuring free development of all the peoples. The achievements of national Soviet Republics and autonomous regions, which formerly were backward provinces, make a particular contrast against the background of the present-day situation in a number of Moslem countries in Asia and Africa and naturally induce the Moslem clergymen of our country to back socialism and to contribute in their way to the success of the new social system. This is confirmed by clergymen in their preachings addressed either to their parish or to Moslems abroad.

Under the conditions of prevailing socialist production relations when the major part of the population has become alien to religion and most believers are convinced supporters of socialism, Islam is able to survive only by adapting itself to the new social and economic system.

The construction of a developed socialist society, the transition of all population strata to the ideological and political position of the working class, the development of the proletariat dictatorship state into a state of the entire people, the formation of a new historical entity of people, that is, the Soviet people, all these factors contributed to increased loyalty and goodwill of the Moslem organizations towards the socialist system and to the social ideals of the working class. The positive appraisal of the socio-economic changes in the country has become an integral part of the official policy of the Moslem clergy.

Now clergymen are searching in their holy books for the possibility and necessity of such changes, and these changes are admitted to be performed by the will of Allah. The clergy no more ignores the fact that all the achievements in our country in all spheres of life result from the character of our social and state system. Moreover, they have begun to look for "their own place" in the socialist society.

On the occasion of the 60th anniversary of the Great October Socialist Revolution the leaders of four Moslem Boards sent on behalf of all the Moslems of the Soviet Union a greetings message to the leaders of the Soviet state. It reads *inter alia* : The Moslems of the Soviet Union are proud of the fact that they took part in the October Revolution and together with the proletariat of Russia fought against the old regime and actively joined in the construction of socialism in the USSR. During 60 years thanks to the selfless labour and friendly help of all the peoples of the USSR former backward peoples of the Soviet East have made great historical progress in their economy and culture and proved to the entire world that Moslems are also capable of achieving the highest degree of progress.

Now the Moslem theologians speak about the advantages socialism enjoys over other socio-economic systems. Further they say that the main principles of socialism were proclaimed by Islam more than 1300 years ago, but they were not understood by the previous generations. Therefore, the modern theologians suggest "that all the social principles in the Koran and Sunna should be thoroughly studied".

The Moslem clergy consider Islam to be a progressive religion keeping pace with the times and helping the Soviet people in the construction of communism. Modern theologians claim that "Islam is the most modern and progressive religion. It shows the peoples the way to peace, friendship, and progress".[10]

Stating that the construction of socialism and communism in the world is predicted in the Koran and is blessed by Allah. Theologians give the following arguments. The Soviet Union is steadily achieving success in all spheres of life, which could not have been achieved had it not been blessed by Allah. Since Allah has blessed the Soviet power and its leaders, therefore the believers must do their utmost to ensure maximum success in building the communist society and consider their work for the benefit of the society as God blessed deeds.

By interpreting the work and other activities for the benefit of the socialist society as God blessed ones, it is possible to conclude that the God blessed deeds can be performed not only by those who devote their deeds and thoughts to Allah but by those who never give a thought to it and even by those who deny any religion. Ecclesiastics draw the following conclusions ... "The Soviet leaders who believe neither in God nor in prophets ... implement laws which take after the will of God and the directions of prophets". (These were the words spoken by Mufti A. Bozgoziev, former deputy chairman of the

Moslem Religious Board for the Transcaucasus in one of his speeches).[11]

Thus, in the end it turns out that everything good done in our country is not only of a God blessed nature, but was also predetermined by God long before. "50 years of the existence of our multinational state with the permission of merciful and beneficient Allah have been the years of development of the national economy, military power, rising welfare and culture of the peoples of our country", said Sheikh-ul-islam Aliaga Suleiman-Zade, Chairman of the Moslem Religious Board for the Transcaucasus in his statement on the occasion of the 50th anniversary of the USSR. "By the will of Allah the Soviet science has crossed the advanced levels of the development of man's thought. Freedom, equality, fraternity, and friendship between nations and nationalities have triumphed. This all is relevant to the Holy Koran and is achieved with the blessing of Allah".[12]

From the positive attitude to the revolutionary processes in certain countries due to the events taking place in the world, theologians come to generalizing conclusions and a "special philosophy of revolution" is being worked out. The idea that social revolutions are God blessed in general and that they are of tremendous importance for the acceleration of social development is now often expressed by Moslem religious workers. "Social revolutions taking place in various countries give rise to new forms of government that undoubtedly is in the interest of a nation and is considered to be the basic principles of Islam," said Ahmedzjan Mustafin, imam-khatib of the Moscow cathedral mosque, on the conference of the USSR Moslems held in Tashkent. History has more than once proved this Islamic principle and the tremendous importance of the social revolutions for the progressive development of mankind. An example of this is the Great October Socialist Revolution and also revolutions in Egypt, Yemen, Lybia and in many other countries.[13]

The process when one socio-economic structure is superseded by another is according to the modern theologians a natural change taking place by the will of Allah who comes out against exploitation and injustice and does not tolerate for a long time a system based on these principles. "Without any hesitation and with an absolute confidence one may state that the capitalist system based on injustice and exploitation is doomed to failure and will be replaced with a socialist system based on just laws," said Agaev A.A., the akhund of the Khachmass mosque of the Azerbaijan SSR at the Moslem conference held in Tashkent in 1970. "The laws of God are inexorable and justice will triumph all over the world !"

Admitting the possibility and inevitability of social changes modern theologians come out against those reactionary forces which try to halt the progressive development of society. "Raising our thanksgiving prayers to Allah we ask Him to grant His holy blessing to all the patriots conducting struggle with arms in hands for the most sacred thing in the world—their freedom which is declared by the Holy Koran as an everlasting and inherent right of every man," said A. Isaev, former imam-khatib of the Leningrad mosque during one of the sermons. "At the same time we ask Allah to send his God's penalty and eternal damnation to all the dark forces trying to stop the wheel of history."[14]

The idea that the establishment of socialism is blessed by God is widely preached by the Moslem clergy. This idea has been formed by the theologians after understanding and reflecting by the theologians on historic reality and in particular of the fact that the rank and file Moslems in the USSR have accepted the targets and goals of socialism as being their own. In the minds of many Moslems the socialist construction has long been associated with the ideals of Islam which appear before them as the cherished ideals of the working people.

Under the new conditions many other problems are considered by the Moslem religious workers with account taken of the changed situation and transformation in the consciousness of the believers. Nowadays theologians suggest that the goal and sense of human life is to be found in the welfare of earthly existence, in aspiration to happiness in this world rather than in prayers to obtain paradise in the other world. Unlike their predecessors who divide the people into those who will and will not be granted happiness by Allah, that is, Moslems, and non-Moslems respectively, the modern theologians declare that all people are created for a happy life.

Moreover, despite the prescriptions of the dogma promising the non-believers only infernal torments the contemporary religious figures state that non-believers also may receive paradise beatitude if they work well for the good of society or defend their motherland with arms in their hands.

In other words the complete equality of the people guaranteed by mature socialism irrespective of their origin, nationality, social status and attitude to religion is thought by the Moslem ideologists to be relevant to the views concerning life in the other world and this is regarded as inevitable. If the clergymen following the Koran continued to refer to all the non-believers as inhabitants of hell doomed to stay there forever, the believers would not understand them because in the conditions of the Soviet way of life the believers' attitude to the non-believers has radically changed. Religious intolerance and confessional self-insulation have vanished into the past. Nowadays, practically each believer has non-believing relatives and friends and traditional contraposing believers against non-believers has lost its former significance.

Therefore, the Moslem religious workers now prefer to avoid using the appeals of the Koran to believers to fight against those who do not believe in Allah (9.29), and to have no Christians and Judaists as friends (5.56). The clergy, on the contrary, state that Islam calls for friendship and co-operation towards all the people irrespective of their nationality and attitude towards religion. Theologians say that following the prescriptions of Islam makes a man a true internationalist and an opponent to the national narrowness and isolation.[15]

The Moslem ideologists have begun in a new way to approach the concepts of war and peace. The Koran dogma of war as a manifestation of the will of Allah gave place to opinions saying that wars depend on the will of men and classes and ousting the necessity to struggle for the security and strengthening of peace. It is well-known that the Moslem religious workers in the USSR have actively joined in the world movement of the supporters of peace. In recent years at their initiative four international conferences were held in the Soviet Union with the aim to unite the efforts of all the followers of Islam in the struggle for peace against imperialist aggressions. The eminent Moslem religious personalities in our country were among those who took the lead in organizing the historic world conference "Religious workers for lasting peace, disarmament and just relations among nations" (June 1977). The leading report at this conference was read by Mufti Ziautdin-khan ibn Ishan Babakhan, one of the Moslem leaders of the USSR.

The lessening of the believers' interest in the dogmatic concepts, the dominating importance of secular ideas in their evaluation of the surrounding world, greater nationalism in relation to the religious orders and rites—all this force clergymen to introduce on a large scale non-religious elements into the religious complex.

In the preaching activity of the clergy dogmatic issues have been replaced by secular problems. One of the most important principles of Islamic dogma—the principle of predetermination—is now neglected by the theologians. The ecclesiastics stress more the existence of laws relating to the development of nature and social life. But to deviate less from dogma they say that all these laws were established by Allah.

Trying to prolong the life of religious rites modern theologians turn to secular arguments rather than to their dogmatic laws. During preceding centuries Moslems were obliged to observe all the rites and carry out all the prescriptions for the sake of Allah and not for the sake of securing better life in this world. It was considered reproachable to look into them for any earthly sense. Abu Khamid Muhammed ibn-Muhammed al-Gazali, the famous medieval theologian, used to declare such findings as the "greatest stupidity and ignorance."[16] Unlike him, the modern clergy applies much effort to convince their listeners that each Islamic prescription or rite is of great importance for man's mundane life and that is why Allah established them. For example, a prayer is said to help man keep himself clean, physically strong and disciplined. Other Moslem religious workers even state that it was *namaz* that laid the foundation of modern gymnastic exercises. The fast during the *ramadan* month is said to promote bodily and spiritual health to improve digestion, to help get rid of excess fat and allegedly to cure diseases. Even the *haj* (pilgrimage to Mecca) turns out to have great political significance. The clergymen say that it is meant not only to obtain God's gratitude in the after life, it is also used for the mundane causes such as social relations among people, exchange of experience between the representatives of various professions, friendship between nations, and strengthening of peace all over the world.

Thus adapting to reality, and to the changed views of the believers the concepts of Islam concerning a number of problems have undergone a certain evolution. Secular concepts find their way in an increasing scale, into the religious ideology which causes shifts in the cult practice of religious organizations.

At present the rites and prescriptions of the Koran and Sunna have become a burden to a considerable part of the believers and they cease to observe them. The fact that believers are losing a number of important signs of religiousness is acknowledged by clergymen. If during the first years of Soviet power such processes caused outright dissatisfaction among the clergy, nowadays they behave differently. They put up with the actual situation. Since their views have changed, believers are allowed to observe many religious prescriptions but not so strictly. The religious centres have published the so-called *fetts* (explanations) which even condemn a number of traditions existing in the Moslem community for centuries, such as: wearing a *paranja* (a woman's veil), paying and receiving *kalim* (ransom for a bride), the pilgrimage of believers to the "holy" graves, etc.

The ecclesiastics find various arguments enabling a man who does not strictly observe the obligatory prescriptions of religion to consider himself a believer. For this purpose they refer to the verses of the Koran saying that God does not want to offer difficulties to the followers of the Koran. He just wants to relieve them of their burden. Proceeding from this, it is concluded that there is a possibility of exercising rites and to implement prescriptions in an adapted form, although to ensure this the clergy must not only revise the century-old traditions but also redraft direct prescriptions of the Koran. For example, the Koran says prayers should be said at a certain time (*Sura* 4, *ayat* 104) and the fast should be observed during the month of *ramadan* (2, 181), during all "counted days" (2, 180). But the clergy because of the circumstances have "to permit" the prayers to be exercised not at a predetermined time but when a possibility exists for it; and not the whole month but only several days at the beginning, in the middle and at the end of this fast. The number of workers of various professions who are allowed to abstain from the fast is increasing.

Observance of some rites may be supplanted by a donation to the mosque. For example, the cattle offering during the Id al Azha (*kurban-bayram*) holiday may quite possibly be suppressed, in the opinion of many clergy, by paying the cost of the offered cattle skin to the cash-box of the mosque. Providing the believers with such kinds of "indulgencies", theologians make it easier for a man to consider himself one of those who has fulfilled a religious prescription, as also an additional way for strengthening the finance situation of religious organizations. To allow the people (especially the youngsters) who do not strictly observe the obligatory requirements of religion (*farz*) a chance to consider themselves Moslems, the clergy resort to special explanations. "We cannot reproach the modern youth with not observing the *urazu* and not excising the *namaz*", said one of the priests at the Tashkent Chupan-Ota Mosque in 1969. The youth honestly attends to its duties before the state and the people and the fulfilment of the duty towards the Motherland is our most important obligation (*vadjib*)."[17]

Relaxations in exercising various religious rites which the clergy had to grant to believers are, alongside with the evolution of other sides of the religious complex, a clear evidence of the religion's decay. By improving the ideology of Islam, introducing changes in the sphere of worship, allowing believers to deviate from the ritual laws of Islam, the clergy try to keep in the fold of religion those who neglect the minimum of religious prescriptions obligatory for each Moslem. Such a position of the clergy contributes to keeping formal relations between a part of the people and religious organizations. Meanwhile among the believers it promotes the opinion that not all requirements of religion should be exercised obligatorily and that the believers have the right not to exercise even some of those prescriptions, non-observance of which less than 50 years ago was considered as a deviation from religion.

Evolution of the social positions of religion, the attempts of the clergy to introduce changes in their moral sermons and worship activity are lawful phenomena characteristic of the whole history of mankind. During all times religion had in one way or another to reflect and retroactively to submit proofs for the changes which took place in the life of society. The modernization of Islam in our country is a result of the objective process in the society, the consequence of tremendous socio-economic and cultural transformations and their reflections in a specific religious form.

Modernization of Islam should be considered as a tactical manoeuvre of separate religious leaders. This also is a result of transformations in the outlook of the broad masses of Moslems and the representatives of the clergy and the ideologists of modern Islam.

Modernization of Islam, its adaptation to the contemporary conditions, aimed at strengthening its vitality at the same time objectively brings about the shattering of the principles of faith renders the contents of religion sterile and results in its degradation.

The fact that the clergy and the rank-and-file believers are convinced that it was Muhammed who declared the socialist ideals and the scientific achievements of today were foretold by the Koran naturally makes no changes in the character of Islam as a religious ideology alien to the scientific and materialistic outlook. However, the realistic position of the religious organizations and complete acceptance of the Soviet reality by believers contributes to the greater possibility of dialogue between secular society and the believers and to a more active participation of Moslems in the construction of the new society. And this, in its turn, cannot but lead to further evolution of the believers' consciousness, to the erosion of illusory ideas from it and to stronger elements of a scientific world outlook.

REFERENCES

1. See I. Djabbarov, *Social progress, Life and Religion*, Tashkent, 1973, p. 82.
2. See *Materials of Scientific Conference 'Modernization of Islam and Salient Problems of the Theory of Scientific Atheism'*, Moscow, 1968, p. 73. 34.
3. See *Salient Problems of Atheistic Education*, Alma-Ata, 1976, p. 73.
4. See *Materials for Scientific Conference 'Moderanization of Islam and Salient Problems of the Theory of Scientific Atheism,'* Moscow, 1968, p. 84.

5. G. Bazarbaev, *Secularization of the Population of Socialist Karakalpak*, Nukus, 1973, p. 50.
6. *To a Society Free from Religion*, Moscow, 1970, p. 174.
7. See G. Bazarbaev, *Secularization of the Population of Socialist Karakalpak*, Nukus, 1973, p. 89.
8. See *Materials of Scientific Conference 'Modernization of Islam and Salient Problems of the Theory of scientific Atheism'*, Outline of reports. Moscow, 1968, p. 96-110.
9. *Ibid.*, p. 90.
10. *Moslems of the Soviet East*, the journal published by the Moslem Religious Board for Central Asia and Kazakhstan in Tashkent in Uzbek, Arabic, English, and French, 1969, Nos. 3-4, p. 37.
11. Quoted from N. Ashirov, *Evolution of Islam in USSR*, Moscow, 1973, p. 51.
12. Quoted from: *Atheistic Readings*, Issue 8, Moscow, 1976, p. 54.
13. *Moslems of the Soviet East*, 1970, Nos. 3-4, p. 33.
14. Quoted from: N. Ashirov, *Evolution of Islam in USSR*, Moscow, 1973, p. 41.
15. For details see: N. Ashirov, *Islam and Nations*, Moscow, 1975, Chapter III.
16. See S.N. Grigorijan, *From the History of Philosophy in Central Asia and Iran*, 7-12, Moscow, 1966, p. 254.
17. Quoted from: N. Ashirov, *Modern Islam and Youth*, Moscow, 1972, p. 20.

17

Survival of Pre-Muslim Beliefs in Islam

V.N. Basilov & K.K. Kubakov

ISLAM as professed by every nation in any country has always had, and still has, its own peculiar features, which are determined by the way of life of every definite society (the State system and social order, economy and customs and traditions). The local features of Islam are also considerably conditioned by the religious beliefs and rights, which originate from religions existing prior to Islam and which were ousted by it.

Pre-Muslim religious traditions were notable in the beliefs and rites of Muslims in the Russian Empire as far back as the late 19th and early 20th centuries. Although many of those beliefs and rites were Muslimized, some of them had nothing in common with Islam even outwardly, retaining the features of their pre-Islam origins. For instance, various religious rites and ceremonies were connected with agricultural activities. In spring, Muslims in Central Asia and the Caucasus celebrated *Novruz* (New Year) with festivities and rites designed to ensure good crops for peasants.[1] Muslims in the same regions had also an ancient custom, the first ploughing rite, which was well known throughout Eurasia. According to it, the first furrows were cut in the land by a well-to-do, experienced, and healthy old man.[2] In Central Asia, the first day-of-ploughing rites were devoted to the saint of agriculture, Boboi-Dehkon (the old Cultivator). It was believed in some areas that the man to begin tillage first was the embodiment of the saint of agriculture during the rite.[3] There were also a number of rites making the harvesting season. Some of them were based on the belief that the soul of the field is concealed in the last ear to be reaped. While harvesting, Tajiks from Karategin and

Darvaz, for instance, sang a ritual song "I'm in mourning" and tried to reap faster and faster in order "to alleviate the suffering of land before it died".[4] Upon threshing corn, Tajiks and Uzbeks drew a line around the heap with the help of a wooden spade and crowned it with a piece of earth or oxen dung. These actions originate in the archaic beliefs of Tajiks in Vahan and Ishkashim in the Pamirs, who considered the heap of corn a symbol of body of the saint of agriculture.[5] Some Tajik groups believed the heap of straw which remained as a result of winnowing to be the grave of the old Cultivator, and nobody was allowed to step over it.[6]

The rites of calling forth the rain or discontinuing bad weather were widespread. In one such rite of calling forth the rain, which was popular in the Caucasus and in Central Asia, a group of women singing a ritual song carried a doll through the village. The rite ended with the doll being drowned in the river. In some areas the doll was substituted by a woman, on whom water was thrown and who was even bathed in the river. A ritual meal of all the participants in the ceremony crowned it all.[7]

Sacrifices completed the construction and cleaning of irrigation canals in Central Asia. As a rule, the animals were killed by cutting their throats with their blood dripping into the water. Even in the last century Uzbeks and Tajiks sacrificed human life as a last resort.[8]

Survivals of the pre-Muslim religious traditions were also characteristic of domestic and family ceremonies. Magic acts and procedures were typical of wedding rites designed to protect the newly-weds against "the evil eye" and other kinds of "spoiling". The bride and bridegroom were thought to be specifically open to witchcraft when a mullah married them. Uzbeks in Khorezm guarded the house, in which the marriage took place, against strangers, and particularly, against childless women. If such a woman crossed the room during the *nikas* ceremony, it was believed that her barrenness would affect the bride.[9] The period following the birth of a child was especially dangerous for the mother. Both of them were believed to be absolutely helpless against witchcraft and evil ghosts. The young mother, therefore, had to observe strictly various rules and regulations.[10] Lezghins, for instance, did not allow her to enter the sheepcot or to approach water. Outsiders were kept at a distance from the mother and child.[11]

The circumcision ceremony is a universal Muslim custom but local traditions have also had their impact on it. As Uzbek ethnographical materials have shown, the circumcision ceremony (*sunnat-toi*) includes the rites rooted in ancient procedures.[12]

Funeral ceremonies were also characterized by pre-Muslim survivals. In some areas burials were different from the rites laid down in the Shariat. Until quite recently, Uzbeks and Tajiks in some villages used to bury their dead in a common vault. The bones of those who had died earlier were moved aside, to a common heap. This tradition, which was widely observed in the Middle Ages (as the excavations of the crypts in the Shahi-Zinda necropolis in Samarkand have shown), go back to the ancient Mazdeist beliefs.[13]

That the dead were revered by Muslims can be seen from the ritual feeding of the dead souls. On certain days, hot meals with grease were cooked whose smell was generally believed to be nourishing to the souls of the dead.[14] It is still believed that the dead can have an influence inflicting illness and misfortune on indifferent relatives. In the Caucasus and the Volga area, people were convinced that the dead control the weather. Epidemic diseases were within the province of the dead. As a result of an epidemic of dysentery, many children died in a village of the Krasnoufimsk district in Bashkiria in 1909. The villagers believed there was a sorcerer involved who fed on children's blood even after his death, getting out through a hole in his grave. Despite the mullah's admonition, they examined all suspicious graves thoroughly and found one in which their stick was stained with blood. So they dug out the grave, took the dead body out of it, dissected it, poured kerosene over it and reduced it to ashes.[15]

Folk medicine contains an abundance of pre-Muslim views and beliefs revealed in various religious and magical methods of treatment. In order to cure epizootics, for instance, Bashkirs and Tatars used fire obtained as a result of rubbing against wood. Pilgrimages to sacred places coupled with various archaic rites were the most widespread methods of "curing" human beings and animals. Irrational folk medicine laid particular stress on belief in ghosts.

Worship of ghosts is the most distinct feature of pre-Muslim traditions. Islam introduced the new terms of *jinn* and *shaitan* (taken mostly as synonyms). These new names were used for the former ghosts in the religions of nations converted to Islam. But pre-Islam demons and ghosts have not only retained their original characteristics, but even their names, such as Pari, Dev, Albasty, Al Pab, Martu, Shurale, Yarymtyk, Oi Iasi, Bichura, Bastryk, Zheztyrnak, and others. The above ghosts are not the common heritage of all the nations preaching Islam. Thus, Shurale, the forest ghost, was worshipped only in the Volga area and Western Siberia. The bloodthirsty Zheztyrnak was the ghost of the Kazakhs and Kirghiz. The features of all ghosts were archaic in nature. Many of them were believed to need food ; others, for instance Pari or Albasty, could have sexual relationships with people.[16]

Certain groups of ghosts were claimed to be capable of, and even inclined, to do harm to people. Therefore, Muslims had a lot of ways to defend themselves against ghosts. Home-made amulets, a knife, and a needle were considered reliable means of protection against evil and were easily obtained. In cases, however, where the ghosts "have already done harm", Muslims had to ask "specialists" who had power over the ghosts for help.

Every nation had its own experts, who, with the help of their assistant ghosts, could foretell one's fortune, cure diseases, and find belongings or animals that had been lost. Peoples in Central Asia and Kazakhstan had a shaman which was a hereditary title for a doctor and magician. The shaman would go into ecstasies appealing to his ghosts, to the accompaniment of musical instruments (such as the tambourine with Uzbeks and Tajiks, and stringed instruments with Turkmens, Kazakhs and Kirghiz). Sometimes they demonstrated their ability, to prick themselves with a knife or a sabre and remain uninjured, or to take and lick, without any harm to themselves, a red-hot object made of iron. This is what witnesses to the performance of Kazakh shamans (*bakshy*) wrote : " . . . He jumped to his feet, sat down, got up again, brandishing a dagger, which appeared in his hands all of a sudden, then, seizing an axe, hit himself with its back with all his might, so that his bones cracked. He fell down exhausted and lying, stabbed himself in the heart with the dagger so skilfully that everybody saw the dagger pierce into his body by half of the blade. Then he acted as if he was dying, and his wheezing produced an impression of a death-rattle" (1848).[17] Yet another witness writes: "He (*bakshy*-authors) girdled himself with a rope and made two Kirghiz (Kazakhs—authors) on both sides of him pull its ends in opposite directions. Then, as if he were a gymnast on a horizontal bar, he started turning around the rope rapidly, which made it tighten more and more around his waist. His eyes became blood-shot and nearly went out of the orbits, his breath was taken away, he was wet with sweat. There was a feeling that the rope will cut him in two in a moment" (1899).[18]

The Muslim clergy tried to discard those traditions and customs that were non-Islamic in origin. In certain localities mullahs and ishans forbade the villagers to observe their ancient traditions and rites.[19] In their struggle against pre-Islam traditions and customs, the clergy were supported by local rulers. Thus, Alim-Khan (killed in 1818), Governor of Kokand, thought it expedient to root out the worship of sacred trees and persecuted those individuals who were known as magicians.[20]

However, clergymen did not confine themselves to the "purification" of Islam, and often their activities were not even aimed at it. Mullahs belonged to their peoples and to their time ; therefore they backed many traditions, which were pre-Islam in origin, and because they sincerely believed them to be Muslim, tried to reconcile them with the ideology of Islam, if they contained certain contradictions and discrepancies. They did much to make Islam and pre-Muslim rites and beliefs influence one another in equal measure reciprocally.

On the one hand, mullahs opposed shamans (contemporary clergymen, as is observed by ethnographers nowadays, still disapprove of shaman practices). There were cases in Karakalpakia, in which crowds incited by mullahs stoned to death shamans who according to certain rites had women's clothes on.[21] On the other hand, some forms of cooperation between the Muslim clergy and shamans were observed, since the acute struggle between clergy and shamans was only typical of the period when Islam was being introduced and established. Later, shamanism was Muslimized. since men and women shamans were Muslims themselves. This was manifest in many aspects of shaman practices. In their ritual songs shamans appealed to Allah and Muslim saints for help. The ghosts, with which they claimed to have contacts, were identified with the *jinns* of the Koran, or subdivided into Muslims and non-Muslims. By the end of the 19th century, shamans throughout Central Asia included the Sufistic rite of *zikr* or *jahr* in their practices with the religious formulas of "La illahi il Allah", "Allah-hu", and so on.[22]

Shamanism was Muslimized and this made it possible for the population converted to Islam, to believe in it. Ishans and mullahs sent the diseased for treatment to shamans, and gave the shamans their blessing to serve their ghosts. There were instances in which the Muslim clergy took part in shaman's rites, in particular, dervishes belonging to various Sufistic orders.[23] Turkmen Chovdurs in the Khorezm oasis thought that shaman activities originated from pilgrimages to the graves of some Muslim saints, or from some saint appearing before a shaman in his dream. The population in Khorezm believed that one of the local saints, Ashkaidyn-Pir, patronized shamans, while Kazakhs thought the saint Korkut to be the shaman's patron.[24] Shamans enjoyed great popularity with the Turkmen population in Khorezm. Addressing a shaman, Turkmen Chovdurs called him reverently "Ishan-aga', as if he were one of the clergy.[25]

Shamanism was especially pronounced in the activities of the clergy of different ranks. To support this fact, an abundance of material has been collected about ishans (*pirs*), who claimed to have contacts with their assistant ghosts. For this reason, they took upon themselves to cure the diseased by "driving away" the ghosts that had caused the disease. Groups of honourable khojas, who posed as the descendants of the Prophet, were considered (for instance, by Turkmens) to possess an "army" of ghosts ; they also tried to heal people allegedly hit by *jinns*.[26] While saying prayers over the diseased in order to protect them against ghosts, many ishans, khojas and mullahs struck them with a whip, just as shamans did. One of the Turkmen mullahs was known as "Mullah with Dutar", because his seance of treatment consisted in calling the ghosts to the accompaniment of a stringed instrument. Shamanistic rites were performed by wandering dervishes (*divanas* or *dubanas*), who had certain outward symbols of their own, such as a hat made of swan's skin, or a crook with rattling metal pendants or clinging bells). Dervishes drove ghosts away, made prophesies and told fortunes.[27] A group of Turkmens had the Sufistic rite changed so much that it acquired all features of a shamanistic performance by the end of the 19th century.[28]

Studies of pre-Islam survivals do not only give us an idea of Islam's local features in the past but contribute to a better understanding of the gradual dying out of religion.

What is happening to pre-Muslim survivals today ? Prior to answering this question, it is necessary to point out that the atheistic education organized by the government and Party bodies, gave little attention to pre-Muslim religious traditions. This was stressed more than once by the ethnographers of the Islamic regions. A.K. Alekperov, an expert in Azerbaijan's ethnography, wrote more than 40 years ago about the "... one-sidedness of the anti-religious activities, which, from the very beginning, were aimed solely at combatting Islam. . . "[29] "The struggle against Islam", he pointed out, "was not meant as the struggle against religion, but against a definite form of religion".[30] This "produced a misleading and extremely dangerous impression of the successes of anti-religious propaganda. In the Kuba district, for instance, the mosques were closed down quite easily, without any resistance from the population, including even the elderly people ; however, the graves of sheikhs (*pirs* and *ustazes*) and other holy graves remained intact, and propagandists did not notice them."[31] Much later, at the end of the '50s, G.P. Snesarev, an ethnographer of Central Asia, pointed out that, in actual fact, things remained the same, since the atheistic educational activities directed against official Islam, did not affect many of the existing forms of religion.[32] "Atheistic activities in Central Asia aim at struggling solely against orthodox Islam ; they leave out all of the pre-Islam survivals", he concluded.[33]

In this way, pre-Islam religious survivals have not been affected directly by anti-religious propaganda. Incidentally, Muslim clergy, who have lost their former influence on the believers during the years of Soviet power, could not help eliminate those survivals. According to ethnographic research of the last few years, believers observe also pre-Muslim traditions and rites, among other types of religious survivals. Various authors note, in particular, conservatism marking burial and funeral rites, which include ancient pre-Islam traditions.[34] In some areas, groups of believers still observe the rite of calling forth rain.[35] Certain archaic features are typical of the saints cult, which is still one of the most stable elements of Islam for believers today. They continue to believe in the evil eye and in the effectiveness of various amulets.[36] Some of them also believe in ghosts, this is why there exist various kinds of witchcraft and religious quack medicine (as well as shamanism in Central Asia). An opinion was voiced that "... (religious) survivals, which originate in pre-Muslim beliefs, live longer than the orthodox Islam survivals degrading at a more rapid pace.".[37] As G.P. Snesarev had justly put it, the long life of pre-Islam traditions was due to their close connection with family life. "Although considerable changes have taken place, specifically, in women's position, a family still remains a closed community, less accessible for progressive changes than, for instance, production collectives."[38]

When speaking about pre-Muslim survivals existing today, mention sould be made of the following facts :

1. At present, only certain groups of believers observe pre-Muslim rites and traditions, mostly middle-aged and elderly people, above all, women. In fact, it is difficult for ethnographers, to find people whom they could consult on relevant problems.

2. Today we can come across only a few pre-Muslim views, customs and rites, which were widely observed by Muslims just a few decades ago. For instance, a complex series of agricultural rites have been abandoned. This was largely due to collectivization in agriculture, which has brought about a new labour organization. Only the older generation remember about the rite of preventive magic ploughing, the first furrow rite, etc. In the 1950s, one could see an animal's skull guarding crops against the evil eye in some areas (in Turkmenia, for instance). Today this tradition has fallen into oblivion. Even the burial rites have lost their archaic features. Thus, in the 1920s Tajiks

from the upper Zeravshan made a doll representing the dead and put it up on the sticks above the grave. "Such dolls were placed by mothers or sisters on the graves of children, youths and girls, as well as young women who had not yet given birth to a child. Very often a doll was placed on a wooden horse. Such dolls sat with their faces to the road, with a whip in their hands. Their dress was made of a shirt or a gown of the dead, and the dolls on women's graves were the hair of the perished women."[39] In the same decade as ethnographers observed, Kirghiz invented, different symbols representing, the dead. For instance, they put a pillow vertically, put a gown of the dead on it and his turban on top of it. Then it was placed in the corner and curtained off from the rest of the room.[40] These customs were forgotten by about the 1930s. More such examples could be cited.

3. Those pre-Muslim traditions that are still observed by believers, have undergone qualitative changes. The rites and procedures become more and more over-simplified, lose their niceties and their former meaning. There is no rite or belief which remains static. (The same can be said not only about pre-Islam survivals, but also about all religious views and rites of Muslims today.)

Materials of the shamanistic cult are a brilliant illustration of the decay of traditional beliefs. In the last few decades, shamanism has receded into the background. There are hardly more than 10 shamans (both men and women) in Turkmenistan. They have become a rarity in Kazakhstan and Kirghizia. Shamanistic traditions are more popular in Uzbekistan and Tajikistan, nevertheless, they have also seen substantial changes. Thus, the older generation had witnessed the decline of shamanism in the Zeravshan Valley, Uzbekistan. Men shamans were active there even before the war, whereas today they are only middle-aged or elderly women. Contemporary women shamans are unable to keep up the former traditions. In the '30s there were shamans (*bakshy*) in those areas, who, when in ecstasy, could take with bare hands red-hot iron and coals and lick them, jump out on to the roof of the yurt, swallow and then hawk out a thread done in knots. Women shamans of today are unable to do anything of that kind. During the "healing" or initiation rites they sing out appeals to the ghosts to the accompaniment of a tambourine. The rite of healing is extremely primitive nowadays, with shamans walking around the patient, touching him with a tambourine and beating him with the lungs of sacrificial animals, and lighting lamps, which are sometimes placed on the head and palms of the patient. Some of the procedures have lost their meaning.[41] The idea of the world of ghosts is becoming vaguer, the images of ghosts are on the wane, and their specific features are fading. As a result, ghosts which till recently belonged to definite groups of different types are confused. Apparently, shamanism will disappear soon even in those regions, in which it is still preserved.

In this way, in our time of the general decay of religion, the existing pre-Muslim beliefs and rites are destined to disappear, just as Islamic views. They are drawing nearer and nearer to their complete end, which is due to the social transformations and greater cultural needs of our society.

NOTES AND REFERENCES

1. See, for instance, G.P. Snesarev, *Relicty domusulmanskih verovaniy i obriadov u uzbekov Horezma* (Relics of pre-Muslim beliefs and rites among the Uzbeks of Khorezm), Moscow, 1969, pp. 205-15; M.R. Rahimov, *zemledeliye, tadjikov basseyna r. Hingow v dorevolutsionniy period* (Agriculture of the Tadjiks in the basin of Hingow river in the pre-Revolutionary period), Stalinabad, 1957, pp. 192-203; R. Kadyrov, *Dorevolutsionniy, obriadoviy folklov tadjkov basseyna Kashka-Daryi* (pre-Revolutionary ritual folklore of the Tadjiks in the basin of Kashka-Darya river), Dushanbe, 1963, pp. 36-41 (in the Tadjik language).
2. O.A. Sukhareva, *Islam v Uzbekistane* (Islam in Uzbekistan), Tashkent, 1960, p. 30; G.F. Chursin, "Prazdnik 'vyhoda pluga' u gorskih narodov Dagestana" (The "First ploughing" festival among the mountain peoples of Daghestan), in *Isvestiya Kavkazskogo istoriko-arheologicheskogo instituta*, v. 5, Tiflis, 1927; I.M. Shamanov, "Narodniy Kalendar karachayevtsev" (The Karachays' folk calendar) in *Sovetskaya etnografiya*, 1971, N 5, pp. 113-14.
3. G.P. Snesarev, *op. cit.*, pp. 216-21; I. Muhiddinov, *Zemledeliye pamirskin tadjikov Vahana i Ishkashima* (Agriculture of the Pamiri tadjiks in Vahan and Ishkashim), Moscow, 1975, pp. 92-3; M.R. Rahimov, *op. cit.*, pp. 183-87.
4. *Tadjiki Karategina i Darvaza* (The Tadjiks of Karateghin and Darvaz), v. 1, Dushanbe, 1966, p. 130.
5. I. Muhiddinov, *op. cit.*, pp. 103-6.

6. *Tadjki Karategina i Darvaza*, v. 1, p. 143.
7. M.R. Rahimov, *op. cit.*, pp. 210-11; L.I. Lavrov, "Doislamskiye varovaniya adygeitsev i kabardintsev" (pre-Islamic beliefs of the Adyghs and the Kabardinians), in *Issledovaniya i materialy po voprosam pervobytnyh religioznyh verovaniy* (Trudy Instituta etnografii Akademii nauka, SSSR, v. 51), Moscow, 1959, p. 202 ; A.G. Trofimova "Iz istorii religioznyh obriadov vyzyvaniya dozhdia i solntsa u narodov Yuzhnogo Dagestana" (On the history of the religious rites of inviting rain and sun among the peoples of Southern Daghestan), in *Azerbaidjanskiy etnograficheskiy sbornik*, 2, Baku, 1966; (S. Gadjiyeva, *Sh. Kumyki. Istoriko-ethnograficheskoye issledovaniye* (The Kumyks, a historical-ethnographical study), Moscow, 1961, pp. 323-24.
8. I. Muhiddinov, *op. cit.*, pp. 100-1.
9. G.P. Snesarev, *op. cit* , p. 83.
10. See, for instance, S.M. Demidov, "K voprosu o nekotoryh perezhitkah domusulmanskih obriadov i verovaniy u yugozapadnyh turkmen" (On the problem of some survivals of pre-Muslim rites and beliefs among the south-western Turkmens), in *Trudy Instituta istorii, arheologii i etnografii Akademii Nauk Turkmenskoy SSR*, v. 6, Ashkhabad, 1962, pp. 202-5; L.A. Firshtein "O nekotoryh obychayah i poveryah, sviazannyh s rozhdeniyem i vospitaniyem rebionka u uzbekov Yuzhnogo Horezma" (On some customs and beliefs connected with the birth and upbringing of children among the Uzbeks in Southern Khorezm), in *Semiya i semeiniye obriady u norodov Sredney Azii i Kazahstana*, Moscow, 1978 (See the bibliography on page 189).
11. G.A. Gadjiyev, "Doislamskiye verovaniya i obriady lezgin. Po materialam Samurskoy doliny" (pre-Islamic beliefs and rites of the Lezghins as based on the materials from Samur valley), Makhachkala, 1977 (manuscript of Ph.D. thesis), p. 180.
12. G.P. Sensarev, "K. voprosu o proishozhdenii prazdnestva sunnat-toy v yego sredneaziatskom variante" (On the problem of the origin of "sunnat-toi" festival in its Central Asian form), in *Sredneaziatskiy ethnograficheskiy sbornik*, III (Trudy Instituta etnografii Akademii rauk SSSR, v. 97), Leningrad, 1971.
13. See, G.P. Snesarev, *Relicty. . .*, pp. 147-56, idem "Bolshesemeyniye zahoroneniya u osedlogo naseleniya levoberezhnogo Horezma" (Big family common graves among the sedentary population of Khorezm on the left bank of the Amu-Dariya), in *Kratkiye soobscheniya Instituta etnografii Akademii nauk SSSR*, No. XXXIII, 1960, pp. 60-71; S.P. Poliakov and A.I. Cheremnyh, "Pogrebalniye sooruzheniya naseleniya doliny Zeravshana" (Burial structure of the Zeravshan valley people), in *Domusulmanskiye verovaniya i obriady v sredney Azii*, Moscow, 1975, pp. 263-67.
14. G.P. Snesarev, *Relicty. . .*, p. 276; T.D. Bayaliyeva, *Doislamskiye*

verovaniya i ih perezhitki u kirgizov (pre-Islamic beliefs and their survivals among the Kirghizes), Frunze, 1972. p. 59.

15. "Rasprava s koldunom" (Outrage upon a sorcerer), in *Turkestánskiye vedomosti* (newspaper), Tashkent, 1910, N 178.
16. O.A. Sukhareva, "Perezhitki demonologii i shamanstva u ravninnyh tadjikov" (Vestiges of demonology and shamanism among the plain Tadjiks), in *Domusulmansktye verovaniya i obriady v Sredney Azit*, Moscow 1975, pp. 13, 45-55; G.P. Snesarev, *Relicty...*, pp. 44-5; Kayum-Nasyrov, "Poveriya i obriady kazanskih tatar, obrazovavshiyesia mimy vliyaniya na zhizn ih sunnitskogo magometanstva" (Beliefs and rites of the Kazan tatars as originated outside Sunni Islam), in *Zaplski Imperatorskogo Russkogo Geograficheskogo obschestva po otdeleniyu etnografii*, V. VI, St. Petersbourg, 1880, pp. 15-16; S. Rudenko and I. Bashkiry. Istoriko-etnogroficheskiye ocherki (The Bashkirs. Historical-Ethnographical Essays), Moscow-Leningrad, 1955, pp, 319-20.
17. A. Novolineyets, "Chary shamana v Kirgizskom aule" (The charms of a shaman in a Krighiz nomadic settlement), in *Orenburgskiye gubernskiye vedomosti* (newspaper), 1848, No. 25.
18. L. Berg, "Iz sonnogo gorda, Kazalinkisya zametki" (From a sleepy town, Notes made in Kazalinsk) in *Russkiy Turkestan* (Newspaper), 1899, No. 94.
19. V.N. Basilov, *Kult sviatyh v islame* (Worshipping of saints in Islam), Moscow, 1970, pp. 95-6, 108-9; S.M. Demidov, "O verovaniyah i obychayah turkmen, sviazannyh s ognion" (On the Turkmenian beliefs and customs concerning fire), in 'Issledovaniya po etnografii turkmen', Ashkhabad, 1965, pp. 176-77; M.R. Rahimov, *op. cit.*, p. 205; M.S. Andreyev, "Kharakteristike drevnih tadjikskih semeynih otnosheniy" (On the character of ancient family relationships among the Tadjiks) in *Izvestiya Tadjikskogo filiala Akademii nauk SSSR*, v.15. 1949, P.7.
20. M (allitskiy), "Odin iz dramaticheskih epizodov Kokandskov istorii (pokushcniye na zhizn Alim-hana)" (One dramatic episode in Kokand history, an attempt upon Alim-Khan's life), in *Turkestanskiye vedomosti* (newspaper), 1905, No. 189.
21. Yu. V. Knorozov, "Mazar Shamun-nabi"—in *Sovetrkaya etnograepa*, 1949,p. 96.
22. G. P. Snesarev, *Relicty...*, p. 53;O.A. Sukhareva, *Islam V Uzbekistane*, pp. 51-2: V. N. Basilov, "Traditsii zhenskogo shamanstva u kazahov" (Female shamanism traditions among the Kazakhs) in *Poleviye issledovaniya Instituta etnografii*, 1974, Moscow, 1975, pp. 121-23.
23. A. Dnayev, "Krigizskiye bolezni i sposoby Sh lecheniya" (Diseases and their treatment among the Krighizes) in *Turkestanskiye vedomosti* (newspaper), 1902, No. 80.
24. V.M. Zhirmunskiy, "Oguzskiy geroicheskiy epos i 'Kniga korkuta, (The Oghuz' heroic epic and 'Dede Korkut kitabi')" in *Kniga moyego*

deda korkuta, Moscow–Leningrad, 1962, pp. 145-74; V.N. Basilov, Kult *sviatyh v islame*, pp. 40-68

25. V. N. Basilov, "Niyazklychev K. Perezhitki shamanstva u turkmen-chovdurov (Vestiges of shamanism among the Chovdur Turkmen) in *Domusulmanskiye verovaniya i obriady v Sredney Azii*, Moscow, 1975, pp. 136-37.
26. V. N. Basilov, *Kult sviatyh v islame*, chapter III.
27. T.D. Bayaliyeva, *op. cit.*, p. 121, "A-ov O.Baksy i duany" (The baksys and the duanas), in *Krigizskaya stepnaya gaseta* (newspaper), Omsk, 1894, No. 36,p. 4.
28. V. N. Basilov, "O proiskhozhdenii turkmen-ata prostonarcdniye formy sredneaziatskogo sufizma)" (On the origin of the Ata Turkmens the popular forms of Central Asian sufism) in *Domusulmanskiye verovaniya i obriady v Sredney Azii*, Moscow, 1975, pp. 157-72, 165.
29. A, K. Alekperov, *Issledovaniya po arheologii i etnografii Azerbaidjana* (Studies in archaeology and technography of Azerbaijan) Baku, 1960, p. 187.
30. *Ibid.*, p. 188.
31. *Ibid.*, pp. 188-89.
32. G. P. Snesarev, "O nekotorih prichinah sohraneniya religioznobytovyh perezhitkov u uzbekov Horezma" (On some causes behind the religious survivals in the everyday life of the Khorezm Uzbeks), in *Sovetskaya etnografiya*, 1957, No. 2, p. 62.
33. *Ibid.*
34. G. P. Snesarev, *Relicty...*, p. 107. yesbergenov, and T. Atamuratov, *Traditsii i ih preobrazovaniye v gorodskom bytu karakalpakov* (Traditions and their transformation among the urban Karakalpaks), Nukus, 1975, p. 167, and others ; *Tadjiki Karategira i Darvaza* (The Tadjiks of Karateghin and Darvaz), v. 3, Dushanbe, 1976, pp. 162-64.
35. A. V. Avksentiyev, Islam na Severnom Kavkaze (Islam in the Northern Caucasus), Stavropol, 1973, p. 151; T. D. Bayaliyeva, *op. cit.*, p. 150.
36. A. V. Avksentiyev, *op. cit.*, pp. 149-50; S. Demidov, Na piostrom shnurke" (On a black-and-white cord), in *Vecherniy Ashkhabad* (newspaper), 16 October, 1973.
37. G. P. Snesarev, *Relicty...*, p. 18.
38. *Ibid.*, p. 20.
39. L. A. Troitskaya, "Nekotoriye starinniye obychai, obriady i poveriya tadjikov doliny Verhnego Zeravshana" (Some ancient customs, rites, and beliefs of the Upper Zeravshan valley Tadjiks), in *Zaniatiya i byt narodov Sredney Azii* (Sredneaziatskiy etnograficheskiy sbornik, III), Leningrad, 1971, p. 241.

40. M. S. Andreyev, "Poyezdka letom 1928 g, v. Kasanskiy rayon (sever Fergany)" [A trip to the Kasan District, a northern part of the Ferghana valley] in the summer of 1928", in Izvestiya obshchestva Tadjikistana i iranskih narodnostey za yego predelami, v. 1, Tashkent 1929, p. 116; and T.D. Bayaliyeva *op. cit.*, pp. 64-5.

41. See, for instance, V. N. Basilov, "Noviye materialy o shamanskom bubne uzbekov" (Some new data on the Uzbek shamanic drums in *Poleviye issledovaniya Instituta ethnografii, 1975*, Moscow 1977.

18

Process of Departure of the Uzbek Population from Religion

S.M. Mirhasilov

THE MODERN status of Islam and the disappearance of religious traditions in the Soviet East, and in Uzbekistan, in particular, is a subject which attracts the attention of a large number of researchers. The present paper deals with those forms in which religious survivals continue to exist in the everyday life of the Uzbek people, and is based on the results of the ethnographic and ethno-sociological research carried out by the author and other scientific research workers.

The process of the secularization of the everyday life and the consciousness of the people in various areas of the Moslem East has found its expression, among other things, in the radical weakening of religion's role in the life of the Uzbek people. Of decisive importance in this respect have been the deep going socio-economic changes. The process has been rendered more effective by the cultural-cum-educational work among the population, liquidation of illiteracy and the creation of a wide network of organizations in the field of scientific education, all already begun in the first years of Soviet power.

A decree dated 1 August 1918 and issued in the Turkestan ASSR of which Uzbekistan was then part, provided for all instruction in schools to be given in the native instead of the Arabic language. In the appeal issued by the People's Commissariat of Public Education (Narkompros) of the Turkestan Republic it was stated : "All the nationalities are hereby granted the right to instruct their school children in their national schools—in their native tongues".[1] This signified the end of the old confessional schools whose graduates were, in fact, half illiterate and could, at best, read Arabic texts without knowing what they meant. Instruction in their native tongues was of great importance for the cultural development of the Uzbek people. But the confessional schools did not agree to surrender its position immediately, the attempts to transform it met with a vehement resistance on the part of the reactionary elements, and "beatings of pupils and their parents, killings of the first Soviet teachers, destruction of the schools were not rare during the first period of the existence of the Soviet power".[2]

At first, the secularization of the schools met with a certain opposition among the believers. Under the influence of the clergy, part of the population even abstained, at first, from sending their children to school. Certain difficulties which took place at that time not only in the cultural but also in the economic and political life of the country also played their part as did the centuries-long influence of Islam on the local population, which had determined a number of local peculiarities in their mode of living. All this called for the exercise of a somewhat gradual approach to solving the task of secularization of the people's education, V.I. Lenin wrote that "the cultural task cannot be solved as quickly as the political and military tasks... The period of time needed in this case is longer due to the very substance of this task and it is necessary to adapt oneself to this longer period, planning one's work and showing a maximum of perseverence and exercising a systematic approach."[3] Therefore, in the years immediately following the October Revolution, the teaching of the basics of religion had to be allowed in the national schools of the Turkestan Republic provisionally, until 1923.[4]

The people soon came to realize, however, the advantages offered by the Soviet national as compared to the confessional schools. One of the chief merits of the Soviet schools was seen by the parents in the fact that in them their children quickly learned to read and received a better grounding in various subjects. Special surveys carried out in that period in rural localities demonstrated that "the population shows an obvious preference for the Soviet schools and in this respect there are no grounds to fear for its future. The poorest strata of the population in kishlaks are thirsting for knowledge and are not so religious as to require that it should be given in religious forms", and that the existence of the old-method schools is "a consequence of the fact that the population is undersupplied by the Soviet schools" and studying in the old-method schools are "mostly children of beys and middle peasants".[5] By the year 1923, the confessional schools which had been one of the seats of the Moslem religion ceased to exist in the Republic.

The following are some other facts that may be cited by way of illustration of how Islam disappeared from the social life of the country. Thus, the number of the Shariat courts functioning on the territory of the Republic dwindled form 220 in the first years of the Soviet power to only 9 in the year 1927. The Shariat courts were not in a position to compete with the new Soviet court. But had the wide masses of believers still considered it necessary to rely on the norms of the Shariat, their liquidation would have been impossible.

Scientific atheistic propaganda also played its part in freeing the consciousness of the people from religion. In November 1928, the First Republic Congress of Militant Atheists was held in Samarkand. It worked out a programme of anti-religious struggle in the conditions of Uzbekistan.[6] In their activities, the atheists did and do rely on the Party's dictum that the struggle against religion is not a struggle against believers but a criticism of the anti-scientific views standing in the way of the formation of the materialist outlook.

However, if the struggle of the Soviet power aimed at moulding a new man armed with a scientific outlook had not been extended to the injunctions regarding the seclusion of women under Islam, it would not have been successful. The task of the emancipation of women in Uzbekistan was beset with grave difficulties, which can be explained by the viability of the patriarchal-feudal structures and the influence of religion which supported the norms of the old way of life.

The year 1927 saw the beginning of the offensive (hudjum) against the old way of life and, in particular, against the injunctions regarding the seclusion of women. It manifested itself in the mass unveiling campaign, or casting the *paranja*, a symbol of the subjugation of women. The unveiling contributed to a further emancipation of women and dealt a heavy blow to the influence of the clergy.

The emancipation of women took place amidst an acute struggle against the zealous adherents of the old way of life. In their hatred for the women who exposed their faces they committed cruel acts of terror. In 1928, 118 women were killed and 63 during the first half of 1929.[7] As for the total number of women killed or heavily wounded in those years by the reactionary elements in Uzbekistan as a whole, it reached almost 300.[8]

However, the process of the emancipation of women was not to be stopped. The participation of women in the socialist construction which went on in all spheres of the national economy, and also in the state and cultural construction created all the conditions necessary for the establishment of the actual equality of sexes. The casting off of the *paranja* and the emancipation of women proved a genuine revolution in the life of the Uzbek people.

Despite the Koranic injunction to show a hostile attitude to people professing other beliefs, the Moslems usually lived in peace with them and the slogan of waging a holy war against the infidels was invoked, in fact, only in some periods in the history of some countries. But the barrier put up by Islam between the Moslems and those professing other beliefs was, indeed, a significant one. Since religious distinctions were identified with national ones, narrow-mindedness was bound to follow and certain obstacles found to arise in the way of communication with the peoples professing other beliefs. But it should be pointed out that the religious intolerance so zealously propagated by the reactionary clergy and the exploiter classes found response usually only among part of the population. The Russian social scientists, who studied the life of the peoples of Turkestan after it was acceded to Russia found that the common people harboured no fanaticism.[9] The origins of the fraternal friendship between the Russian and the Uzbek peoples which came to flower in the years of the Soviet power can be traced back, in fact, to the good relations of friendship formed by many Russian and Uzbek families already before the October Revolution.

At the present time, representatives of dozens of ethnic groups live and work side by side in Uzbekistan. Thus, at the Tashkent Textile Combine, there are representatives of over 40 ethnic groups, at the Uzbek Metallurgical Works named after V.I. Lenin in the Andijan region over 30, in the V.I. Lenin Collected Farm of the Syr-Daryinsky District 17. The joint work of the representatives of various ethnic groups promotes their drawing closer together. In the last decades, this process of drawing closer together of the Uzbeks and other ethnic groups has been considerably intensified. Inter-ethnic contacts have become a regular norm not only at places of work but also in everyday life. Research conducted by the Sector of Concrete Sociological Studies, Institute of Ethnography of the Academy of Sciences of the Uzbek SSR, in 1974 showed that about 30 per cent of Uzbeks worked in the collectives in which representatives of other ethnic groups made up no less than half of the total membership.[10]

The study of the results of the public opinion polls goes to show that in the view of about 78 per cent of Uzbeks, aged 20-50, it is immaterial, in terms of communication at work, to which ethnic group their co-workers may belong. Sixty-six per cent of the urban Uzbeks maintain friendships with people belonging to other ethnic groups and 32 per cent have relatives who have entered into ethnically mixed marriages. These are becoming more frequent not only in towns but also in rural localities, especially in state farms with highly diverse populations. Ethnically mixed marriages were looked upon with favour by a majority of the interviewed.

The ethnographic study of the Uzbek rural population has demonstrated that the lowest number of the ethnically mixed marriage are of those in which the partners of the Uzbeks come from families which, in the past, practised a religion different from that of Uzbeks.[11] This can be accounted for by a strong ethnic heterogeneity of the rural population and by the fact that its ethnic distinctions in the mode of living have been retained to a considerable extent.[12] There can be no doubt that the religious prejudices do play their part, too. Uzbek women still rarely marry men belonging to other ethnic groups. In the ethnically mixed marriages, the husband is usually an Uzbek while the wife is sometimes a Russian.

As the conjugal (consisting of the married couple and their offspring, sometimes with the parents of one spouse) becomes the most widespread type of family, more and more newly wed couples now live separately from their parents, maintaining good relations with them, and their ethnically mixed marriage do not cause them those inconveniences which are connected with the need to adapting to new modes of living, which arise in the extended families. The life-style of mixed families bears the imprint of the ethnic distinctions characteristic of both spouses. The non-Uzbek women, especially in rural families, usually have a good command of the Uzbek language, assimilate the subtleties of the life-style and ethics of the ethnic group to which their husbands belong, and they in their turn, make their own ethnic contribution to the life-style of their families. The children are usually given their father's nationality, which is documented. If the wife is Russian, the children are bilingual. They are usually given Uzbek names, but sometimes double-barrelled ones (Uzbek and Russian).

The radical changes that have taken place during the years of the Soviet power in all spheres of the economy, way of life, and culture of the Uzbeks have contributed to the departure of the wide masses of the working people from religion and to the dissemination of an atheistic outlook among them. But various religious traditions and beliefs connected with them are still found to exist to a certain extent in the everyday life of the people.

As is known, it is obligatory (*farz*) for every Moslem to follow such main pillars of Islamic worship as the verbal profession of the unity of Allah and the prophethood of Mohammed, the five obligatory daily prayers (*namaz*), the payment of the alms tax (*zakat*), the fasting (*ruza*), and the pilgrimage to Mecca (*hajj*). Even prior to the October Revolution, these Islamic injunctions were followed by the Uzbeks far from fully. Today, the older generation still retains the knowledge of the main duties and various prescriptions and rites of the Moslem ; some of them are practised by the representatives of the older generation. The youth do not know, as a rule, or have a very hazy idea of either Islamic mythology or norms of everyday life prescribed by Islam or its ceremonies. The young people do not know the meaning of religious rites, but if they do participate in them, they are prompted to do so not by their religious convictions but by the desire to avoid a conflict with their devout parents.

The knowledge of the symbol of faith by part of the youth can also be explained by the same reasons. Anxious for the "fate" of their children who have no idea about the basis of faith, devout parents consider it necessary, at least, to have their children learn the symbol of faith—the *Kalima*. Brought up in the spirit of the Uzbek traditions, calling for instilling respects for parents and older people from very childhood, young people learn this in order not to offend their parents.

The pilgrimage to Mecca is observed today by a very small proportion of the believers, mainly by the workers of the religious establishments. In the past, there was a widespread belief that visiting the graves of some of the most reserved saints could be recognized as equal to the pilgrimage to Mecca. The *zakat*, a pious deed, according to which one sacrifices one-fortieth of his wealth for the poor lost its original meaning and was turned into a State tax prior to the October Revolution, though, our materials show that in Tashkent itself and in a number of the Tashkent and other regions it was continued to be given to poor families in pre-revolutionary times.

The observance of some Islamic prescriptions cannot always be viewed today as a manifestation of religiousness. Thus, the *fitr-ruza*, a pious charity for mullahs in the period of fasting or for poor single persons, is given by the elder people in the family. The non-believers do not interfere in order to avoid gossip, accusations of stinginess, and so on. The young people agree, sometimes, to go through the Moslem marriage ceremony not out of any conviction, but out of respect for their elders who insist on inviting the mullah.[13]

A certain part of the population still performs the five daily prayers and observe fasting. This however, does not apply to the young people. The sociological research carried out in the period from the end of the sixties till the beginning of the seventies showed that, out of the total number of the interviewed, those aged 18-30 do not observe the fasting and the five daily prayers at all but these prescriptions are observed by 5 per cent in the 30-40 age group, by 12 per cent in the 40-50 age group, and by over 70 per cent in the over 50 age group. Ninety per cent of the mechanizers and 94 per cent of the workers replied that they observed neither the fasting nor the *namaz*.[14]

The five daily prayers are performed, as a rule, only by people belonging to the older generation, who sometimes do not even know the full text of the prayers. There are many old people who either do not perform any prayers at all or participate only in the prayer of the assembly once a week in a mosque (the Friday *namaz*). The youth do not perform the prayers, do not know them, and show no desire to learn them.

This mass non-observance of the acts of worship prescribed by Islam even by the believers can be explained by the fact that the mullah has lost his importance and influence as a spiritual mentor, while the mosque has lost its former role as the centre of social life.

Already in the period from the end of the twenties and the beginning of the thirties, the number of mosques dwindled in Uzbekistan by 1,500. In such wards of the city of Tashkent as Kator terak, Khofiz, and Pushtihamon the attendance in the mosques declined by more than half. It should be noted that even in these years those who attended the mosques for prayers were mostly in the over 40 age group.[15] The number of mosques has now dwindled still more. As an illustration, I would like to cite some data from my field notes. According to what I heard from older people, in the Niyazbashi settlement (the Yangiulsky District in the Tashkent region) there were prior to the October Revolution, about 1,000 households and 12 mosques while in the Baitkurgan kishlak (the Ordzhonikidzevsky District in the Tashkent region) there were 300-350 households and seven mosques ; now the settlements have only one functioning mosque in each, which are attended by a rather narrow circle of people belonging to the older generation. The preserved buildings of other mosques are used by the collective farmers for economic purposes.

The mosques, bazaars, and chaikhanas have now given way as centres of social life to the cultural-educational and administrative offices, the Soviets, management boards of collective farms, schools, clubs, houses and places of culture.

Still at the end of the forties and the beginning of the fifties one could meet people who fasted in the month of Ramadan. Among them, were not only the old but also middle aged people. Among the youth, there were, practically none who fasted. In recent years, the number of those fasting has dwindled appreciably also among the people belonging to the older generation. It is difficult to find today those who fast throughout the whole month. There is a widespread practice among most believers to fast in a token fashion—for three days at the beginning and for three days at the end.

While in our days fasting is found to be observed by a lesser and lesser number of people the custom of *iftor* connected with it is more persistent. *Iftor* is held by some families periodically once in several years, while in others annually. It is a regular part of the cycle of annual events held in commemoration of the dead. *Iftor* is a solemn assembly of old people for a feast to break the fasting and for performing the evening *namaz*, which is gathered once a year on any day of the month of fast. In his prayer during the *iftor* the mullah consecrates the Koran which he recites wholly before the gathering in response to a request of its organizers to the spirits of their dead parents and relatives.

Though most old people attending the *iftor* do not fast, the festival is now even more ostentatious than before. Sometimes, many guests are invited (relatives, neighbours from the districts), festival dishes (*pilav*, *manti*, *norin*, and others) are cooked, guests are also served sweets and a special dainty called *nisholda* which is prepared, in accordance with tradition, only in the month of Ramadan. The *iftor* is attended also by the young people who are seated in a separate room where they are offered food, sometimes with wine, contrary to Islamic prohibition. The youth regards the festival simply as an occasion to make merry with the religious importance attached to it. Among the reasons which promote the existence of this custom, one can mention the growing well-being of the people, and, however paradoxical it may seem, the decline of religiousness. Holding the festival with their children participating in it, parents look upon it as a chance to expiate for the "sins" of their children. The holding of *iftor* is considered to be a pious deed, as an atonement for neglecting fasting.

Thus, the very reasons for performing even the obligatory Islamic prescriptions have undergone a change. Most believers are motivated to perform them not by their conviction but by the desire to pay tribute and "honour the traditions of their parents"

The most persistent custom among Moslems is that of circumcision (*sunnat*). It is performed in all Uzbek families under some pretext or other. Many already recognize the uselessness of the custom and of the onerous expenses involved in holding a feast to mark the occasion. However, under the influence of their parents, relatives, and neighbours many people allow the operation to be performed on their sons. Even the most devout believers while looking with indifference upon the neglect of the obligatory prayers and fasting by their children, relatives, and acquaintances, insistently demand that circumcision be performed and the occasion marked with a sumptuous feast.[16] The religious meaning of circumcision has lost much of its importance ; it is known mainly to the older generation. A majority of the population considers it a necessary sanitary and hygienic norm. Nevertheless, this custom still gives rise to nationalistic prejudices and alienates Uzbeks (and other peoples who formerly professed Islam) from peoples who do not practice circumcision.

In the first decades of the existence of the Soviet power, in a number of industrial enterprises and collective farms there were cases of absenteeism from work which took place under the influence of the clergy during the religious festivals and the month of fasting. For example, in the "Red October" Collective Farm in the Yangiulsky District as many as 6,000 mandays were lost in 1932. According to a report of the *Pravda Vostoka* in those years there were some cases of absenteeism from work and refusals to work in the evening shifts in the period of fasting in a number of industrial enterprises in Tashkent. Prompted by the mullahs and devout parents, some school children in the city of Samarkand did not attend school during the religious festival Kurban-hait. At the same time, in many towns and villages of Uzbekistan, meetings were held, at which workers, collective farmers and employees called upon the population not to observe religious festivals and not to stop work during these.[17]

In the last decades, there were still cases of absenteeism from work during religious festivals in some collective farms. Thus, in one of the collective farms of the Yangiulsky District, in the Tashkent region, on the first day of the Kurban-Hait festival (Id-ul-Adzha), which fell on June 5, 1960 some brigades stopped work almost altogether. Many men attended the festival *namaz* which was held near the grave of the saint Sultanbuv. But today such cases do not take place. The festival prayers are still attended by a large number of men including also young people. Attendance at the congregational festival *namaz* far exceeds attendance at the five daily prayers or of the Friday prayer in mosques. There exists an opinion that the performance of the festival *namaz* is a pious deed (*savob*) and it expiates all the sins. It is also believed that the knowledge of the text of the prayer is not obligatory for those who attend the festival *namaz*. Imitation of the movements of those at prayers can suffice to reckon the *namaz* performed. Therefore, people who are not devout believers usually perform the festival prayer "just in case", for their own peace of mind. Some unbelievers also attend the festival *namaz* in order not to offend old people from their ward or *kishlak* and retain their reputation in their eyes.

The ethno-sociological research has demonstrated that the Ramazan-hait and the kurban-hait festivals are celebrated mainly by people in the age group over 60 while people in lower age groups who do celebrate them are predominantly those who are engaged in unskilled manual work.

It should also be noted that, according to the results of the surveys carried out at the end of the sixties, the religious elements on the ceremonial side of these festivals have decreased in number. For as many as 80 per cent of the people celebrating these religious festivals, they are strictly a family affair and an entertainment ; they deck their homes to suit the occasion prepare treats, visit relatives and the sick, congratulate friends, take strolls, play games, take rest and so on.[18] In contrast to former times when the important Moslem festivals of Kurban-hait and Ramazan-hait were grand occasions with masses of people going out into the street, today they are held only in places of worship or in the family circle.

New festivals have taken the place of religious festivals, which has proved to be a significant factor in the secularization of social life.[19] It is important to note that the all-Union revolutionary festivals—the October Revolution, May, Day, International Women's Day, Victory Day, Constitution Day and some others, have long since been universally observed also in the family circle. The decking of homes, the custom to put on new clothes, the laying of the festival table, visits to relatives and near ones have also become the indispensable elements of Soviet festivals.

Extremely picturesque are such people's festivals as the Pahta Bairam (the Cotton Festival) which has been introduced on popular initiative at the beginning of the sixties, the traditional festival Kovun Saili (the Melon Festival), the ancient people's festival Nauruz marking the spring New Year, and others. All these festivals preserve the national colouring and exhibit many elements of the traditional non-religious rites. The origins of the pre-Moslem festival Nauruz signifying the rebirth of nature, and accompanied by merry-making and people's games, goes back many centuries but is still alive among the people. The Moslem clergy strove to use this manifestation of popular feeling to strengthen their influence among the masses and held sermons during the festival. However, the Nauruz did not become a Moslem festival. Its purely temporal and at the same time traditional features have attracted the attention of the wide public who still consider it necessary to preserve and develop it in our days.

The religious obsequial rite and the custom of commemoration of the dead still live on. These rites exhibit the interlacing of the Islamic prescription with those of ancient animism. The believers consider it necessary to perform the Moslem funeral service (*janaza*), the ceremony of expiating the "sins" (*dovra*), and so on. The ancient belief that the souls of the dead remain on earth and visit homes finds its expression in such customs as holding funeral repasts on 7th, 20th, and 40th day and on the first anniversary of the death of the deceased, and also in consecration sacrificies to the souls of the dead, commemoration prayers, kindling of lamps, and recitation of the Koran.[20]

However, the people have come to realize the uselessness of many elements of the commemoration and funeral rites. Thus, the ancient custom of burying the dead on the family plot is disappearing. The old ceremonies which are out of accord with the modern life-style are gradually replaced by the new ones with no religious connotations.

Among the pre-Islamic religious beliefs and cults, which still exist, one should point out to some survivals of animism which are rather indefinite in their content. Only some representatives of the older generation, especially women, believe in good and evil spirits, and understand the meaning of some rites connected with their worship or protection against them. Some women still believe in witchcraft-bewitchment (*sovutma*) and disenchantment (*isitma*). Sometimes, women resort to ancient magic when in doubt regarding their husbands' affection towards them.

Worshipping of the holy places in the form of pilgrimage or sacrifices still continues.[21] Sometimes, groups of people perform a sacrific (*darveshana*) as a way of soliciting God for a good agricultural year. In the spring of 1965, the unending rains damaged the collective farms and personal properties and some old people decided then to perform this age old ritual in the hope that the weather might improve.

There still persist some elements of the chilla ritual according to which for 40 days after delivery the mother and child are subjected to a strict regimen by taboos and prescriptions because it is considered that during this period they are susceptible to the influence of evil spirits. It is considered undesirable that they should communicate with strangers and even with near ones, go out or visit the near even in the necessary cases. The mother should not shake hands with women who come to congratulate her, The *Beshik-toi*, a solemn festival to mark the birth of a child, is held after the *chilla* period is over.

Superstitions connected with *chilla* are departing from the scene more and more. Partially, this can be explained by the fact that mother and child stay in a hospital for a few days after delivery. However, certain prescriptions not conflicting with the sanitary and medical rules of caring for the health of the mother and her newly born child do remain in force.

As an illustration of the dying out of the ancient beliefs, we can cite the following fact. On the territory of one of the collective farms of the Yangiulsky District (the Kishlak of Chinaz), one could see in the beginning of the sixties the changal bushes, an object of veneration, growing in the middle of a cotton field. From time immemorial, the bush had been looked upon as an abode of spirits and when the field was ploughed the bushes were left untouched for fear that the spirits might do harm. In 1965, I could note that such sacred places in the middle of fields were ploughed up here and also in a number of other collective farms. Similar processes of the dying out of religious survivals in some or other form go on also among other peoples of our country including those who professed Islam.[22]

In the course of the ethno-sociological survey conducted in in Uzbekistan in 1974 some concrete materials were obtained, which show the attitude of the population to religion and religious customs. According to these data, a majority of the interviewed placed themselves in the category of unbelievers. In the towns, the position of religion is weaker than in rural localities. For example, in Tashkent, the percentage of believers is one-third less than in smaller and medium towns and in rural localities. As has been noted by researchers, the national milieu in towns is more heterogeneous in respect of its ethnic and religious attributes[23] and the social and ethno-cultural processes are more intensive.

Among other conditions which influence the attitude of the population to religion, an important role belongs to education, the socio-occupational status of the people and also their age. Most believers are over 40 and with lower educational levels and occupational skills are lower than unbelievers. The believers are mostly made up of illiterate people or those with only an elementary education. In respect of their socio-occupational status, the believers are mostly engaged in unskilled manual occupations.

Socialist transformations that have taken place in the country, social progress, and the wide scale of the cultural-cum-educational work have all contributed to the departure of the wide masses of the population from religion and resulted in the secularization of the social and everyday life of the Uzbek people.

NOTES AND REFERENCES

1. The Central State Archive of the Uzbek SSR, archival collection p-17, document entry 1, file 1062, leaf 21.
2. Kh. Sh. Inoyatov, *Oktyabrskaya revolutsiya v Uzbekistane* (The October Revolution in Uzbekistan), Moscow. 1958, p. 222.
3. V. I. Lenin, *Works*, the 4th edition, pp. 55-6.
4. The Central State Archives of Uzbek SSR, archival collection p-34, document entry 1, file 35, leaf 7. See also: K. E. Bendrikov, *Ocherki istorii narodnogo obrazovaniya v Turkestane* (1865-1924) (Historical Sketches of the Public Education in Turkestan, 1865-1924), Moscow, 1969, p. 417.
5. *Sovremennyi kishlak Srednei Azii, vip. I Niyazbekskaya volost, Tashkentskaya oblast Uzbekskoi SSR* (The Modern Central Asian Kishlak, Issue No. 1. the Niyazbeksky District the Tashkent region). published by the Sredazburo TsK VKP (b), Tashkent, 1926, p. 157-58.
6. For more details see "*Khudosizlar*" (Atheist) magazine, 1929, No. 3, p. 38.
   (Also G. Pulatov, *Uzbekistonda ateistik kharakat tarikhidan* From the History of the Atheistic Movement in Uzbekistan), Tashkent, 1960, p. 67.
7. P. H. Aminova, *Oktyabr i reshenie zhenskogo voprosa v Uzbekistane* (The October Revolution and the Solution of the Women's Question in Uzbekistan), Tashkent, 1975, p. 98.
8. M. A. Bikjanova, *Semya v kolkhozah Uzbekistana* (The family in the collective farms of Uzbekistan), Tashkent, 1959, p. 38.
9. See, for example, A. P. Khoroshin, *Sbornik statei, kasayushchikhsya do Turkestanskogo kraya razdel-* "*Ocherki Tashkenta* (Collection of articles about the Tashkentsky Territory—section entitled "Sketches of Tashkent) SPb, 1876, p. 101; and also *Istoriya Uzbekskoi SSR* (A History of the Uzbek SSR), Vol. I, book II, Academy of Sciences of the Uzbek SSR, Tashkent, 1956, p. 198.

10. Regarding the programme and methodology of these researches, see: Yu. V. Aruthunyan, *Sotsialno-kulturnye aspekti razyitiyai sblizheniya natsi v SSSR* (The socio-cultural aspects of the development of the nations and their drawing together in the USSR), *Sovetskaya Etnografiya* (the Soviet ethnography) magazine, 1972, No. 3, pp. 3-24.
11. M,A. Bikzhanova, *Semya v Kolkhozakh Uzbekistana* (Family in the Collective Farms of Uzbekistan), Tashkent, 1959. *Etnograficheskie ocherki uzbekskogo selskogo naseleniya* (Some ethnographic sketches of the rural Uzbek population), Moscow, 1969; S.M. Mirkhasilov, *Sovremennaya semya selskogo naseleniya Usbekistana* (The modern family among the rural population in Uzbekistan), *Obshchestvennye mavki v Uzbenaukistane* (The Social Sciences in Uzbekistan) magazine, 1977, No. 4.
12. This has been noted by the researchers on the subject of family among other peoples. See, for example, A. E. Ter-Sarkisyantz, *Sovremennaya semya u armyan* (The moderm Armenian family), Moscow, 1972, p. 121.
13. See also, V. Basilov, *Islam i sovremennost*, "*Politicheskoe sambobrazovanie* (The political self-education) magazine, 1969, No. 10, pp. 96-8.
14. M. Abrarov, *Preodolenie perezhitkov shariata v Sovetskom Uzbekistane* (The overcoming of the survivals of Shariat in the Soviet Uzbekistan). The author's abstracts of a dissertation submitted for the defense of a scientific degree of Master of Science (Ph), Tashkent, 1970, p.16.
15. For more details, see: G. P. Snesarev, *Dukhovny oblik uzbekskogo krestyanina* (The ethical profile of the Uzbek peasant). *Etnograficheskie ocherki uzbekskogo selskogo naseleniya* (The ethnographic sketches of the Uzbek rural population), Moscow, 1969, pp. 244-291.
16. For more details, see: G. P. Sensarev, *K Voprosu O proiskhozhdenii prazdnestva sunnat-toi v ego sredneaziatskom variante—"Zanyatiya i bit narodov Srednei Asii"* (*Sredneaziatsky etnografichesky sbornik, vip. III*), *Trudi Instituta Etnografii*, (Regarding the origins of the sunnat-toi festival in its Central Asian variant —"The pursuits and the way of life of the peopies of Central Asia"— "A Central Asian Ethnographic Collection, issue III—Transactions of the Institute of Ethnography), vol. XCVII, Leningrad, 1971.
17. G. Pulatov, see his work indicated above in paras 6 and 16, p. 69.
18. K. Aripov, *Povishenie kulturi bita trudyashchikhsya mass v period kommunisticheskogo stroitelstva i ego znachenie v preodolenii religioznikh perezhitkov (an materialakh Uzbekskoi SSR)* (Raising the cultural standards of everyday life of the working people masses in the period of the communist construction and its importance in overcoming the survivals of religion—on the materials of the Uzbek SSR), The author's abstract of a dissertation submitted for the

defense of a scientific degree of Master of Science (Ph), Tashkent, 1970, p. 18.

19. For more details, see: N. P. Lobacheva, *Formirovanie novoi obryadnosti u uzbekov* (The formation of new ceremonials among the Uzbeks), Moscow, 1975; N. P. Lobacheva, L. A. Tultseva, *Traditsii v sovremennoi obryadnosti uzbekov* (The traditions in the modern ceremonials among the Uzbeks), *Sovetskaya etnografiya* (The Soviet ethnography) magazine, 1977, No.6, pp. 32-44, and other.
20. For more details, see: O. A. Sukhareva. *Islam v Uzbekistane* (Islam in Uzbekistan), Tashkent, 1960; G. P. Snesarev *Relikti domusulmanskikh verovanyi i obryadov u uzbekov Khorezma* (The relics of pre-Moslem beliefs and rites among the Uzbeks of Khorezm), Moscow, 1969.
21. On the topic of worshipping saints, see: V. N. Basilov, *Kult svyatikh v islame* (The cult of saints in Islam), Moscow, 1970.
22. G. P. Vasilieva, *Preobrazovanie bita i etnicheskie protsessi v Severnom Turkmenistane* (The transformation of the life-style and the ethnic processes in north Turkmenistan), the part written by V. N. Basilov, Moscow, 1969.
23. N. P. Lobacheva and L. A. Tultseva, see para. 20, p. 34.

19

Formation of New Unreligious Rites as one of the Manifestations of the Secularization of Social Consciousness

N.P. Lobachyova

RADICAL changes in the social and economic system and affirmation of new ideology necessarily bring about changes in all spheres of life. They inevitably affect the family and every-day life, all that makes up the spiritual culture of a nation. Ritualism or a complex of customs and rites connected with this or that event in social or family life and related to all spheres of human activity likewise undergoes change.* However, ritualism, particularly of the family cycle, is a very conservative social institution and changes in it come about much later than changes in other spheres of material and spiritual life. The creation and popularization of new festive occasions and civil rituals corresponding to the new way of life and world outlook process in our country has stimulated this and resulted in deep going social and cultural transformations.

Using the examples of the peoples of Soviet Central Asia and Kazakhstan, this report will elucidate the formation of new family rituals, a process developing in a more complex way than the formation of new social ceremonies and holidays. This is due largely to the fact that the creation and holding of these festivities is the competence of various organizations which rely in

* Thus, the loss of many elements of traditional ritualism, folk customs and folk art under the influence of capitalist relations in town and country and urbanization of the life of smaller towns were more than once noted in ethnographic and philosophical literature. [1,2]

their activities on the wishes and recommendations of the population and the new customs that arise. Though the introduction of this category of public ceremonies in the everyday life of the people requires time and has its difficulties, it does not run counter to old social rites, for new festivities are connected with different dates and take place in different periods than the old rites. Traditional religious holidays and ceremonies lost their obligatory character with the separation of the Church from the State and ceased to be national, while their observance has shifted to the family and places of religious worship. Their impact on the masses has and continues to weaken as religiosity is overcome.

A different situation arises when new family rites appear. Naturally, the official part of celebration (the registration of a marriage or of a newly born) takes place in a state institution. But the rite itself is performed by members of the family (with the participation of relatives, friends and neighbours) and not by representatives of public organizations and can therefore be deliberately changed only to the extent to which people themselves want to accept innovations.

Traditional family ritualism within its framework reflected the legal, moral, and religious guidelines of the people for some particular period. At the same time, it preserved, in a relict or transmuted form, traces of customs, rites, and beliefs of particular historical periods beginning with the primitive communal system within which it began to emerge. This distinctive feature predetermined religious syncretism which is the basis of this social institution. A more ancient layer of ritualism consists of survivals of early forms of religion, chiefly, black magic, the cult of nature and fertility, natural phenomena, worship of fire, the cult of the hearth and ancestors, demonological conceptions, and so on, but all of them are preserved in forms which lose their original shape or are adapted to different social conditions. Official religions like Islam found reflection in the performance of one or two rituals for example, reading of Moslem prayers when concluding some ceremonies of an obviously non-Moslem origin, and in the treatment of the ritual complex as a whole. [34] In marriage ritualism the peoples of the region display one Moslem ritual, that of wedlock (*nikkah*). Islam also manifests itself in prayers during name-giving and in the rite of circumcision, which has become a symbol of accession to the Moslem religious community. A purely Moslem ritual is the memorial service (*janaza*), but many conceptions and rites of pre-Islamic origin have been Moslemized and are now treated by the population as Islamic (for example, some specific features of the ideas about the soul, the rite of the transfer of the sins of the deceased—*fidiya*, etc). Thus, traditional family ritualism of the beginning of this century combined survivals of ancient religious beliefs and Moslem rituals. Apart from religious traditions, family ritualism included a number of customs reflecting the specifics of social organization. In this sphere one could observe also many surviving phenomena which have a new ring today. Despite the fact that the group of customs (exogamic bans, the custom of avoidance, money paid for the bride, dowry, etc., if we take the marriage cycle) is not connected with religious ideology, it was an inseparable component of the ritual complex viewed as a single whole and hallowed in this form by Moslem religion and established by public opinion. Therefore, when we speak of the process of formation of new non-religious rites on the basis of the transformation of their religious forms, we have to bear in mind not only rituals with a religious content but the entire complex of customs and rites connected with this or that family event.

The regions of Central Asia and Kazakhstan, like others, belong to regions of the country where traditional forms of family ritualism which have by now undergone notable changes, are still rather tenacious, for the influence of the traditions of the patriarchal-feudal pattern, dominant before the revolution, is still felt to some extent. Therefore, the process of formation of a new rite can be observed in all details.[5]

At present we see the co-existence in this region of diverse variants of family rites of one and the same function. Thus, still in existence are : traditional variants of ritualism which have undergone certain changes compared with the pre-revolutionary period ; various transitional forms ; new ceremonies which have got rid of religious rites and *kalym* but still retain some elements of traditional ritualism, which have lost their former meaning ; and even rituals which are completely free from elements of folk ceremonial (*e.g.*, the usual party of the urban type given on the occasion of a particular family event). Arranging all existing variants of family rites in an evolutionary series, we shall obtain a picture of stage-by-stage development of a rite from the old to the new. These stages in the development of the rite are observed also in other regions, among peoples of a different ethnic group, culture, and religion, which testify to the typical character of the process of formation of new ceremonies of the family cycle among different peoples (see the materials on the North Caucasus, Dagestan, Latvia, Udmurtia, the Altai region, etc).[6] But this process develops with different speed among different peoples due to a large extent to the specific features of their historical past (the level of social, economic, and cultural development, the influence of official religion, etc.). The process of formation of non-religious ritualism in the country as a whole has not yet been completed, though all peoples already have new family ceremonies. Only among some peoples they have attained more or less consummate forms. The degree of the spread of new rites differs among different social groups, but on the whole they gain foothold more rapidly in the urban environment.

Let us describe in greater detail the ritual forms existing at present in the given region. As an indicator let us take the marriage ritual which displays sufficient tenacity in everyday life.

Thus, the modern Uzbek marriage in the traditional variant has preserved almost the entire cycle of ancient customs and rites, beginning with match-making and ending with the post-marital visit of the groom to the house of the parents of his wife. It is accompanied also by a religious rite of marriage and transmuted forms of *kalym*. It also retains the tradition of a festive feast (separately for men and women grouped according to ages), in which the groom and bride do not take part. Nonethelesss, its content has changed considerably. For example, the match-making ceremony is now an act whereby the bride is acquainted with the relatives of the groom, an act of mutual aquaintance of the relatives and, when the relatives already know one another, a formal announcement of marriage, since young people usually themselves agree to marry and notify their relatives who then perform the entire or almost the entire ritual ceremony according to the tradition. Formerly, the question of marriage was decided by the relatives of future husband and wife, and at the basis of this act lay a business transaction.

By tradition, to discuss organizational questions of the coming marriage, respected people are invited to partake of food offering, but the determining principle of their choices is now not kinship or community, but respected people of the office institution, collective farm, or neighbourhood (*makhallya*) where representatives of the family work or live. The range of persons invited to attend the marriage ceremony has changed too. Apart from relatives and neighbours, invitations are sent also to those with whom the groom and bride work or study. Thus, though the old tradition of holding such festivities in large collectives still persists, the range of their participants has changed. Kinship and communal ties and obligations have been broken and the principle guiding invitation to family festivities is the personal wish of the masters of the ceremony and not their unchallenged duty of including members of a definite collective, or relatives. Different too are now the gatherings of the bride's girl friends and coevals of the bridegroom : now they are joyous meetings of young people who come to spend the time with a girl or boy friend and to help in the marriage preparations.

Kalym, prohibited by the Soviet law, still exists in some areas, but in a modified form, often in the shape of rich presents, "payment for the milk of the mother", and so on. Its value is fully absorbed by the expenditure on the dowry and the marriage ceremony itself, that is, the element of "sale and purchase" disappears in such type of marriages. Nonetheless, even in this form it may become an obstacle to marriage, for it is its condition.

If in the past all details of marriage ceremony were obligatory, today young people refuse to comply with this or that custom as they wish. Many actions determined in the past by religious ideas have lost their former religious significance and are taken as a game. This applies, for example, to torchlight parades, groups of horsemen prancing around the marital cortege during the bride's journey to the house of the groom, showering of sweets and so on. Formerly they were associated with the protective or stimulating magic. A new civil ritual of wedlock, in this variant of marital ceremony is separated from the marriage proper by two, three, or even more days. Occasionally the marriage ceremony includes a new element—solemn feasting according to the urban pattern for young people.[7] And so, even the traditional marriage ceremony shows elements of the coalescence of old and new traditions.

The character of changes in the traditional marriage of Kazakhs is in principle the same. In most cases, young people, reaching agreement about marriage in advance, inform their parents and then comes the match-making ceremony which has lost a number of customs that were obligatory in the past and, in particular, those connected with various redemptions. In rural areas, groups of match-makers consist of three to five people headed by the father or senior relative of the groom. Usually they bring with them presents for the parents or other members of the bride's family. On the arrival of the match-makers the father of the bride organizes a feast to which close relatives are also invited. After the conclusion of the talks the match-makers are by tradition offered a ritual meal—*kuiryk bauyr*. This ancient custom has lost its former legal meaning (in the past the partaking of the meal served as a guarantee of the inviolability of marriage arrangements by the parties concerned). The match-makers are then asked to sing, play the dombra, or to make presents instead. Merry-making which accompanied the proceedings and degraded the dignity of the match-makers has become a thing of the past. On their departure the guests are offered presents.

Still extent is the custom of the groom's visit to the bride's house before the marriage (called formerly *uryn baru*). It has completely lost its former meaning (in fact, it is a relic of the ancient marital ritual and in the 19th and early 20th century it opened the pre-marital meetings of the groom and bride) and even its name. This visit is now called *korzhin aparu*, meaning the delivery of presents by the groom to the bride's family in a special bag (*korzhin*) made of home-spun woollen or carpet fabric. Presents are often brought in suitcases, but the term still exists.

Festivities are usually held first at the bride's and then at the groom's house. If people uniting in wedlock come from the same village, marriage festivities are held in one of the family houses or in public premises where all are brought together irrespective of age. When they are held at home, feasting is organized in several stages and by age groups. A special party is organized sometimes for the coevals of the groom. For young people the table is laid out in the urban manner, while older people are hosted preferably according to the national tradition. Feasting is followed by merry-making opened always with a song—*toi bastar*.

Among traditional customs observed to this day are the inspection of the dowry (*korimdik*), showering of sweets on the bride and groom (*shashu*), the pouring of oil in a fire by the bride and groom (*otka moi kuyu*), offering of a dish with a piece of breast meat (*tos*) to the groom and meat from the leg of an animal (*zhambas*) to the match-makers, performance of ritual songs (*zhar-zhar* and *betashar*), present-offering by match-makers, and so on.

Registration of marriages in village Soviets, town registration offices, places of marriage ceremonies is likewise an obligatory part of the marriage ceremony.[8] Thus, in the traditional Mazakh marriage one observes the same phenomena as in the Uzbek : reduction of the rite as a whole due to the dropping of some of its links ; revision of old ritual actions ; and inclusion of new elements characterizing rituals of the Soviet era. The same changes have taken place in traditional ritualism also in other Central Asian republics.[9]

At the next stage in the development of the ritual a number of transformed elements of the traditional wedding, which as a rule have become either elements of game or symbols of good wishes (*i.e.*, devoid of their ancient religious-magic content) are combined with characteristic features of a new national non-religious wedding—solemn registration of marriage, marriage festivities attended, contrary to tradition, by the groom and bride, their parents and other relatives, friends, men and women together. However, the above-mentioned *nikokh* still takes place, but, in contravention of the tradition, in isolation from the wedding, in secrecy as it were. Usually the performance of this act is explained as a tribute of respect to older relatives who still entertain religious convictions.

Lastly, there is a new form of national wedding known in the region under the name of "red wedding" (*kizil-tui*) or "wedding in a new way" (*yangicha tui*). It retains in a modified form a number of features of the traditional wedding in the customary congratulations and felicitations with their traditional symbolism, in the artistic decoration of ceremonies in the order of their sequences, and so on. However, the basis of the ceremony is the ritual of solemn registration of marriage ; the wedding feast has new forms and takes place with the participation of people of different ages, men and women, with the groom and bride sitting at the head of the table. The Moslem ritual of marriage is already gone, as are the social life survivals of the *kalym* type and the custom of avoidance.

There are marriage ceremonies in which there is a smaller connection still with the old wedding : YCL youth and student weddings taking place mostly at public premises. Their national colouring is expressed more in the national professional forms of art and partly in the national meals during feastings. They are non-religious and do not contain any negative social and everyday survivals.

Thus, the series of wedding ceremonies described here testifies to the gradual disappearance of the religious element from marriage ritualism and its transformation into a non-religious ritual, which is one of the manifestations of the secularization of social consciousness. Old elements of the ritual are replaced by new ones. Thus, at first the solemn registration of marriage takes place in isolation from the wedding ritual and then becomes its organic component. The case of the religious rite is reversed—being an organic part of the traditional wedding, it gets divorced from the ritual and is totally absent at the last stage in the development of the ritual.

The transformation of the traditional wedding ritual takes place at the grassroots—people themselves abandon archaic customs and seek new forms of the ritual. Purposeful activity aimed at evolving new festive occasions and civil rituals and spreading them in everyday life merely contributes to the process.

As already mentioned, special work in the field of ritualism conducted in our country is explained by the fact that old forms of ritualism have come into contradiction with new relations in the family, the changed status of women, the cultural level, and the entire pattern of modern life. Here are a few examples to illustrate the point in the case of Uzbekistan.

In Uzbekistan the house is no longer divided into the *ichkari* and *tashkari*, that is the men's and women's halves. In the family and in production men and women are not isolated from one another. But traditional festivities of the family cycle meals were served separately for men and women. Equally discordant with new family relations was the custom to separate the bride from the guests by a ritual curtain during the wedding. Uzbek women have long ago parted with the *paranja* and *chachvan* as well as other veils with which they concealed their faces during meetings with men in the street or at home in the presence of the husband's senior relatives. These discrepancies called for a speedy formation of new rites.

The first experiments in the development of new rites were undertaken after the revolution, when "red weddings", "October celebrations" and other festive occasions began to be held. They greatly differed from traditional rituals and therefore were not popular among the masses. Nonetheless, they gave an example that family celebrations could be held in a different way than earlier.

The activity to develop and popularize non-religious rites continued in subsequent years. It was particularly stepped up in the 1950s and 1960s, when, following the rehabilitation of the war-ravaged national economy, there was a revival of ritual life, especially in old traditional forms. It was guided by special methodological councils, usually under the auspices of the "Znaniye" Society and under the control of the Ministries of Culture. These activities in towns and the countryside were carried on by special ritual commissions. These commissions included party, YCL and trade union workers and representatives of the scientific and intellectual community. They worked in close contact with Houses of Amateur Folk Art, Palaces of Culture in towns, district, and regions. Commissions worked out scenarios of new red-letter days and civil rituals which were put to the test at Palaces of Culture and Wedding Palaces (opened at that time in many towns) and so-called Homes of Happiness which were more abundant in rural areas. New rituals were widely reported in the press, over the radio and television, and also in fiction. Not only members of commissions but also anyone who wished and who made his suggestions could participate in the creation of new rituals. Many enthusiasts came forward. A considerable role in this work was played by scientists, especially ethnographers.

In the 1950s and 1960s the main attention was paid to developing new public festivities and rituals. In Central Asia and, in particular, in Uzbekistan, they included the harvest festivity (*khosil bairami*) or cotton festivity (*pakhta bairami*), musk melon celebration (*kavun saili*), various public ceremonies (issue of the first passport, send-off for service in the army, the ceremony of worker qualification, etc.) and civil rituals related to family life (solemn registration of a marriage, birth of a child, civil funeral). They have become part and parcel of everyday life, forming the foundation of new family festivities. But each ritual of the family cycle, apart from the official act, is a festive feasting which was formerly accompanied by various customs and rites and specific entertainment.

In those years the press propagated YCL youth weddings with the aim of fostering new forms of festivities differing from traditional forms. The ceremonial of such weddings was created by the participants themselves or commissions mentioned earlier. Weddings were held at town Palaces of Culture, collective-farm orchards, Homes of Happiness, and so on. In their procedure they differed sharply from traditional weddings and did not reproduce the old ceremonial. Naturally, they were free from any religious elements. Entertainment was provided by participants in amateur art groups. It was at such weddings that feasting round a common table began to be introduced according to a custom widespread among the majority of the population of the country. At these weddings the bride and the groom sat at the head of the table. YCL weddings were organized by representative of management and public organizations of enterprise, collective farm or educational institution where the newly-weds worked or studied. But these weddings gained ground with difficulty as at the instance of the older relatives such weddings were preceded, or followed, by a wedding according to the traditional rules.

Studies show that the majority of the population in the national republics have declared in favour of the new non-religious ritual, a ritual without *kalym* and other customs of the past but which preserved a certain national colouring.[10] Thus, the example of ritualism clearly shows a tendency towards the ultimate overcoming of the religiosity of the population and simultaneous preservation of national features of culture.

Summing up, let us formulate the basic aspects characterizing the formation of new ritualism. As can be seen, the formation of new non-religious family ritualism consists of two basic interconnected processes. One of them is the transformation of traditional ritualism carried out by the population itself under the impact of social, economic national, political, and cultural changes in our society. These transformations signify the gradual disappearance of many elements of traditional ritualism (above all, those connected with religion) which have come into contradiction with the new social pattern of archaic traditions, and also reconceptualization of many persisting ritual actions. Another process is the rise and gradual incorporation into a transformed ritual of new customs and rituals established in course of socialist construction and created to a large extent, thanks to the purposeful activity of public organizations. The interplay of these two processes gives rise to new ceremonies in content and form which, however, retain national specifics and, at the same time, have features common to all peoples of the USSR. National specific features of new ceremonies embrace progressive elements of traditional rituals incorporated into new rites, while their common features embrace civil rituals and new customs appearing in the first place in urban culture and based on new morality reflecting the equality of people of different nationalities, equality of the sexes, and on a new world outlook which has no room for religious ideology. The process of formation of new non-religious rituals passes through a number of stages reflecting the gradual liberation of the consciousness of the masses from the influence of religion, that is, the process of secularization of social consciousness.

These stages are as follows (as exemplified by wedding ritualism): first the traditional wedding ritual is gradually transformed ; at the next stage observance of the traditional wedding ceremony is accompanied by parallel celebration of weddings according to a new pattern ; then the elements of the traditional wedding gradually merge with new customs born in the Soviet age when further loss is observed of old traditions which lose their social foundation parallel to the erosion of religious rituals, both Islamic and surviving earlier forms of religion ; and lastly, a new non-religious ritual emerges, which retains national colouring but includes elements of the folk ritual in its local variant. The next stage will evidently consist in the elaboration of unified forms of national ritual.[11] On the basis of the general trends in the development of modern culture in our country, it may be assumed that simultaneously further loss will be observed of traditional features of ritualism coupled with the multiplication of new country-wide features, first of all in towns, which is bound to lead ultimately to the creation of country-wide ritual forms.

In this report an attempt has been made to examine the process of formation of new rites through the example of wedding ritualism. It should be pointed out that the intensity of this process differs in different cycles of family ritualism. The greatest persistence of old forms is observed in the ceremonies of the funeral-memorial cycle.

NOTES AND REFERENCES

1-2. See L.A. Anokhina, M.H. Shmelyova. *Kulturn i byt Kolkhoznikov Kalinikskoi oblasti* (Culture and Everyday Life of Collective Farmers of the Kalinin region), Moscow, 1964; *Byt gorodskogo naseleniya Srednei polosy RSFSR v proshlom i pastoyashchem* (Everyday life of the Urban Population of the Central Zone of the RSFSR in the Past and Present), Moscow, 1977, pp. 282-93 ; I.V. Sukhanov, *Obychai, traditsii i preyemstvennost pokoleniy* (Customs, Traditions, and the Continuity of Generations), Moscow, 1976, pp. 100-1 ; I.A. Kryvelev, Sovremenniye obryady i rol etnograficheskoi nauki v ikh izuchenii, formirovanii i vnedrenii (Modern Rituals and the Role of Ethnographic Science in Their Study Formation and Introduction)—*Sovetskaya ethnografiya*, No. 5, 1977.

3-4. See G.P. Snesarev. *Relikty domusulmanskikh verovaniy i obryadovykh perezhitkov u uzbekov Khorezma* (Relics of Pre-Moslem Beliefs and Rites among Uzbeks of Khorezm), Moscow, 1969, pp. 334 O.A. Sukhareva, *et.al.*, *Islam v Uzbekistane* (Islam in Uzbekistan), Tashkent, 1960.

5. G.P. Snesarev ; O nekotorykh prichinakh sokhraneniya religiozno-bytovykh perezhitkov u uzbekov Khorezma (On Some Causes of the Preservation of Religious Everyday Survivals among Uzbeks of Khorezm)—*Sovetskaya etnografiya*, No. 2, 1957 ; I. Dzhabarov. *Borba idyot za cheloveka* (The Struggle is Going on for Man)—*Do uma i serdtsa kazhdogo* (Reaching the Mind and Heart of Everyone),

Tashkent, 1968 ; *Obschestvenny progress byt i religiya* (Social Progress, Everyday Life and Religion), Tashkent, 1973.

6. Y.S. Smirnova, Traditsii i innovatsii *v* razvitii semeinoi obryadnosti (po materialam Severnogo Kavkaza) (Traditions and innovations in the Development of Family Ritualism/On the Basis of the Materials of the Northern Caucasus/)—Report at the Ninth Congress of Anthropological and Ethnological Sciences (Chicago, 1973), Moscow, 1973 ; B.M. Alimova, Brak i svadebniye obychai kumykov *v* proshlom i nastoyashchem (konets XIX-XX vv.) (Marriage and Marriage Customs among Kumyks in the Past and Present/the End of the 19th and 20th Centuries/), Moscow, 1977, synopsis of candidate's thesis ; M.Y. Endzele, Someiniye obryady latyshskogo gorodskogo naseleniya v XX v. (Family Rituals of the Lettish Urban Population in the 20th Century), Moscow, 1973, (synopsis of candidate's thesis) ; L.S. Khristolyubova, Semeiniye obryady udmurtov (Family Rituals of Udmurts) (Experiment in Quantitative Characterization), Moscow, 1970 (synopsis of candidate's thesis). N.I. Shatinova, Semya narodov Yuzhnoi Sibiri V svete Sovremennykh etnicheskikh protsessov (na primere altaitsev) (Family Among the Peoples of Southern Siberia as Exemplified by the People of Altai), Moscow, 1978 (synopsis of candidate's thesis).
N.P. Lobachyova, O. formirovanii novoi obryadnosti u narodov SSSR (on the Formation of new Rituals Among the Peoples of the USSR)—*Sovetskaya etnografiya*, No. 4, 1973.
7. I. Dzhabarov, Obshchestvenny progress, byt i religiya ; N.P. Lobachyova, Formirovaniye novoi obryadnosti uzbekov (Formation of New Rituals Among Uzbeks), Moscow, 1975 ; T. Tashbayeva, Traditionniye komponenty v sovremennoi uzbekskoi svadbe (Traditional Components of the Modern Uzbek Wedding). Thesis of reports at a session devoted to the results of field ethnographic and anthropological investigations in 1974/1975, Dushanbe, 1976.
8. Kh. Argynbayev, Semya i brak u kazakhov (Family and Marriage Among Kazakhs), Alma-Ata, 1973 (in the Kazakh language) ; Svadba i svadebniye obryady u kazakhov v proshlom i nastoyashchem (Marriage and Marriage Rituals Among Kazakhs in the Past and at Present)—*Sovetskaya etnografiya*, No. 6, 1974.
9. See A.T. Bekmuratova, *Byt i semya karakalpakov v proshlom i nastoyashchem* (Everyday Life and Family of Karakalpaks in the Past and at Present), Nukus, 1970 ; Kh. Esbergenov, T. Atamuratov. *Traditsii i ikh preobrazovaniye v gorodskom bytu karakalpakov* (Traditions and Transformation in the Urban Life of Karakalpaks), Nukus, 1975, etc.
10. N.P. Lobachyova, L.A. Tultseva, Traditsii v sovremennoi obryadnosti uzbekov (Traditions in the Modern Rituals of Uzbeks)—*Sovetskaya etnografiya*, No. 6, 1977.
11. D.M. Ugrinovich, *Obryady, Za i protiv* (Rituals. Pros and Contras), Moscow, 1975, p. 158.

The Orthodox Church in the USSR*

L.A. Tultseva

THE ORTHODOX Church was the official religion in Tsarist Russia, being practically part of its state apparatus. It possessed enormous wealth, including land, of which, by 1905, there was over 6.02 million acres. That is why it was no surprise that the decrees of the revolutionary government of the Soviet State, which annulled the privileges the Russian Orthodox Church enjoyed over other religions, had seriously affected the Church's economic and political interests.

"The Decree on Land" (26 October (8 November) 1927), one of the first adopted by the Soviet State, abolished the right of private property with regard to land and declared all land, including that of the church and the monasteries, to be the property of all the people.[1] The decree declared that the most just and equitable solution of the land problem was as follows : "All land, whether state, crown, monastery, church, factory, entailed, private, public, peasant, etc. shall be confiscated

*The present paper's basic aim is to describe the Orthodox Church of the Russians, the Ukranians and the Byelorussians, who comprise the majority of the Orthodox Christian believers in the USSR. The Russian Orthodox Church also includes the believers living north of the European part of the USSR and the northern Urals (the Karelians, the Veps, the Komi and others), in the Volga area (the Udmurts, the Maris, the Mordavians, the Chuvashes), in Siberia (the Khakasses, the Yakuts, the Shortses, part of the Altains, the Buryats), in Moldavia (the Moldavians, the Gagauses), in the Caucasus (part of the Ossetians and of the Abkhasians), as well the gypsies, small numbers of Estonians, Latvians, and others The secularization processes which are at work among the above mentioned peoples are identical with the processes which are currently affecting the Orthodox believers among the Russians, the Ukranians, and the Byelorussians.

without compensation and become the property of the whole people, and pass into the use of all those who cultivate it".[2] "The Decree on Land" reflected the peasantry's age-old dream to achieve full ownership of the land they cultivated.

By its "Declaration of the Rights of the peoples of Russia" of 2(15) November 1917, the Soviet State abolished each and every national and religious privileges and restrictions, thus putting an end to the policy designed to divide the peoples by means of religious and nationalistic ideology and propaganda.

The State-proclaimed equality of the rights of the peoples regardless of their attitude to religion put the other religious communities in the country on an equal footing with the Russian Orthodox Church, thus helping implementation of the principle of religious tolerance and equality frequently put forward by the masses at different stages of history.

From its very inception, the revolutionary Soviet State embarked on a course to make freedom of conscience a reality. An important legislative milestone in this respect was the decree "On the Separation of the Church from the State and of the School from the Church" of 23 January 1918, in whose elaboration V.I. Lenin took an active and direct part. The decree contained a clear definition of the Church's status in the socialist state, setting up a state system of legal guarantees for the exercise of freedom of conscience. The decree's fundamental provisions were as follows:

(1) The Church was separated from the State.

(2) Within the bounds of the Republic, it was prohibited to issue any local laws or ordinances which may hinder or restrict freedom of conscience, enjoyed equally by all citizens, or create any advantages or privileges on the basis of a faith-belonging to citizens.

(3) Every citizen may profess any religion or none at all. All restrictions on the rights of citizens because of their professing or not professing any religion at all were abolished.

The decree made the profession of religion a private matter for each citizen. That is why the decree categorically prohibited any reference to the religion of citizens in official documents.

It also abolished some state functions of the Church (*e.g.*, registration of births, marriages, or divorces), which had formerly been its domain.

Article 9 stated: "The school is separated from the Church". Removing the religious and clerical element from the state system of school education, the decree thus deprived the Church of the possibility of exercising its religious influence on the upbringing of the younger generation.

The young socialist republic inherited from the old Russia not only most involved social but also pressing confessional problems. The democratic principles, respect for the faith and everyday traditions of the people, and concern for the rights and individual freedom of each citizen, proclaimed by the Soviet State in its legislative acts, deprived the Orthodox Church of its erstwhile privileged position. All this could not but affect both the ideological and political orientation of the Orthodox Church.

The loss by the Church of its former wealth and privileges caused the clergy to be hostile to the Soviet State. This opposition in its extreme counter revolutionary manifestation included calls for an active struggle against Soviet power and was headed by Tikhon who was elected Patriarch on the eleventh day following the October Revolution. The Restoration by the Local Council of the institution of Patriarchate, abolished by Peter the Great, was one of the ways to rally the Orthodox clergy in their struggle against the Socialist State. On election day of the Patriarch (5 November 1917, old calendar), an official preacher of the Council spoke of the scope and functions of the new Patriarch as follows: "He is called upon to bring together all the actively believing forces of the people, inspiring them to exploits in the service of the centuries-old precepts on which Russia had been built and lived."[3] These "precepts" are well-known: they are the orthodoxy, absolute monarchy, nationality and exploitation of all non-Russian peoples.[4] The activities of the new Patriarch turned out to be politically oriented towards restoring the monarchy: he contributed to turning the Church into a political organization, which fought Soviet power under the banner of the Orthodox Church, actively supported counter-revolution and anathematized Soviet power, opposing the Soviet government's decree on the confiscation of a part of the Church's wealth to purchase grain to feed the fourteen million famine-stricken population of the Volga area.

These compromising activities of the church leaders caused an active resurgence of the so-called Renovation movement which had, prior to the revolution, put forward some principles of religious reformation, which, however, had been denounced by the Church.[5] Under the new conditions, the followers of the Renovation movement came together to form the so-called "Zhivaya Tserkov" (Living Church) under the Higher church administration headed by Archbishop Antonin (Granovsky). "The Living Church" demanded Tikhon's resignation, an end to the Orthodox Church's counter-revolutionary activities, and recognition of the new state system. It also proposed to update the church canons. The loyal political attitude of the "Living Church" to Soviet power gave rise to sympathy among believers and representatives of the Orthodox clergy. But as regards religious reforms, there was lack of unanimity among the Renovation followers. Some of them favoured radical changes in the doctrine and practices of the Orthodox Church, while the moderate wing sought to avoid an intra-church schism. The most viable element within the Renovation movement proved to be the "Union of Communists of the old Apostolic church "headed by Metropolitan A.I. Vyedensky. The Union's programme provided for updating the canons and reforming the ethic principles of the Orthodox Church as well as simplifying its complicated liturgical procedures.

In the spring of 1923, in the conditions of a schism within the Orthodox Church, the Local Council of the Renovation Church was convened. The decisions adopted by the Council proved to be symptomatic in many respects. In the first place, the Renovation Church Council adopted an appeal to the Soviet government declaring the Church's readiness to do its utmost to implement the great beginnings of the October Revolution.[6] The Renovation Council annulled Tikhon's anathematising of Soviet power and announced to its adepts Tikhon's removal from the post of Patriarch. With regard to the reform programme of the Living Church the Renovation Local Council in the conditions of 1923, did not dare to approve them. The reason was that the overwhelming mass of the rank-and-file believers and the lower clergy was not ready to accept canonical and liturgical innovations. Besides, Patriarch Tikhon's new tactics undermined the position of the Renovators. In his messages of 1923 and 1925, Tikhon dissociated himself from counter-revolutionary forces and proclaimed the necessity to depoliticize the Church, thus, contributing to the return to the old Orthodox Church of many of its followers. Tikhon declared the decisions of the 1923 Renovation Local Council to be non-canonical. In subsequent years there emerged a trend towards narrowing the gap between the Renovators and the Patriarchate, which brought about their final reunification after the Great Patriotic War.

In assessing the historical significance of the Renovation trend in the Russian Orthodox Church in the twenties, researchers correctly state that it stimulated the process first of political and then of ideological evolution of the Orthodox Church in adjusting itself to the socialist society. The Church reformers of the twenties were the first to formulate the required basic adjustment for the Church under socialism, which were subsequently developed and implemented by the Russian Orthodox Church when it had overcome its Renovation schism.[7]

Complex processes were also at work among the rank-and-file believers in the twenties. First, one must point out that by the time of the October Revolution, the Church had already compromised its reputation as the owner of enormous wealth and a major exploiter. The clergy's open greed satisfied through imposition of high taxes and unbridled high interest money-lending caused a sharp anti-clerical sentiment among various strata of the population. The counter-revolutionary activities pursued by a part of the clergy in the civil war further intensified the anti-clerical feeling. V.D. Bontach-Bruevich, a prominent figure of the Soviet State, gave a vivid description of the attitude to the clergy in the first days following the October Revolution :

> Everywhere, without exception, the representatives of the Orthodox Church, all these numerous priests and senior priests, metropolitans, church hierarchs, ordained and non-ordained monks, all of them immediately came to feel the burning breath of a genuine proletarian revolution. Nobody

> now paid them even a token respect. On the contrary, they were openly and definitely called the enemies of the people, for centuries long they resisted and suppressed any cultural stirrings, especially among the masses. The fact was emphasized by all the socialist newspapers and magazines, by speakers at numerous meetings. The struggle was waged everywhere to expel these greedy "community spongers" from all public organizations ...[8]

The October Revolution and the civil war had seriously undermined the prestige of the Church as a social institution.

> "Millions of people lost faith in the Church as a perceptor and counsellor in social and political matters. For the believers, the role of the Church as the carrier of a certain world outlook, morality and some specific forms of emotional experience had by now become separated from that of a preceptor in worldly affairs. The latter, first of all, included matters of state power, home and forign policy and of the social undertakings. But it was being realised in the course of socialist construction".[9]

In everyday life of the people the gap between the old patterns of behaviour, relying on religious and patriarchal traditions, and the new principles of collective activities, based on a new non-religious world outlook, was mostly felt.

The social and class structure of the population of that time was another major factor adding to the complexity of the situation. One has to take account of the important fact, that the early post-revolutionary years did not produce a radical qualitative change in the traditional alignments of the various social strata within the peasant class. The age-old traditions of life of the pre-revolutionary village came into complex relationship and interaction with the revolutionary transformations and the new trends in social, economic and cultural life. Observations of the local lore students of those years reveal the desire of some groups of believers to assess socialist transformations from a Christian point of view. The following is a report from the district of Kasimov, dating back to 1924 :

> Now, one hardly hears any talk about the saints of the events from the sacred history... In everyday life, it is, perhaps, some of the older persons who would, though rarely, refer to the life of a saint... It seems as if the older people are obeying an 'urge' to comprehend our times which baffle them by recalling one religious prophecy or another.[10]

The attempt to comprehend the new life from the position of Christianity was natural for peasants, whose world outlook had been shaped by the reality of old Russia. This general tendency has deep historical roots consisting of socio-religious utopias, and some of the ideas of Christian socialism.

The attitude of people to the Church and to religious rites has been complex and very often contradictory. The younger generation, highly receptive to everything new and progressive, were frequently, apt to follow centuries-old traditions. Cultural and economic transformations could not instantly affect everyday life and change people's consciousness. That is why in rural areas such traditions as baptizing, church marriages and funerals, were still generally practised, religious holidays were widely observed, and cross-bearing processions and public prayers were organized to mark the beginning of the cattle-grazing or sowing season as well as in case of droughts, epidemics or epizootics. Such public prayers were more frequent in agricultural areas. But very indicative are the local lore students' observations that, for example, a public prayer in the fields was marked by "a lack of inner conviction (among the participants—L.T.) as to the usefulness of the ceremony" (1923), and that during such prayers "the younger people feel ill at ease being obliged to walk across the field" (1928).[11]

The agrarian calendar rites, being closely interlinked with the Orthodox cult, have preserved some magic and sacral elements. The calendar rites in the twenties were practised in varying degrees by the various peoples of the USSR. They were, perhaps, most diffused among the Russians, while being preserved in their most traditional form by the peoples whose Christianization was less obvious (the Karelians, the Veps, the Komi the Komi-Permyaks, the Udmurts and others). In the twenties a relative decline is observed in the conduct of religious rites. A partial preservation of the calendar rites, syncretized with the Orthodox cult and some of its canons, was mainly due to such a socio-economic factor as the fragmentation of small-scale peasant households each of which had an economic life of its own thus contributing to the preservation of the traditional way of life with its prejudices, rites, and notions.

By 1929, while socialist forms of production were already dominant in industry, agriculture still remained predominantly a small commodity economy, based on private small-scale farms. The limited possibilities of small-scale commodity production in agriculture did not keep pace with the rates of industrial growth. That is why agriculture's transition to large-scale, socialized production (through co-operation and collectivization) became an objective necessity. It was through such a transition that the contradiction could be eliminated between socialist industry and small-commodity agriculture, and a rise in agricultural production could be ensured.

Religion became the chief ideological weapon for the groups which opposed the socialist transformations. It is in this period that the so-called "holy letters" began to be spread in rural areas with the purpose of obstructing the progress of civilization or hindering a particular collective farm activity like the storing of forge and harvesting, or even against a campaign to protect people's health (*e.g.*, vaccination against small-pox, or other epidemic diseases). In their struggle against collectivization, the anti-social forces widely resorted to the fabrication of "miracles". Rumours were spread about auto-renovation of church cupolas and ikons, of weeping or singing ikons, appearances of the Virgin, various saints and Christ himself, of crosses falling from the skies, unusual lunar eclipses, inextinguishable icon lamps, etc.[12] As a rule, however, all of this failed to produce the desired effect.

The construction of socialism in the twenties and the thirties, involving large numbers of believers, became the major factor contributing to undermining the social roots of religion. The successes scored in the twenties in the propagation of the materialist weltanschauung and of atheism or "godlessness" (as was the term employed in those days) were quite significant.

The dynamics of departure from religion and the propagation of atheism amongst the peasantry during the reconstruction of the national eonomy can be seen from the following table.[13]

Age groups	Percentage of persons observing religious rites and holidays			
	Males		Females	
	Individual peasants 1922-23	Collective farmers 1934	Individual peasants 1922-23	Collective farmers 1934
Up to 24 years	62.6	1.0	71.5	12.2
25-39 years	71.4	3.2	100.0	26.5
40-59 years	100.0	14.5	100.0	47.9

The general decline in the numbers of believers, in the observance of rites (such as baptizing, church marriages, communions, etc.) and in the observance of the patron saints, days and other religious holidays caused a sharp reduction in the incomes of the church parishes. In these conditions, some churches were closed down, particularly in those areas where their numbers exceeded the requirements of the local population.

It happened sometimes that the matter of closing down local churches was not given adequate consideration. At times, misjudgement of the real religious situation caused church closures when these could have been avoided. But here one has to take account of the pent-up anti-religious feeling in the masses. A.V. Lunacharsky, the first people's commissar for education and a prominent figure in the Soviet State, justly pointed out that "a people's revolution cannot help being accompanied by outbursts of revengeful feeling pent-up in the long-exploited and plundered people against the dominant classes. Hence, the natural and spontaneous resentment with regard to the life style of these dominant classes".[14]

The spontaneous resentment of the people was also directed against the Church which was a true servant of the exploiting classes. This, however, does not imply an intentional line in the use of violence with regard to religion. On the contrary, the party and the Soviet government repeatedly condemned violations of legislation on cults. Here is, for example, an extract from a resolution adopted by the 13th Congress of the Russian Communist Party (RCP(B) 1924) on the work in rural areas : "It is necessary to resolutely do away with any attempts to fight religious prejudices by administrative measures such as closure of churches, mosques, synagogues, Roman Catholic churches, prayer-houses, etc. Anti-religious propaganda in rural areas must be exclusively conducted through materialistic explanation of the natural and social phenomena the peasant comes in touch with".[15] In this connection, it should be remembered that one of the first decrees promulgated by Soviet power was on the preservation of the cultural heritage of the past. Protection of cultural monuments (including those of religious architecture and arts) was assumed by the State. This principle is now enshrined in the new Constitution of the USSR : "Concern for the preservation of historical monuments and other cultural values is a duty and obligation of citizens of the USSR" (Article 68).

The new socio-historical and cultural-ideological situation served as a basis for restructuring social and family life to liberate it from religious traditions, customs, and rites. The religious holidays and rites were replaced by new, civic holidays and rites which reflected the revolutionary enthusiasm of those days, the powerful labour upsurge and the successes scored in socialist construction. Gaining wide recognition at that time were such rites as the "Octoberist" rite, that is, when newly borns were registered without being baptized, the "Red" weddings (outside the church) and civic funerals. Anniversaries of the Great October Socialist Revolution, May day and the Red Army Day came to be widely observed. From 1929, the rural population began marking Collectivization Day and the Harvest Day. Industrialization Days, that is 6 August and 25 December 1929, were marked by great labour achievements (the latter was organized on the initiative of workers of major enterprises on Christmas Day).

In those tense times, imbued with the spirit of revolutionary romanticism, young people took an active part in the work of liberating the consciousness of the people from religious ideas and traditions. Participation of young workers and peasants in industrialization, collectivization of agriculture, the cultural revolution, and in all the major projects of the early five year plans was of no small importance in spreading mass atheism among the young people of that time.[16]

The successes of the Soviet State both in the international arena and on the home front (including the achievements of collectivization), also profoundly influenced the Orthodox Church and the thinking of the clergy. In these circumstances, some of the clergy made an attempt to adapt religion to the new form of life: "Collective farms are created according to the holy writings and to God's will and we are not against your participating them", the Orthodox priests were saying to their parishioners, "but you should not forget the Church".[17] The new socialist reality also caused some reassessment of values in the content of prayers. The Church adopted a new approach to such questions as the importance of labour, woman's role in social life, and religion's attitude to the social order.

Further softening of the earlier frictions between the Orthodox Church and the Soviet State followed in the period of the Great Patriotic War. From the very start of the war, the Church authorities and all the clergy took a patriotic stand. The Church launched a major propagandistic campaign contributing to the country's defence : it spread patriotic messages among believers, organized church services for the triumph of Russian arms, thus boosting the morale of believers, and organized collections of offerings for the needs of the front. Representatives of the Russian Orthodox clergy, including Metropolitan Nikolai of Kolomna and Krutitsy, took an active part in the work of the Extraordinary State Commission, set up in 1942 to investigate the crimes perpetuated by the fascists on the occupied territories.

However, there were some clergymen who betrayed their motherland and collaborated with the enemy. This was mostly the case on the territories temporarily occupied by the fascist invaders. The fascists opened up nearly 10,000 churches intending to use them as a political weapon in the war against the Soviet State. But they failed. The majority of the Orthodox clergy on the occupied territories either remained neutral or secretly sympathized with and assisted the liberation struggle waged by the Soviet people.[18]

The enormous hardships of the war years and of the period of reconstruction of the national economy somewhat slowed down the process of the withering away of religion. There was even some partial resurgence of religious feeling among some sections of the population who sought consolation because of the loss of their near and dear ones in the war. Nonetheless, the erosion of the religious consciousness of orthodox believers continued which is borne out by a number of sociological studies undertaken in recent years.

The essential difference in the composition of the Orthodox parish in the twenties and at present is worth noticing. Formerly, the membership of the orthodox community was highly heterogeneous in its social and demographic composition, whereas, today the body of believers is rather homogeneous : these are mostly old people, the majority of whom are women. As a rule, these people have little or no education and are mostly employed in unskilled jobs.

On the whole, for instance, according to the findings of a 1968 study undertaken in the Penza Region, "28.4 per cent of the people surveyed preserved, to a greater or lesser degree, their ties with the Russian Orthodox Church. Their share is reduced to 10-12 per cent if one considers active faith respondents (*i.e.*, those who observe regular fasting ; confessions, or daily praying both in church and at home)".[19] Basically, the situation is similar in other regions. Of interest, for example, is the data characterizing the dynamics of the religiousness in the Voronezh region from 1917 to 1972 : 1917—81 per cent believers ; 1927—73 per cent ; 1937—47 per cent ; 1945—37 per cent ; 1961—26 per cent ;[20] 1972—about 20 per cent.[21] It is well known that there are many more believers among the rural population as compared to the urban. Thus, the study conducted in the Penza region revealed that about 18 per cent of the population of the city of Penza were either full believers or believers with some reservations as compared to nearly 40 per cent in the rural areas.[22] A survey conducted in the city of

Pskov revealed that 87 per cent of citizens rejecting religion had diversified social interests and spiritual requirements and took an optimistic view of life.[23] Similar data were characteristic of other regions of the country.[24] Despite the specific local conditions in each of these regions, the general trends in the process are more or less uniform.

Of some importance in assessing these general trends is such a charcteristic as the degree of conviction on the part of the believer in the truth of his views. Studies on the present level of religiousness suggest different classifications of believer groups.[25] A simple classification, adequately reflecting the real situation, distinguishes between confirmed, ordinary, and hesitant believers. The first are consistent believers whose behaviour is determined by religious principles. The religious and non-religious notions of an "ordinary" believer are interwoven and, in a sense, mutually balanced. The consciousness of such believers combines a belief in the after-life with the reality of this world, a belief in God with real life orientations, and reliance on their own abilities, knowledge and practical experience. The world outlook of hesitant believers contains some religious notions but the place they occupy in their consciousness is insignificant. The distribution of Orthodox believers in these groups is very indicative : the first group comprises about 10 per cent the second 55 to 60 per cent whereas third 30 to 35 per cent.[26] These figures are very important. They testify to the erosion and instability of religious beliefs among the Orthodox Church followers. In fact, the present-day believers practically lack any canonical knowledge (no definite notion of the idea of God and the trinity, no knowledge of the lives of the saints, vague notions of Christian demonology, etc.). At present, religious beliefs have more to do with everyday life than with the knowledge of Church dogmas. Another essential fact is that each new generation reproduces less religiousness than the previous. This brings about a progressive secularization of the Orthodox cult. Take for example the icon, the indispensable attribute of the Orthodox cult. Its perception in the last several decades has significantly eroded (among the believers), bringing about a complete rejection (among the hesitant) of the iconographic symbols. At present the owners of icons, are, as a rule almost completely ignorant of the sacral symbolism of the sacred images they keep. But the most important fact is that a considerable part of today's believers do not think it necessary to worship them.

Another indication of the qualitative erosion into religious feeling is that fewer numbers of people fast. "The non-observance of fasting by most believers reflects the weakening of their faith in after-life and God-preordained destiny, which narrows the sphere of religious motivation".[27] Believers themselves are sometimes inclined to justify the non-observance of an obligatory religious precept by a reassessment of their moral values (adducing, for example, the argument that fasting may be dispensed with since food does not corrupt man and that observance of the moral principles of collective life is most important). Also important for an adequate evaluation of the secularization processes is the fact that the new social and cultural forms have penetrated even the sacral periods of fasting. For example, in March, the International Women's Day often coincides with Lent, which, however, does not prevent people, regardless of their attitude to religion, to mark the occasion in ways hardly reminiscent of fasting.

Also significant is the changed role of such traditional precepts of the Orthodox cult as attending church, communion and confession, saying prayers, and so on. Adherence to these is now limited to the framework of some families and within them to some individuals mostly of the older generation.

Perhaps the most important Orthodox rite is that of baptism because through it man joins the Orthodox community. A significant feature is that, compared with the past, the religious notions that go with this rite have grown rather dim. Now it is very rare for a participant in the rite to have even a vague idea of its chief sacral purpose, that is, of purifying the newly-born of "original sin". Still vaguer is the knowledge of the end purpose of baptizing which according to the Orthodox doctrine is to enable one to enter the "kingdom of heaven". The findings of sociological studies reveal that of the rite's participants only 8 to 12 per cent are true believers baptizing their children out of religious convictions.[28] The findings of a study conducted among workers in the city of Gorky show that people perform the rite because they perceive it as an ancient national custom or a tradition which should be preserved.

This was the opinion expressed by 25.5 per cent skilled and 33.1 per cent unskilled workers polled.[29]

A prominent place is still occupied by customs and rites connected with funeral ceremonies and repasts. The influence of some phenomena of traditional social psychology is especially felt in this sphere. On the other hand, church weddings, another church rite of a different emotional character is now performed rarely.

At present, the religious content of holidays has, in many respects, been lost, but there still lingers the tradition of family meetings and feasting on religious holidays. This circumstance is an important factor keeping alive the tradition of religious holidays not only among the believers but also among those who have no contact with religion. Some elements of the agrarian calendar and church-proper holidays, are not only preserved but also endowed with a new content. They are perceived not as religious holidays but rather as those emerging out of popular tradition, as rites to be performed on certain days of the year. That is why the elements of entertainment and emotional and aesthetic features are predominant in them. Examples are the facetious fortune-telling, young people indulge in on Christmas Eve or on the Twelfth day, the ritual feasts during Easter, adorning homes with birch-tree branches, flowers or grasses on Whitsunday, ablutions on Ivan's Day, and so on.

On the whole, Russian Orthodox Christianity, while upholding its stand of traditionalism, has nevertheless reflected the present-day social reality in its canonical sermons, instructions and evaluations. Influenced by the rapid socio cultural transformations occurring in our society which has built a developed and mature socialism, Christianity is stepping up its efforts to elaborate the concept of "the Church's social activities". According to this concept, the church is called upon to support and propagate the social principles of socialism and communism. From a historical viewpoint, such a concept is not new or original since the religious systems at various historical stages had as a rule absorbed the prevailing socio-political and, partly, scientific doctrines, which helped them to a certain extent to keep pace with the times.

Under mature and developed socialism, there dominates a scientific-materialist, atheist weltanschauung. The profound and broad processes of secularization at work in socialist society exercise their influence on the world outlook, psychology and behaviour of all believers, including the Orthodox followers. But religion has still managed to retain some of its influence over certain groups of the population.

Finally, we would like to stress an important conclusion which may be deduced from the actual process of the socio-cultural construction in the USSR, namely, that neither racial, national, language, religious, nor any other difference has become a barrier obstructing the socio-economic and cultural development of the peoples of our country. Internationalism and equality of peoples, proclaimed as principles of state policy have strengthened the spiritual unity of the nations and nationalities of the USSR. And this unity is the guarantee of the Soviet State's further progress along the path of social development.

NOTES AND REFERENCES

1. It should be noted that the confiscation of the property of the church and monasteries in favour of the State was not an isolated case in the history of the Orthodox Church. On numerous occasions the church's property had been secularized by the Tsars, *ukases* (*i.e.*, edicts). Thus, in 1764 Catherine II annexed from the Church for the State over 900 thousand serfs with their land.
2. 'O religii i tserkvi. Sbornik vyskazivanij klassikov marxisma-leninizma, dokumentov KPSS i Sovetskogo gosudarstva, (the classics of Marxism-Leninism, documents of the CPSU and the Soviet State), Moscow, 1977, p. 91.
3. 'Denyaniya Svyaschennogo Sobora pravoslavnoj tserkvi, (Acts of the Holy Synod of the Orthodox Church), Book III, Petersburg, 1918, p. 116., cited from: Platonov N. F., Pravoslavnaya tserkov' v 1917-1935 gg.—*Ezhegodnik Muzeya istorii religii i ateizma* (The Orthodox Church in 1917-1935. Annals of the Museum of the history of religion and atheism), V, Moscow-Leningrad, 1961, p.212.
4. *Ibid.*
5. For more details see: Titlinov B. V., *Tserkov vo vremya revolutsii* (The Church during the Revolution), Petrograd, 1924; Kurochkin P.K., *Evoljutsiya sovremennogo russkogo pravoslaviya* (Evolution of the contemporary Russian Orthodoxy), Moscow, 1971, p. 55-84.

6. Deyaniya II Vserossijskogo pomestnogo cobora pravoslavnoj tserkvi' (Acts of 2nd All-Russian Local Council of the Orthodox Church),. Moscow, 1923, p. 4, cited from: P.K. Kurcchkin, *op. cit.*, p. 72.
7. P.K. Kurcchkin, *op. cit.*, p. 76.
8. V.D. Bontch-Bruevich *Izbrannye sochineniya* (Selected Works) T., I., Moscow, 1959, p. 255-56.
9. E I. Lisavtsev, *Kritika burzhuaznoy fal' sifikatsii polozheniya religii v SSSR* (On bourgeois falsifications of the status of religion in the USSR) Moscow, 1975, p. 134.
10. Ryazanskiy oblastnoj kraevedcheskiy muzej. Etnlogicheskij arkhiv Obschestva issledovatelej Ryazanskogo kraya (District lore museum of the Ryazan' oblast. Ethnological Archive of the Society of researchers of the Ryazan krai). Book I, No. 10.
11. *Ibid.* Book III, No.61; Book VIII, No. 188; Book XII, No. 289.
12. V. Shishakov, Religiozno-kulackcye vreditel, stvo v derevne (Religious-Kulak sabotage in the village) in *Antireligioznik* (Anti-religious journal), 1930, No.8-9, p. 26.
13. G.V. Vorontsov, Strcitel' stvo socialisma v SSSR i massovij otkhod trudyaschikhsja ot religii (Construction of socialism in the USSR and mass falling back of the toilers from religion), in *Voprosy nauchnogo ateizma* (Questions of scientific atheism), Issue 4, Moscow, 1967, p. 47.
14. A.V. Lunacharsky Pochemu nel 'zya verit' v boga? (Why is it impossible to believe in God?) in *Izbrannye ateisticheskiye proizvedeniya* (Selected atheistic works), Moscow, 1965, p. 373.
15. Cited from: 'O religii i tsrkvi. Sbornik vyskazivaniy klassikov marxisma-leninizma, dokumentov KPSS i Sovetskogo gosudarstva' (On the religion and Church. A collection of quotations from the classics of Marxism-Leninism, documents of the CPSU and the Soviet State), Moscow, 1977, p. 63.
16. For more details see: I.A. Galitskaya, E.G. Filimonov, R.V. Ghekryzheva, Objektivniye i subjektivniye faktory formirovaniya massovogo ateizma sovetskoj mologyezhi (Objective and subjective factors of mass atheism among the Soviet youth); in *Molodyezh i ateism*) (The youth and Atheism), Moscow, 1971, p. 6-21.
17. *Bezbozhnik* (Atheist), July 30, 1931.
18. For more details see: V.E. Titov *Pravoslaviye* (Orthodoxy), Moscow, 1967, p. 117-18.
19. P.K. Kurochkin, *op. cit.*, p. 93.
20. M.K. Teplyakov, *Problemy ateisticheskogo vospitaniya v praktike partiynoj raboty* (Problems of atheistic upbringing in the Party's practice), Voronezh, 1972, p. 123.
21. A.I. Gerasimov, N.I. Martynenko, *Ideologiya i deyatal'nost, sovremennogo pravoslaviya* (Ideology and practice of contemporary orthodoxy), Voronezh, 1972, 3.
22. A.A. Lebedev, *Sekulyarizatsiya naseleniya sotsialisticheskogo goroda — K obschestvu svobodnomu ot religii* (Secularization of the socialist

urban population— Towards a society without religion), Moscow, 1970, p. 144.

23. N.P. Andrianov, *Evolutsiya religioznogo soznaniya* (Evolution of the religious consciousness), Leningrad, 1974, p. 25.

24. See the following works N.P. Andrianov, R.A. Lopatkin, V.V. Pavlyuk, *Osobennosti sovremennogo religioznogo soznaniya* (Specific features of modern religious consciousness), Moscow, 1966; *Konkretniye issledovaniya sovrenennykh religioznykh verovaniy* (metodika, organizatsiya, rezul'taty) (Concrete studies in contemporary religious beliefs, methods, organization, results), Moscow, 1967; *Chelovek. obschestvo, religiya* (Man, society, religion), Moscow, 1968 ; A.N. Mukhin, *Daninika religioznosti veruyuschikh i ideologicheskaya deyatel' nost' pravoslavnoj tserkvi.* (Dynamics of religiosity among the believers and the ideological practice of the Orthodox Church). Cand. of phil. essay, Moscow, 1969; *K obschestvu, svobodnomu ot religii* (Towards a society without religion). Moscow, 1970 ; E. Duluman, B. Lobovik, *Tancher v. Sovremenniy veruyuschiy* (Contemporary believer). Moscow, 1970 ; *Ateizm i sotsialisticheskaya kul' tura* (Atheism and socialist culture), Moscow, 1971 ; Yu.F. Borunkov, *Struktura religioznogo soznaniya* (Structure of the religious consciousness). Moscow, 1971 ; N.I. Puchkov Vliyaniye vnutriklassovykh izmeneniy v sotsialisticheskom obschestve na razvitiye ateizma mass (Influence of the intra-class changes in socialist society on the development of atheism among the masses). In *Voprosi nauchnogo ateizma* (Questions of scientific atheism), Issue 13, Moscow, 1972 ; L.A. Tultseva, Sotsial' naya struktura i voprosi tradittionnogo povedeniya (Social structure and questions of traditional behaviour). In *Poleyiye issledovaniya Instituta Etnografii* (Field research of the Institute of Ethnography), 1974, Moscow, 1975 ; A.A Lebedev, *Konkretniye issledovaniya v ateisticheskoy rabote* (Concrete research in atheistic work), Moscow, 1976; V.A. Saprykin, *Sotsialisticheskij gorod i ateisticheskoye vospitaniye* (Socialist city and atheistic upbringing), Alma-Ata, 1976; V.V. Pavlyuk, *Psikhologia sovremennikh veruyuschikh i ateisticheskoye vospitaniye* (Psychology of modern believers and atheistic upbringing). Lvov, 1976.

25. See, for example: N.P. Alekseyev, Metodika i rezul 'taty izucheniya religionznossti sel' skogo naseleniya (na materilakh Orlovskoj oblasti) (Methods and resu'ts of studying religiosity among rural population on the materials of the Orel oblast) in *Voprosi nauchnogo ateizma* (Ques/nostion of scientific atheism), Issue 3, Moscow, 1967, p. 135 ; A.A. Lebedev, Sekulyarizatsiya naseleniya sotsialisticheskogo goroda, — *K obschestvu, svobodnomu ot religii* (Secularization of the socialist urban population,— Towards a society without religion), Moscow, 1970, p. 134-36.

26. E. Duluman, B. Lobovik, V. Tancher, *Sovremenniy veruyuschiy* (Contemporary believer), Moscow, 1970, p. 38-51.

27. L.N. Ulyanov, Opyt issledovaniya motivatsii religioznogo povedeniya (Research experience in the motivation of religious behaviour), in *Voprosy nauchnogo ateizma*, (Questions of scientific atheism), Issue 11, Moscow, 1971, p. 226.
28. D.M. Aptekman, Prichiny zhivuchesti religioznogo obryada kresche-niya v sovremennykh usliviyakh (Causes of tenacity of the religious rite of christening in modern conditions). In *Voprosy filosofii* ('Questions of philosophy'), 1965, No. 3, p. 8 ; L.N. Ulyanov, *op. cit.*, p. 228-29.
29. V.A. Smirnov, Issledovaniye religioznogo obryada kresheniya sredi rabochikh (Studies in the religious rite of Christening among the workers), in *Voprosy nauchnogo ateisma* (Questions of scientific atheism), Issue 5, Moscow, 1968, p. 92.

21

Evolution of Protestant Confessions in the USSR

E.G. Filimonov

SOME few church and sect-type confessions represent Protestantism in the USSR. These are, primarily, the Lutheran Church, the churches of Evangelical Christian Baptists, Methodists, Reformists and the religious bodies of Adventists, Pentecostals and Jehovah's Witnesses.

Lutheranism is mostly spread over the territories of our Baltic republics and, mainly, in Estonia and Latvia where it sprang up as early as in the first quarter of the 16th century. In the second half of the 19th century, which witnesses the process of formation of the Latvian and Estonian bourgeois nations, the influence of Lutheranism grew particularly strong. And, with the bourgeois-democratic revolution of 1917, the semi-feudal Lutheran churches of Estonia and Latvia became bourgeois ones. According to bourgeois statistics, in the early forties 78 per cent of the population in Estonia and 56 per cent in Latvia thought themselves Lutherans.[1] On the eve of World War II the German population of the Baltic republics was repatriated to Germany with the result that on the strength of the changed composition of the believers the Latvian and Estonian churches became national.[2]

Apart from Estonia and Latvia, there are Lutheran communities in Kazakhstan, Kirghizia, and in the Omsk and Novosibirsk regions. Having come into being in the process of migration of the German colonies, these communities consist of Germans.

As the capitalist relations developed and the peasants were introduced to the commodity-money relations, there appeared in Russia some Protestant sects of the Mennonites (at the close of the 18th century), Baptists (in the latter half of the 1860s), Evangelicals (in the 1870s), Adventists (in the 1880s), Pentecostals (in the opening decades of the 20th century) and others. Their proliferation was greatly helped by the missionaries from England, Germany, and the USA.

In the process of their evolution and class differentiation in pre-revolutionary Russia the Baptists, Evangelicals and others lost many of the inherent characteristics of sects and became specifically bourgeois churches. On the eve of the revolution there were over 200,000 Baptists, Evangelicals, and Adventists in this country.[3]

The Evangelical Christian Baptist Church took on its present form in 1944 through uniting the organizations of the Baptists and the Evangelical Christians. In 1945 and 1947 the Union of the Evangelical Christian Baptists was joined by some communities of the Pentecostals, that is, by the Christians of the Evangelical belief and the Apostolic Christians. In 1963, some of the Mennonites joined the Union too. According to the church administration, the organization of the Evangelical Christian Baptists number, at present, more than 500,000 members of many nationalities,[4] including Russian, Ukrainian, Byelorussian, German, Latvian, Estonian, Georgian, Armenian, and Ossetian believers. The Evangelical Christian Baptist, communities are to be found in many regions of the Russian Federation (RSFSR), the Ukraine, Moldavia, Latvia, Estonia, Kazakhstan and other republics of Central Asia, and elsewhere. The church is headed by the All-Union Council of the Evangelical Christian Baptists (AUCECB), whose printed organ is the *Bratski Vestnik* (the Brotherly Herald).

Outside the Union of the Evangelical Christian Baptists there are some Baptist and Evangelical Christian societies which function autonomously (the so-called "Free Baptists"). In the early sixties some of the Evangelical Christian Baptist bodies refused to recognize the AUCECB as their head and set up their own "spiritual centre", namely, the Council of Churches of the Evangelical Christian Baptists (ECB).

Adventism in the USSR is manifest in two main trends, that is, the Seventh Day Adventists and the Reformist Adventists. The Adventists do not have a single centre and their communities, which function on an autonomous basis, are mainly spread over the territories of the Ukraine, Moldavia, Kazakhstan and the Baltic republics, numbering some 19 to 20 thousand members altogether.[5]

Apart from the Pentecostals, who have joined the ECB Union, there are also some of their communities functioning autonomously (in the Ukraine, Byelorussia, and elsewhere).

The Mennonites (both brotherhoods and churches) are mainly found in the Orenburg, Omsk and Novosibirsk regions, the Altai krai, and in the republics of Central Asia and the Baltic Sea area.

Small communities of the Methodists exist in Estonia and in the Trans-Carpathian region of the Ukrainian SSR. In the same Trans-Carpathian region there are also several reformed Church societies whose members are the Hungarians.

And, finally, the followers of the sect of Jehovah's Witnesses are found in a number of provinces in the Ukraine, especially in the western ones, and over the territories of Moldavia, the Northern Caucasus, Kazakhstan, the Irkutsk province, the Krasnodar krai, Estonia and elsewhere.

By virtue of their ideological content, the Protestant churches and sects represent in the USSR the bourgeois form of the Christian religion and function in the conditions of the socialist society, as a socio-historical and ideological survival.

The ideology and activities of the Protestant confessions are deeply affected by the process of secularization which, being conditioned by the totality of the objective and subjective factors, is called upon to free various aspects and spheres of the society's and the individual's life from religious influence and to assert the atheistic world outlook, based on scientific materialism.

It is under socialism that the secularization process, which is called forth by the general social, scientific, technological and cultural progress of today's world, develops most profoundly and extensively.

The deepest transformations in the economy and social relations, brought about as a result of the victorious Great October Socialist Revolution and the building of a developed socialist society, and the improvement in the educational and cultural standards and material well-being of Soviet people have undermined the deepest socio-economic and class roots of religiosity and caused the development of crisis phenomena in the Protestant and other religious confessions. These changes could not help having their influence on the weltanschauung, religious views, moral principles and beliefs of the followers of the Protestant churches and sects and caused some of them to turn away from religion and the church.

The loyal political stand of the Protestant confessions is based on the social views and political convictions of believers. The overwhelming majority of the leaders and ordinary believers in the Protestant communities give their support to the home and foreign policy of the Soviet State and the Communist Party, they are of a patriotic turn of mind and work together with the atheists to build a communist society.

Followers of the Protestant faiths or any other religious trends enjoy and are guaranteed by the USSR Constitution the right to profess their religious beliefs and to practise their religious worship. The socialist State does not interfere with the religious and canonical activities of the Protestant confessions.

The intensity and depth to which the process of secularization affects the consciousness, psychology, behaviour and way of life of the followers of the Protestant churches and sects, are in many ways dependent on the inherent features of their dogma and organization as well as on the peculiarities of the historical development of every particular Protestant trend in the conditions of the socialist society.

Crisis phenomena in the evolution of the Protestant confessions in the USSR find their expression, first of all, in the steadily diminishing sphere of the latter's religious influence, in the lessening of the number of Protestant communities especially, of the rural ones, in the slackening religiosity among the up-and-coming generations, as well as in the radical changes in the socio-demographic structure and social functions of the religious communities.

In the bourgeois Estonia of 1922, 94 to 95 per cent of the population had their children christened, 95 to 96 per cent were wedded and 98 to 99 per cent of the funeral ceremonies were held in a church. In the Soviet Estonia of 1957, the church christened 55.8 per cent of the new-born, wedded 29.8 per cent of the married, and serviced 64.5 per cent of the funeral ceremonies. Fifteen to twenty years later the popularity of the ceremonial rites sharply dropped, which testified to the decreasing influence of the Lutheran church and to increasing secularization. In 1973, 10.4 per cent of the children were christened, 3.2 per cent of the wedding and 40.4 per cent of the funerals were in a church.[6]

In Vorenezh province in 1926-27 there were over five thousand Baptists and Evangelical Christians, but by 1970 their number fell to 2,378.[7] From the beginning of the sixties the number of Baptists in Western Siberia decreases and their share in the overall population of the area becomes twenty times less than in the mid-twenties.[8] In 1975 as against 1929 the number of Baptists in the Altai krai decreased by more than five times.[9]

As against the late twenties, the number of the Evangelical Christian Baptists decreased by 39 per cent and their community by 26 per cent, while their share in the population of the Ukrainian SSR became twice less by the mid-sixties.[10]

During the post-war year the Baptists in Byelorussia had decreased by 30 per cent.[11] In Moldavia in 1944 there were more than 17,000 Baptists, but by 1975 their number had fallen by 1.7 times.[12]

The decreasing numbers and influence of the Baptists and Adventists are particularly noticeable in rural areas in the central regions of the RSFSR, in Siberia, Estonia, Latvia, the Ukraine and Byelorussia. Sociological research carried out in these regions has shown, for example, that the rural communities of Baptists and Adventists are fairly weak and small in number, and include very few young people, if any. These communities and groups, where new members are rarely baptized, gradually become weaker and eventually break up altogether.

According to the statistics of the All-Union Council of Evangelical Christian Baptists, from 1969 to 1974 twenty-two rural communities of ECB ceased to exist as a result of the natural casualties of its members, and the migration to the towns and workers' settlements.[13] Thus, in the Central Volga area in the fifties and sixties "most of the historically formed rural communities of ECB ceased to operate. Out of the ten rural communities in the Chuvash Autonomous Soviet Socialist Republic, for example, six broke up..."[14]

The loss of support for the rural religious communities in many regions throughout the country, the growing crises in them and the diminution of their numbers are a natural result of secularization, of the fact that fewer and fewer new members are forthcoming to swell the ranks of these communities. It is common knowledge that new members of Protestant communities were and still are : (1) children brought up in believers' families, in other words, in religious families ; (2) new proselytes won over during missionary activities from believers of other confessions, very rarely completely new converts, and also former "excommunicants"; and (3) migrants, members of Protestant communities who have moved from other places (for example, from the village to the town, and so forth).

In a socialist society all these sources of swelling the religious communities have weakened considerably, and are not always sufficient to compensate the natural loss of believers. Sociological studies show that the family no longer plays such an important part in passing on religiosity. Despite the strict upbringing that children receive from parents who are believers, these parents can no longer retain a religious influence over their children, bring all the children up in a religious spirit and make them members of the religious community. The religious family now consists of members with differing views. Under the influence of school, the army, and fellow workers, young people break with religion and the community. The very attitude of parents to a religious upbringing and education of their children also changes under the influence of socialist reality and prevailing public opinion. Parents begin to be more restrained and tolerant with regard to this question and listen to the advice and opinions of teachers. Among the Baptists asked in Byelorussia 62.6 per cent consider that belief should not be thrust upon small children.[15] In the Lvov region of the Ukraine among the Baptists and Adventists questioned 45.5 per cent were of the same opinion.[16]

At present, the basis for the missionary activities of the Evangelical Christian Baptists, the Seventh Day Adventists, the Pentecostals and others, has considerably narrowed. In the years of Soviet power new generations have grown up which have been educated in the spirit of a scientific world outlook. As a rule, the generations of unbelievers and convinced atheists are unreceptive to religious influence. The growth of political consciousness, the improved level of education and culture of the Soviet people, and the atheistic upbringing—all serve to firmly oppose religious influence. In a society where a scientific, materialistic, atheistic weltanschauung holds sway, the religious propaganda and missionary activities of the Protestants preachers do not, in most cases, find any response. It is an exceptional case, the outcome of extraordinary circumstances, when a non-believer takes to the faith.

The missionary activities of the Baptists, Adventists and so on are mainly aimed at believers of the Orthodox, Catholic, Lutheran and other churches. As a result of the religious propaganda of the Baptists, Adventists and Jehovah's Witnesses, believers still find themselves disappointed in these confessions, and thus continue to swell the ranks of the former communities. The number of members of the Protestant communities is also affected by migration of believers. An analysis of the population of urban communities and also of communities in regions such as Kazakhstan, the republics of Central Asia, and the Northern Caucasus showed migration processes to have a marked effect. In these regions the migration processes play an important part in the passing on and redistribution of religiosity.

Important changes have taken place in the social and demographic structure of the religious communities. Sociological research carried out in the central regions of the RSFSR, in the Ukraine, Byelorussia, Kazakhsthan, Moldavia, and the Baltic republics reveal a common tendency in the dynamics of the Protestant communities' socio-demographic structure over the last fifty years.

This tendency is reflected, firstly, in the fact that religious communities consist more and more of elderly people and include fewer and fewer young people : secondly, that the standard of education is considerably lower than that of other strata of the population ; thirdly, the member of the Protestant communities are mainly people not involved in social production and the numbers of those engaged in socially productive labour are dwindling ; and fourthly, this tendency is reflected in the sharp drop in the number of men and the growing number of women in the Protestant communities.

Most members of the Lutheran Church are women and elderly people.[17] In 1965-66 in 49 regions of the country 60 per cent of the Evangelical Christian Baptists were over 60 years of age. Of them 79.2 per cent were women, and 42 to 43 per cent were semi-literate and had only primary education.[18] In the urban communities of Baptists in Byelorussia 60 per cent of the believers were over fifty in 1974 (in 1964—58 per cent).[19] In the Ukraine the number of believers with primary education, or semi-literate or illiterate was 75-95 per cent of all the believers. Among the Baptists in the Central Volga area 81 per cent of those asked had V to VIII class education, and only 3 per cent had secondary education. The rest were semi-literate or illiterate.[20]

In the ECB communities in the Penza, Voronezh, Gorky and other regions women accounted for 70 to 85 per cent of the members. Similar phenomena are being observed among Seventh-Day Adventists, Pentecostals, and Mennonites. For example, in the community of "Brotherly" Mennonites in the town of Karaganda 75.6 per cent of the members were women in 1975, and 54.1 per cent of the members were people over fifty.[21]

Definite steps forward in overcoming the sectarian estrangement and seclusion have been noted among Jehova's Witnesses. It is commonly known that a typical feature of this category of believers was that they restricted and reduced to a minimum their civic and social obligations, for instance, they refused to serve in the Soviet Army, to take part in electing the organs of power, to work in voluntary public organizations, and so on.

At present, the Jehovah's Witnesses, especially the younger generation, are coming to regard their civic and social obligations in a different light, and are reviewing their attitude to Soviet society and to its socio-political institutions.

More and more Jehovah's witnesses are becoming trade union members. Many of them take part in the elections of the organs of Soviet power. These phenomena have been noted in the Ivan-Franko, Chernovtsy and Rovno regions of the Ukraine, in the Stavropol and Krasnodar krais, and in the Moldavian SSR.

The change in the Jehovah's Witnesses' orientation and aims has been recorded in sociological studies conducted, for instance, in a number of western regions of the Ukraine (Ivan-Franko, Trans-Carpathian regions). Among the Jehovah's Witnesses the researchers discerned several types of believers who differed in their social aims and in their views of society. It became clear that a religious outlook is by no means the only element in Jehovah's Witnesses' consciousness and is not always the main factor in determining their attitude to society and to life in a socialist country. For 19 per cent of those asked the religious idea was the most important and they regarded the world about them in a negative light through the prism of Jehovistic ideas ; for 28.8 per cent their religious outlook was a neutral one, not involving social negativism ; for another 52.2 per cent their religious views were of less importance and they took an interest in life about them, in socialist society, and their moral appraisals and views of society were positive ones.[22] The fact that there are believers of this type among the Jehovah's Witnesses shows that the orthodox ideas of the Jehovah's Witnesses, the Brooklyn propaganda, is gradually losing its hold over believers.

Byelorussian researchers note that the social orientation, apprisals of social phenomena and attitudes to people among Baptist believers involve a positive attitude to the socialist social system and a sense of patriotism and civic duty. Among Baptists in Byelorussia, besides the 7.7 per cent anti-social ones, and the 55.5 per cent indifferent ones, a type of "sympathizers" (33.5 per cent) and "active ones" (3.3 per cent) were found.[23] Sympathizers show an interest in the affairs of the labour collective and in the fate and affairs of their country. They acknowledge social progress and recognize the importance of the social transformations that have taken place in this country in the years of Soviet power. They are tolerant of non-believers and do not force their children to become religious. As for the "active ones", they do, according to Byelorussian researchers, represent positive social orientation and are objective in their attitude to the life of society. They associate with non-religious people, have a wide variety of interests, attempt to improve their cultural level, and condemn their fellow-believers for their "narrow" views on these questions. They are well thought of by their fellow workers and neighbours.[24]

The fact that these groups do exist among the Baptists, although they do not form the majority, indicates the weakening influence of the religious community on the believer's consciousness. In their attitudes to culture, non-believers, and so forth, they are not guided solely by religious ideas and norms, but independently, by reason and experience.

The weakening influence of religious ideas not only applies to the sphere of social orientation, but also to that of moral consciousness.

The collectivism and humanism of the Soviet way of life cannot fail to affect the attitude of believers to work, to their homeland, to influence their understanding of the sense and purpose of life, and of their social obligations. In these spheres many believers are seen to be moving away from religious views and breaking with the traditional religious norms of morality.

Questions put to Evangelical Christian Baptists showed that 81 per cent of those asked explained the main purpose of their labour according to the Baptist conception, which interprets the social significance of labour in a religious way. However, 19 per cent of those asked not only looked upon labour as a means of sustaining life, but also spoke of its importance for society. Among the Baptists there are people who work with a high sense of responsibility, with an understanding of their labour and civic duty, and who receive diplomas and bonuses. These form the most active part of the believers, who have got away from the influence of the Baptists or have not experienced it in general in the question of their understanding of the social significance of labour.

Thus, the active participation of believers in socially productive labour, work in the labour collective, and the spiritual and moral atmosphere in which the believer moves, constrict and do away with the traditional religious views formed by a religious environment, parents, and the community, and inculcate in the believer a sense of the social importance of his labour.

The scientific and technological revolution taking place in the world, the transformation of science into a direct productive force, the introduction of the achievements of scientific and technological progress in industry and agriculture, and in people's everyday life are compelling the adherents of the Protestant confessions to meditate upon the correlation of the scientific and the religious picture of the world, and upon the part played by science in the world today. It is characteristic of the consciousness of most members of the Protestant communities today that it no longer harbours negativism and a negative attitude to scientific and technological progress. On the contrary, these believers tend to take an interest in the achievements of science and technology, they understand their importance for the life of society and each individual, and are seen to make attempts to link scientific advances with the religious picture of the world and with the principles of religious belief.

This applies, first and foremost, to representatives of the younger and middle generations, who are better educated and possess a certain amount of scientific knowledge and ideas. Among the Baptists asked in Byelorussia 81.5 per cent recognized the attainments of science and the benefit it brings to society.[25] Fifty-one per cent of the Jehovah's Witnesses asked apprised the achievements of modern science positively and recognized its usefulness for society. This attitude is the result of the growing authority of science and the part it plays in socialist society. This is particularly typical of the group of believers who have a seven-year or an incomplete secondary education and participate in social production. Only 5.4 per cent expressed negative or sceptical attitudes to scientific achievements.[26]

Important changes are taking place in the attitudes of members of the Protestant communities to cultural values of the mass media, and so forth. It is commonly known that the traditional ideas of the Baptists, Adventists, Pentecostalists and other churches, which attempt to cut the believer off from the world and isolate him within the framework of the religious community, imposed various prohibitions and limitations in questions regarding the reading of secular literature, pursuits in art and science and so on, as factors interfering with religious belief and preventing the believer from giving himself up completely to God.

Social and scientific and technological progress, the improvement of education and culture, the development of the mass media could not fail to have an effect on the consciousness of sectarians especially those of the new generations of believers, who have grown up in a socialist society, been educated at Soviet schools, and work at socialist enterprises and institutions.

According to a questionnaire circulated recently in the Lvov region, although 84.8 per cent of the believers of Protestant confessions, mainly young and middle-aged people, read religious literature, they are displaying a growing interest in fiction, science fiction and popular science literature ; 42 per cent of the believers read non-religious literature, 88.2 per cent regularly read newspapers, 72.5 per cent magazines, 50 per cent visit museums, 43.1 per cent go to the cinema and 31.4 per cent to the theatre.[27]

In the ECB community in the town of Baranovitch in the Brest region of the Bylorussian Soviet Socialist Republic each family subscribes to a newspaper. More than 20 per cent of the members of the community read newspapers regularly, 96 per cent have radios and receivers, and 10 per cent have television sets.[28]

Research carried out among Jehovah's Witnesses in the Ukraine showed that 38.5 per cent of those asked had a realistic attitude to culture and did not deny its importance for the spiritual development of the personality ; 36.2 per cent tolerated culture and only 5.8 per cent were ill-disposed to it. Besides their interest in religious literature, 59.6 per cent of the believers subscribe to and read newspapers and magazines. This is typical of almost all literate believers.[29]

Jehovah's Witnesses readily read articles published in the *Literaturnaya Gazeta* (Literary Gazette) and *Za Rubezhom* (Abroad) and books with a historical-philosophical and natural science content.

Of late, more and more TV sets have been appearing in the homes of Jehovah's Witnesses (both urban and rural inhabitants). News and political and science broadcasts and programmes about nature, history and the culture of peoples in foreign countries are most popular among them.

Young Seventh-Day Adventists in the town of Karaganda particularly enjoy historical literature and articles and essays on world history. They read the magazines *Nauka i Zhiza* (Science and Life), *Znaniye-Sila* (Knowledge is Power), *Semya i Shkola* (The Family and School), *Rebotnitza* (Woman Worker),

Za Rubezhom (Abroad), and *Zdorovie* (Health) ; they subscribe to the newspapers *Pravda*, *Izvestiya*, *Trud*, *Nedelya*, *Komsomolskaya Pravda* and so on, and also atheistic literature.[30]

Thus, we see that Evangelical Christian Baptists, Seventh-Day Adventists, Jehovah's Witnesses, and so on, are displaying a definite interest in science and culture. There are fewer and fewer fanatics who are blindly convinced of the verity of religion and are intolerant and opposed to society. In the Protestant communities there are growing numbers of believers who reveal tolerance, a tendency to rationalism, to dialogue with atheists, positive, social and moral orientation, and who have a positive attitude to the values of science and culture. Many believers are beset by doubt, and one observes a passive attitude to worship, a moving away from the norms of religious life and dogma, and a cooling off of religious belief. Regarding the state of religious and spiritual life in the communities, the magazine *Bratski Vestnik* wrote : "We have to live and work with people for whom belief has no meaning. This is having a bad effect on the fervour of Christians. Therefore, the belief of many of them has taken on a somewhat neutral tint. In this state they lose their spiritual cast of mind and become passive people". According to the author, this passiveness and inertness among believers have reached such proportions that they are calling forth "anxiety and even fear".[31]

Thus, in defining as a whole the essence of the changes, which are occurring in the consciousness of believers of the Protestant confessions, and which testify to the increasing secularization and the growing crises, the following tendencies should be noted :

1. These changes are of a comprehensive nature and envelop everything without exception, although they touch the sphere of consciousness and behaviour of believers to different extents. Changes are occurring in the sphere of ideas (religious, ethical, and so on), in the sphere of the emotions as well as in the spheres of behaviour and way of life of the believer.

2. The ever increasing divergence between the official religious doctrine, the dogma content and ideas of one or another Protestant current, on the one hand, and the everyday consciousness of the believer on the other.

3. The widening gap between the *religious consciousness* and behaviour of the believers, which indicates that religious ideas and principles are losing their grip and that there is no cohesion between the believer's consciousness and his behaviour. The Bible is ceasing to be a means of regulating the behaviour of believers in their everyday life, in their families or in their labour relations. At every turn of his life the believer faces problems which cannot be resolved from the viewpoint of his belief, that is, from a religious standpoint. The actual behaviour and activities of believers are not always motivated by religious ideas. The latter are not decisive in determining choice in professional or educational training, nor do they have a crucial impact on the socio-political views, work attitudes or on cultural and scientific attitudes.

4. The believers' consciousness is seen to have a complex and contradictory intertwining of religious and non-religious (*i.e.*, secular) elements, the latter of which are coming to play an increasingly important part. Their consciousness is enriched by new ideological and social information which invades their spiritual world by various channels, despite the opposition and restrictions of the religious community heads. As a result the modern believer's consciousness is far from being integral. Religious values are constantly being reappraised, as a result of which a number of elements of the religious complex either disappear or are interpreted in a new way. The signs of religiosity in the consciousness and behaviour of the believer become few, and mainfestations of those signs of religion that have been retained, become less intense.

5. Changes in the religious consciousness of the believer occur unevenly. Research shows that attitude to the world, to society, to the state, to labour, and socio-political and moral views, and so on, were most mobile and subject to change among believers of the Protestant churches and sects. It is precisely in this sphere that the most positive advances are observed, the beneficial effect of socialist reality. Believers are found to be most conservative in their religious views and concepts.

The growing, deepening secularization, which is leading to profound changes in the consciousness and behaviour of believers, is causing serious anxiety among the ideologists of the

Lutherans, Baptists, Adventists, and Pentecostalists, and the heads of the Protestant communities are faced with some inexorable questions : Is it possible to find a way out of the situation that is taking shape ? Can belief be protected and its existence ensured in the epoch of social progress, scientific and technological revolution, when the bases of the religious weltanschauung are being undermined ? How can the growing and accelerating process of secularization be withstood ?

In attempting to slow down the inevitable decline of religion and overcoming the crisis in belief, some of the heads of the Protestant communities are trying to contain the changes occurring in the believers' consciousness in a religious vein. They are attempting to modernize religious teachings and adapt them to the conditions in a socialist society. They are trying to bring together the social and moral principles of Communism and those of Christianity and to proclaim the harmony of science religion, and substantiate the topicality of Christian humanism today. The adherents of this course wish to form a new, more subtle religious consciousness, to educate a believer of a new type who acknowledges and approves the ideals of communism, who is loyal to the Soviet State, who strives to attain a definite educational, professional, and cultural standard, who takes an active part in the life of society, who takes an interest in the topical problems of life today, in science and art, and who, at the same time, unites all this with a devotion to religious ideals and a belief in God.

This trend towards modernization and religious reform is most marked in the activities of the All-Union Council of Evangelical Christian Baptists. While remaining faithful to the principles of Protestant fundamentalism in apprising and interpreting the "holy scriptures", the heads of the Evangelical Christian Baptist Church could not help taking into account the new needs and aspirations of believers born of the Soviet way of life, of socialist reality, and of modern scientific and cultural progress, and are attempting to respond to them in a certain way. Hence, the new trends of interpreting the problems of "Christianity and Motherland", "Christianity and Science", "Christianity and Culture", the extenuation of pietism and rigour, and the attempt to achieve a more up-to-date understanding of the Bible and its significance in the spiritual life of the believer.

However, not all memebers of society approve of these tendencies. At the beginning of the sixties, a schism occurred in the Union of the ECB, and the so-called "initiative group" was formed which subsequently became the Council of Churches of the ECB.

The supporters of this opposition group are seeking a way out of the crisis by more persistent religious propaganda and missionary activities, stricter observance of the norms of morality which are traditional to the Baptists, Adventists, and other confessions and enforcement of the various prohibitions aimed at shielding the believer from the influence of the world. This means intra-community self-isolation, "purification" and "consecration" of the whole way of life of believers, stricter religious upbringing and education of children, activization of religious propaganda, a militant campaign against materialism and advocation of the "salvation significance" of religious belief in the spiritual life of modern man.

Over the last few years the conflict between the conservative and fanatical elements in the Protestant sects and the adherents of a moderate, more flexible adaptation to the world, has heightened considerably. This conflict, which has become a characteristic feature of religious life in the Protestant sects, primarily relates to the content and form of religious activities in a developed socialist society. It involved questions connected with the legislation on religious cults, with the religious upbringing and education of children, with the attitude to secular culture and science, to the ever growing process of secularization and so forth.

Neither the modernization of religious ideas and cults for the purpose of adapting them to the conditions in socialist society, nor religious extremism or more intensive religious propaganda, is in a position to prevent the effect of secularization on the Protestant confessions, to halt the development of the crisis in them which are called forth by deep rooted social factors.

In a socialist society there are a number of objective and subjective factors facilitating the dying out of religious consciousness and religious attitudes and accelerating the process of secularization of the population, of overcoming religion and of shaping a scientific, materialistic, atheistic world outlook in all Soviet people.

Firstly, there are socio-economic and cultural factors linked with the level of the social, economic and cultural maturity attained by socialist society, and with the character of socialist social relations as the educational, cultural and living standards of the Soviet people improve.

Secondly, there is the Soviet way of life typified by social optimism, the collective character of relations between people, political awareness, high standards of culture and social activities, and a great sense of social and civic responsibility.

Thirdly, there is the influence of the scientific and technological revolution, whose achievements are making a substantial impact on believers' world outlook, their psychology and thinking and what impels them to regard the religious picture of the world in a critical light.

Fourthly, there is the process of internationalization of the life of society and the drawing together of nations. In a socialist society the influence of micro-media and patriarchal relations is lessened, and national prejudices and religious isolation disappear. Intensive ethnic assimilation takes place in multinational labour collectives and in families whose members are of different nationalities. There is intensive language and cultural interaction between the different ethnic groups. The development of relations between people of different nationalities, the growth of personal contacts between them facilitate the formation of internationalist views and the overcoming of ethnic and religious narrow-mindedness.

Finally, there is the predominance of socialist ideas, the high level of political, moral and international consciousness among the Soviet people, which are in turn, the result of the systematic and purposeful educational work carried out by the Communist Party and public organizations.

All these factors determine the depth and intensity of the secularization process, its necessary and natural character in the conditions of a developed socialist society.

NOTES AND REFERENCES

1. *Vaike Entsuklopeedia*. Tartu, 1937-1938, 294, 930.
2. K A. Vimsaare, Osobennosti ideologii i deyatel 'nosti sovremennogo lyuteranstva. (Peculiarities of ideology and activity of modern Lutheranism). In: *Aktual' nye voprosy ateisticheskogo vospitaniya* (Actual problems of atheistic education). Alma-Ata, 1976, str. 188.
3. See: *Sovetskaya istoricheskaya entsiklopediya* (The Soviet Historical Encyclopaedia), t. 12, M. 1969, str. 706.
4. See: *Bratskiy vestnik* (Fraternal News), 1966, N 5, s 17. "Tochnoi statistiki nashe bratstvo nikogda ne imelo, eno ne immeet eye i segodnya. Tsifra 500 tysyach, kotoruyu my nazy-250 tysyach kreschennyh po vere ne vyzyvayut ni v kom iz nas somneniya, to ostal' nuyu polovinu nashego bratstva sostav-lyayut veruyuschiye, no poka eschye ne poluchivshie krescheniya. Eto chleny evangel' sko-baptistskih semey -- veruyuschie deti, podrostki, yunoshi i devushki, a takzhe vse te, kogo my nazyvaem priblizhennymi ili priblizhayusch-imisya". (our fraternity never had definite statistics, and has none even to-day. The figure 500, 000 which we list, may seem somewhat untrue, but if 250, 000 christened by religion, are beyond our doubt, the rest half of our fraternity are believers but not yet christened. They are members of Evangelical-Baptist families—children, teenagers, young men, boys and girls, and also all those, whom we call retinue or going to be retinue).
5. V. Seredine, 60-x godov kolichestvo adventistov 7 dnya sostavlyalo 21-5 t. chelovek (In the middle of sixties, Seventh Day Adventists numbered 215, 000). See: F. Fedorenko. *Sekty, ikh veia n dela* (A Sekts, their beliefs and actions). M., 1965, s. 191.
6. K.A. Vimsaare, Osobennosti ideologii i deyatel, nosti sovremennogo lyuteranstva. (Peculiarities of ideology and activity of modern Lutheranism) i — In : *Aktual 'nye voprosy ateisticheskogo vospitaniya* (Actual problems of atheistic education), Alma-Ata, 1975, s. 188.
7. M.K. Teplyakov, *Problemy ateisticheskogo vospitaniya v praktike partiynoy raboty* (Problems of atheistic education in practice of the party work). Voronezh, 1972, s. 156.
8. A.P. Andreev, Ideologiya i praktika sovremennogo baptisma (po materialam Zapadnoy Sibiri) : (Ideology and practice of modern Baptists (on materials of Western Siberia). Avtoreferat (Synoposis of thesis), M., 1973, s. 16.
9. N.M. Rudakova. *Evoluytsiya sovremennogo baptisma i problemy ateisticheskogo vospitqniya* (Evolution of modern baptism and problems of atheistic education). M., 1976, s. 8.
10. A.I. Klibanov, Religioznoe sektantvo i sovremennost'. (Religious sectarianism and the present) *Nauka* (Science), M., 1969, s. 76.
11. Baptizm i baptisty. (Baptism and Baptists, Minsk, 1969, s. 76.

12. V.F. Gazhos, *Evoluytsiya religioznogo sektanstva v Moldavii*. (Evolution of religious sectarianism in Moldavia). Krishinev, 1975, s. 13, 23.
13. *Bratskiy vestnik* (Fraternal News), 1975, N 1, s. 48.
14. G.E. Kudryashov, Dinamika polisinkreticheskoy religioznosti. (Dynamics of polysinkretic religiousness), Cheboksary, 1974, s. 228,
15. See: *Baptizm i baptisty* (Baptism and Baptists). Minsk, 1969, s. 143.
16. *Nauka i religiya* (Science and Religion), 1977, N 4, s. 63.
17. *Aktual'nye voprosy ateisticheskogo vospitaniya*. (Actual problems of atheistic education). Alma-Ata, 1976, s. 188.
18. G.S. Lyalina. Baptizm: Illyuzii i real'nost' (Baptism: illusions and reality). M., 1977, s. 13.
19. G.M. Filist, *Nekotorye osobennosti ateisticheskogo vospitaniya gorodskogo naseleniya* (Some peculiarities of atheistic education of city population). Minsk, 1977, s. 21.
20. G.E. Kudryashov, *Dinamika polisinkreticheskoy religioztosti* (Dynamics of polysinkretic religiousness), s. 229.
21. A.N. Ipatov, *Mennonity*. M., 1978, s. 160.
22. *Iegovizm i Yegovisty* (Yegovism and Yegovists). Kiev, 1974, c. 98-9 (Ukrainian).
23. *Baptizm i baptisty* (Baptism and Baptists). Minsk. 1969, s. 157.
24. *Ibid*, s. 159-60.
25. *Ibid.*, s. 139.
26. *Iegovizm i iegovisty* (Yegovism and Yegovists), s. 140, 128.
27. *Nauka i religiya* (Science and Religion) N 4, 1977, s. 64.
28. G.M. Filist. *op. cit.*, s. 14.
29. *Iegovizm i iegovisty* (Yegovism and Yegovists), s. 132.
30. See: B.A. Saprykin. *Sotsialisticheskiy gorod i ateisticheskoe vospitanie* (A socialist city and atheistic education). Kazhakhstan. Alma-Ata, 1976, s. 69.
31. See: *Bratskiy vestnik* (Fraternal News), 1975, N 6, s. 27, 28.

Index

Name Index